Anna Reynolds
OR Tambo Airport
Johannesburg
5th November 2022

BAMBOOZLED

In search of joy
in a world gone mad

MELINDA FERGUSON

mf

Melinda Ferguson Books,
an imprint of NB Publishers, a division of Media24 Boeke (Pty) Ltd
40 Heerengracht, Cape Town, South Africa
PO Box 879, Cape Town 8000, South Africa
www.nb.co.za

Cover design and typography: Wilna Combrinck
Editor: Sean Fraser
Proofreader: Riaan Wolmarans
Set in Sabon LT Pro
Printed and bound by CTP Printers, Cape Town

First published by Melinda Ferguson Books 2022
First edition, first impression

ISBN: 978-1-990973-52-9
ISBN: 978-1-990973-53-6 (epub)

"Perhaps one did not want to be loved so much as to be understood."
– George Orwell, *1984*

To my boys: Dan, James, Joe and Mat.
To all the Light Keepers in search of Truth, Joy and Freedom.

CONTENTS

AUTHOR'S NOTE

Bamboozled (definition): to deceive, to hoodwink, to mystify

I started writing this book in 2017. And then I stopped. Blocked. Distracted. Diverted.

One year passed. Then two. In year three of avoidance, 2020, we found ourselves in the middle of what felt to me like something out of a godawful episode of the dystopian *The Handmaid's Tale*.

Although it had always been lurking in the background, Death now became the front-row theme of our lives. It smirked at us when we awoke and masked ourselves, adhered to curfews, Covid tests, Covid jabs, PCR swabs, as we watched endlessly ticking numbers and stats dipping and climbing, were told of new variants, travel bans, quarantines – it was Death who greeted us and said: "Howdy. I'm here."

Time took on a sinister new meaning, with ever-changing calendars of lockdown levels, restrictions and viral waves.

Within the first months of The Pandemic, I started taking notes again. I published – and wrote short essays for – three books in that first year, all on the impact of lockdown. Shuffling around in my slippers, I went back to my old writing from 2017 and reread it, and while I liked some of it, I was ruthless, deleting reams that no longer seemed relevant.

By early 2021, in the second year of The Plague, I started talking myself into getting back to serious writing. I began to feel growing birth pangs, an urge to explore what was going on both in my own inner sphere and this unrecognisable new world into which we'd been catapulted. I was consumed: asking questions, uncovering answers and searching for patterns, but also driven by an obsessive quest to find joy and freedom in the midst of it all.

Writing a memoir can be brutal. Not writing it can feel much worse.

An unfinished book is a lot like an unattended, untreated tumour. It grows and nudges and leaves you disturbed. It never lets you forget. It gnaws at your soul, grinding away at you from within.

Oh, I know all the excuses us writers sell ourselves. I'm an ace at telling other authors not to listen to that monkey-mind voice: "This is shit", "Who cares?", "Who do you think you are?"

Yackety-yackety-yak.

The avoidance tricks are never-ending, but they seldom alleviate the mental scratching, like the claws of a mouse trapped under a piano.

Someone once said, "Writing a book feels like banging your head against a wall until you finish it." Trust me. It does.

With that said, though, I am not being entirely honest here. There is a far more significant reason why I froze, unable to proceed. It's the one that aborts many a creation.

The truth is I let myself grow increasingly terrified about what everyone might think. Of me. Of what I had done. Of what I thought. I gave my power away to the voice that whispered: *What will they say?*

Strange, I know, coming from someone like me, who usually has absolutely no filters, who is a shameless confessor at heart, who, in my first book, *Smacked,* had no issue telling the world that I had used drugs as a twice-pregnant mother, had traded sexual favours for crack, stolen my mother's engagement ring and pawned it, that I'd forged signatures on cheques and had bled on the pavement, screeching for a fix – that I'd literally sold my soul and morality for heroin and crack.

In my second book, *Hooked,* without even the hint of a blush, I went on to describe the insanity of love addiction and the lengths to which I'd gone: how I'd stalked my then-boyfriend, steaming open envelopes to track phone bills in a pathetic attempt to find "proof" of an affair, how I'd leopard-crawled up a rain-soaked mountainside to check whether the car of "the other woman" was parked in his drive.

In *Crashed* I brashly told the world of my inglorious collision in which I totalled a R3.2-million Ferrari, how I found my previous lover in bed with a Dutch lesbian and how I managed to snap his dick after clumsy make-up sex.

I, the queen of comeback and confession, with zero shame, could write three whole books about a mountain of scandalous experiences, yet when I tried to write about my fears for myself and our world, about my desperation to unravel the mindfuckery of the "new normal" in which we found ourselves, about my controversial spiritual quest to fix myself, to find freedom, forgiveness and joy, for *this* book, I froze.

Intellectually, I found this fascinating. That I would find it so challenging to write about vulnerability, about loss and confusion, about searching for truth and deeper compassion for myself and the world.

And so I leapt off the precipice of the unknown. And I wrote.

People are strange, and never have I seen that more clearly than in the last two years. Never have I been more stupefied and, simultaneously, more mystified. What a strange bunch of broken and beautiful idiots we human beings are.

Melinda Ferguson
July 2022

PART ONE

A ROOM OF MY OWN

"Lock up your libraries if you like; but there is no gate, no lock,
no bolt that you can set upon the freedom of my mind."
– Virginia Woolf, *A Room of One's Own*

Chapter 1

MURDER IN PARADISE

On 26 March 2021, a woman is murdered two houses from the safe haven I've miraculously managed to purchase as an escape from The Pandemic. The brutal killing takes place just a week before my magical log cabin, built on stilts in a private nature reserve, is transferred and registered in my name.

I will learn more about The Woman only after her death. My elderly Dutch neighbours, just one house from mine, who I've waved to a couple times, are tied up, gagged and robbed the same night that The Woman's life is snuffed out. The wooden rhinoceros that's been lazing on their veranda is used to smash through their bedroom window.

I am not at the new house that Friday night when The Woman is killed. I'm in Cape Town, because the next day I'll be hosting my first real-life writing workshop in The Pandemic. I've just given the group of nine writers, gathered around my 10-seater cedarwood dining table, a prompt: "The first time I realised that things were not as they seemed ..." when a message pings through on WhatsApp.

Usually photos of sunsets, sunrises, proteas and fynbos paper the feed of the homeowners' group. Now and again there are pictures of goats, tortoises, birds, and screenshots of weather reports or rain-gauge levels.

I'm hardly paying attention to my phone, but then I glance at the message again. It's in Dutch.

The words *"ingebroken"*, *"vastgebonden"* and *"vermoord"* catch my eye.

I stare blankly at the writers around the table. They are elbowed down in their prompt.

I read the message over and over again: *"vermoord"* … *"vastgebonden"* … *"vermoord"*. The words quiver on the screen.

What's *"vermoord"*? Isn't that murdered?

My heart freezes.

"I think someone's just been killed on the estate at my new house." The words drop out of my dry mouth. They obliterate the writerly quiet.

The crime changes everything.

Chapter 2

THE "ESCAPE FROM THE PANDEMIC" HOUSE

On the day we find the new house, Soul-Mat and I have decided to travel to Tulbagh to look at a thatched, gabled place I've favourited on Property24. I have always enjoyed staring at houses, but during the first year of The Plague I become obsessed. The search for an "Escape from The Pandemic House" becomes a much-needed distraction from infection numbers and global death stats.

By 4 January 2021, the day we set off on our house-searching mission, I've trawled thousands of places online. We've already visited quite a few in real life, in out-of-town places like Suurbraak, Villiersdorp, Grabouw and Montague.

As we head out of Cape Town, there are few cars on the streets. The world seems drugged.

I don't know much about Tulbagh. I vaguely recall reading something about an earthquake in the late 1960s that left the town severely damaged. In fact, there are no plans to see the house I end up buying. The advert, with its hazy pictures and vague details, had not made the place come across as promising. The copy alluded to some remote-sounding wooden cabin in the sticks. There was mention of the Mostertshoek mountains. I'd never heard of them.

I knew I'd want to go to the house alone sometimes, so this place sounded far too isolated for a woman on her own.

Dangerous even. But since we are in the area, we decide to take a look anyway.

We follow the estate agent, who I've disturbed on her Christmas break, out of Tulbagh, along a seemingly never-ending gravel road. She's told us the cabin is about 10 kilometres out of the sleepy town of Wolseley. It seems much longer.

"Where the hell are we going?" I say to Soul-Mat.

About eight kilometres in, after navigating around a flock of bored sheep chewing up a field of green, we turn a bend ... and everything changes. Nothing prepares me for the majestic haven that unfolds as we close in.

With a vista of mountains, fynbos and otherworldly magic, the place looks like a Swiss alpine village perched somewhere in Africa. As we approach, the hairs on my arms start to rise.

We get to an automated gate. Once through, we make our way up a gentler gravel road. About a dozen houses are dotted across the terrain of a private nature reserve, each more beautiful than the last. They are clearly designed to blend into the scenery. There is only one house that seems eerily out of place. A huge dark-grey, metal-clad, container-like structure, perched two houses from the one we're viewing. It appears to jut out of the landscape like some Nordic house of horror.

"It looks a bit like a coffin," I say to Soul-Mat. We wonder who lives there.

Once parked, we walk past unruly bushes of lush lavender. Honeysuckle twists around the wooden posts that frame the front door.

The silence is almost deafening.

We marvel at the quiet and the quality of the clear, clean, fynbos-infused air.

Within minutes after crossing the wooden-floored open-plan interior of the cabin, onto the deck that reveals a majestic palette of fynbos, mountains and vineyards, and after absorbing the beauty of the sparkling azure pool to the right that reflects the mountain range on its shimmery surface, I know it must be mine.

Without a single doubt, I instantly make an offer.

Soul-Mat tries to lure me aside, to dissuade me from acting too impulsively. That's what soulmates do. They try to protect you. But I already know. I know – like when you meet The One, like when I met Soul-Mat on that dating app – that I belong to this house. After what feels like a lifetime of searching, I have found it. My place of Joy and Freedom.

✳

Three days earlier, we'd had a sinister New Year's Eve. Our first in lockdown. Celebrations had effectively been outlawed, the curfew imposed by the National Coronavirus Command Council banning people from being on the streets. I think, if I recall correctly, it was "home by 9pm" that night. Clearly, the homeless would have needed to hide under a bridge or make themselves invisible in the bushes.

As the clock ticked midnight, we stood alone on our balcony overlooking the city, watching pathetic little puffs of fireworks spluttering on the dark horizon. Somewhere in the black sky, military helicopters thundered, patrolling the mice below by searchlight and drowning all attempts of festivities.

I thought I heard gunshots. They could have been firecrackers. But in all likelihood they were the pop of bullets exploding. An ambulance wailed in the distance.

"We are under siege," I whispered to Soul-Mat. "I can't take this much longer. We need to get out … We have to find somewhere else to go. This shit is just going to get worse. It feels like we are living in an old Soviet state, the 1980s; it's the State of Emergency all over again. It's Gilead, like we're in the fucking *Handmaid's*

Tale. I need to be free, darling. What happens if this never ends, if it goes on like this forever …?"

✳

Within minutes of seeing the house, I sign the offer to purchase. I have no niggling doubt, no wavering. Just absolute clarity.

And so this cabin on stilts, perched in paradise with a mountainside for a back garden, a huge hunk of eons-old rock that reflects the sun's pink, virginal glow in the early morning and fiery orange deep kisses at the end of the day, becomes my "escape from The Pandemic" house.

They say money can't buy you love, but as I stare into the pristine yonder, catching sight of three black eagles soaring overhead, silhouetted against the endless vista of the Matroosberg, at this point I would have argued with that. I am besotted. If money is the ticket to owning this miracle, I am up for the ride.

I'd been saving for something like this for years, working obsessively, like a packhorse, in book publishing. I had recently, somewhat fortuitously, retrieved a sizeable sum of cash that I'd naively lost due to someone else's bad business decisions. In 2020, I'd produced like a demon, and though I am not quite sure how, managed to post my best financial year yet – all in the midst of a bloody pandemic. I clearly thrive on crises.

While millions are suffering, I now strangely find myself in the financial flow of abundance. I shrug off my guilt. This is as good a time as any to spend my unexpected windfall. I now have the means to put down a sizeable deposit and approach my bank to grant me a bond for the rest. Although I hate owing money to institutions, these are strange and sinister times. Death is swaggering in the shadows, swaying her hips and licking her lips on every corner. And, besides, that guy Klaus Schwab, chairman of the World Economic Forum and the big wig of Davos, has been freaking me out lately by blabbing on about the "Great Reset" on the horizon. He seems to take perverse pleasure in proclaiming "you will own nothing and be happy". I mean, what exactly does he mean by that?

Fuck him, I think. I *will* own this piece of land, Mr Creepy Schwab, because I have worked hard for it and I *will* be fucking happy!

Besides, if I die before my bond is paid, what the hell are they going to do about it anyway? At this point, feeling like I do, clod-brained, with the walls of lockdown closing in, I am prepared to pay for my freedom.

Less than three months later, after the news came in that The Woman two houses away had been brutally attacked and strangled to death, I wondered whether Soul-Mat had been right that day on the deck, when he'd warned me to wait. Had I made a crazy, impulsive Covid-brain-numbed decision buying the cabin? Was freedom just an illusion? Was joy a passing fad? Had I backed the wrong horse? It was hard to tell. Ever since a year before, in late March 2020, when things changed overnight, mindfuckery had become the order of the day. And it felt like no one was more bamboozled by it all than me.

Chapter 3

LOVE ISLAND

Had there been buckets of blood in that charcoal-grey box house the night The Woman died? Like in *Carrie*?

Did she hear them as they stole in under the cover of darkness? Was she washing dishes? Getting ready for bed? Was she wearing a paisley nightie? Or boxer shorts and her husband's old T-shirt? Had she bathed yet? Applied her pricey night cream to ward off old age? Or was she more of a shower girl? I myself like deep submersion.

Had she been asleep? Or watching Netflix on the couch? Maybe *Black Mirror*? *The Blacklist*? *Emily in Paris*? Perhaps she was streaming Showmax and watching *Love Island UK*.

I become glued to that show in the first few months of 2020.

After the president announces the extension of the initial three-week lockdown, I try to distract myself from the insanity that's unfolding all around us. Over the next year I will be enthralled by this dreck. I don't only mean The Plague – I also mean *Love Island*. I become a withered vegetable as I watch endless seasons of the tacky reality show back to back. On average there are 40 episodes a season, 57 minutes apiece. That's close to 40 hours a season of toilet-paper viewing. Now multiply that by five seasons. You do the maths.

I become unnaturally attached to *Love Island* hopefuls

like Josh and Emily, John and Abigail, Sarah and Matthew, who squabble, make out and make up in the "love house" in Majorca. While I know that many of the inconsequential conflicts are manufactured to manipulate story line and that I am in fact being played, as I become progressively engaged in my *Love Island* fix, I feel increasingly marooned from Soul-Mat, from the rest of humankind.

It's a lot like addictive crack cocaine. I can't get enough of the inanity. It's my antidepressant, my antipsychotic, my antidote to escape the everyday death-ness of pandemic life. Embarrassingly, these bikinied, jock-strapped airheads appear to give my sad, trapped existence deeper meaning.

Research has shown that relationship reality shows like *The Bachelor/ette* and the *Love Island* franchise cause actual visceral arousal in the viewer, increasing heart rate and releasing pain-suppressing and pleasure-inducing endorphins in the brain. Very similar, in fact, to drug stimulation.

I revel in watching the wall-to-wall dramas and knife-in-the-back betrayals between these wannabe celebrities. From the confines of my bed, I feel something akin to Schadenfreude as devious plans of treachery play out and people are voted off like skittles that come crashing down. Not only do I watch each episode like a hungry hawk eyes its prey, but I also google some of the contestants and follow them on Instagram. As it's a competition to see who will become the ultimate *Love Island* couple, I sometimes "cheat" to find out who will win before that season's grand finale.

I am particularly drawn to an older woman, a Scottish girl called Sophie Gradon. A former Miss Great Britain, Sophie seems a little more intelligent than the rest and appears genuinely broken when contestants turn on her. She obviously suffers from depression and is clearly being tested to her emotional limits as her relationship with barman Tom falls apart. It's scintillating viewing.

Then I make a shocking discovery as I trawl the internet for salacious details of whether Sophie and Tom are still together. In June 2018, two years after she appeared on *Love Island UK*, Sophie commits suicide by hanging herself after imbibing cocaine and alcohol. Three months earlier, she'd revealed in a radio interview that ever since her appearance on the reality show, she'd been a victim of intense cyberbullying and internet trolls.

✳

Did they rape her before they killed her? The Woman, I mean, not Sophie. Did she struggle, scream, shout? Did she try to fight back, rasp and gasp when her final breath exited her body? Were there buckets of blood? Did a scream pierce that silent night, or did they gag her before her terror could shatter that godly peace?

Much like my fascination with the *Love Islanders*, I become obsessed with the details surrounding The Woman's death. Unlike Sophie Gradon, whom I felt I knew intimately, I did not know The Woman who lived just two houses away. Not at all. I see her face for the first time in the Sunday newspapers that report on the murder two days later. I discover that she was an impressive businesswoman: beautiful, statuesque, powerful, at the top of her game in IT at a successful retail chain. She was from a good, well-respected Afrikaner family.

From what I gather by trawling through her Facebook account, she was happily married to The Husband. From their pictures on social media, they look like a couple that had everything, including a multimillion-rand premium SUV. By all appearances, they might even have stood a chance to make it into the finals on *Love Island*.

Chapter 4

RETURNING TO THE SCENE OF THE CRIME

On Sunday, the day after I hear about the murder, I teeter between panic and numb. I am fist-clenched in anxiety. At this stage I know very little about what has happened, besides what I've read on the WhatsApp group and in the newspaper. I don't know any of the estate's homeowners well enough yet to ask for details. I don't even officially own my house yet.

I call my estate agent, who tells me that the caretaker, whom I've mostly dealt with on WhatsApp, is the one who discovered The Woman in her blood-spattered bedroom. I can't bring myself to reach out to him. I am sure he must still be in deep shock.

By Sunday night I am not coping with the not-knowing. There are so many straggling questions. They keep multiplying in my mind, all in a desperate attempt to piece together the sketchy details I've gleaned from the estate agent. What I do know is that there were three men.

Who were they? Where did they come from? Tulbagh? Wolseley? Ceres? It's been a hard year for people who, already destitute, have now been pushed to even deeper levels of indigence and desperation in lockdown. Was it hunger that drove them? Did they see all this wealth and splendour, nestled in the hills of this little private and privileged enclave? Was it envy that drove them, or hunger, or anger, or hatred?

I imagine that all the money they must surely have tried to get for the goods they stole – state-of-the-art flatscreens, the latest iPhones and iPads, all those fancy gadgets they gathered in murderous panic – will soon be spent, and it won't be long before their bellies will groan empty again. The hunger will never cease.

Sometime later I discover that instead of selling or hanging onto their loot, they dumped it in a nearby cemetery – a twist that makes this whole "robbery" and murder a very strange one indeed ...

I try to imagine how they entered our little piece of heaven, our little haven of safety. How did they even get to the estate? Did they walk? I know that they stole my neighbours' car to make their getaway. So they must have arrived on foot. Or did they? Perhaps they got a lift, although I can't imagine that Uber operates in this remote mountainous area. More than anything, I find it hard to understand how they even found this secluded space in the first place, an estate that's completely off the grid, off the map, off any kind of approachable path ... unless you already know that it exists.

Which house did they enter first? Surely, if they had just killed The Woman, would they not have wanted to leave as quickly as possible rather than head to the next property and rob my sleeping next-door neighbours? Perhaps they started there and then moved on to The Woman?

Was it a robbery gone wrong or was her death intentional?

When they forced their way into that big, dark-grey, metal-clad house, was she asleep? *Did they panic did she struggle did she shout did they panic did she fight back did they panic?*

When the rope came out (I have since discovered this detail), did they intend to strangle her or was there a struggle and did they freak out as they pulled it tighter? Did they leave her alive, and did she grow increasingly lifeless as they made their way down the road to rob the elderly couple next door?

At first, I tell myself that they did not mean to murder her, that they made a terrible mistake. If they were cold-blooded killers, surely they would have murdered the couple too? Later, when more details emerge, I find out that they did indeed go to The Woman first. Then they simply walked next door, tied up my neighbours and locked them in the bathroom. I will find it strange when I discover that they treated the elderly woman gently, picking her up so she would not cut her bare feet on the shattered glass of the window broken by the wooden rhino.

Later I will ruminate on this detail many times. That, after brutally killing The Woman, they entered the second house, the one next door to mine, and gently carried their next victim over shattered glass so that she wouldn't injure her bare, just awoken feet? That part of the story seems eerily strange. Like two sets of criminals carried out two entirely different crimes …

※

Around 6pm on Sunday night, I know what I must do. I tell Soul-Mat I need to go back – and I need to go alone. I have to. I know that if I don't return soon, there is a chance that I will never go back to the new house. I know that the longer I stay away, the harder it will be to re-enter the space. I haven't even taken official ownership of it yet, and I'm already wanting to hand the keys back and pull out of the deal. Is there a loophole in home-purchasing legal protocols that allows the buyer to get out of an acquisition if someone is murdered close by?

A few friends I have told are horrified that I am going back alone.

"Don't! You're crazy! They might still be there or come back. Take Mat!"

But I know I must go. Just me.

My dream has been battered, bludgeoned like a wife beater's victim. So I pack a small bag and a few supplies.

On Monday morning, at 5am, when it's still dark and cool in Cape Town, I reverse down our steep driveway and head out on the N1.

I should be stressed.

I should be petrified.

I am strangely calm.

The world is ink-black as I make my way up Du Toitskloof. The 19-kilometre pass, still swathed in pre-dawn mist, is one of the most beautiful carved-out roads into mountains in South Africa. Once used as an animal track reaching into the interior, there were apparently a number of attempts over the centuries to turn it into a pass before it finally got done.

Road building has always fascinated me and, once I'd put in the offer on the new house, I'd read up as much as I could about this one. As I scale up in pre-dawn pitch-blackness, it feels as if I'm having a 19-kilometre-long panic attack, so I try to distract myself from thoughts of murder by thinking of how men built this masterpiece of road engineering.

I know that in the summer of 1941, two years into the Second World War, the building of the pass finally commenced after many years of planning. The workforce came primarily from the 10 000 Italian prisoners of war being held in nearby Worcester. As I steer the car towards the 820-metre summit, I imagine brutally cold winters high up in the mountains, often hampered by snow and freezing winter rain. I'm sure they must have lived like animals in cramped, damp living quarters. It took nine long years to complete the pass and it was officially opened in March 1949 by that racist, Dr DF Malan, the one who would go on to screw up the lives of so many South Africans as he set about implementing his government's policy of racial segregation.

Now I can see nothing in front of me. The mist is so thick it absorbs my car's harsh bright headlights. I'm unsure where the edge of the narrow, winding road ends and where the drop into the deep valley below begins, a long and merciless fall into a bottomless black death trap. Images of the men who blasted rocks and broke their backs, who sweated and toiled to carve out this track, swirl through my mind. Men frozen to the bone in the long winters. I force myself into a place of gratitude. At least I have a car. At least I am not a prisoner of war – just a prisoner of Fear.

Once I've cleared the summit, the black sky slowly transforms, turning grey, then the orange rays of the emerging sun work their magic on the palette of night to day.

It's just before 7am when I arrive on the estate.

It's morgue quiet.

The mansion of murder is now a charcoal-grey coffin, a dark tomb catching the sun's early-morning rays … I half expect to see yellow police tape bound around it, announcing "Crime scene".

I park the car. Heart thumping, I slowly tread the perimeter of my new house. What if they had broken in here and, in the ensuing chaos, no one had checked? What if I discover a huge gash in one of my white, green-rimmed American shuttered windows?

The swallows tweet their morning songs, oblivious to the seething fear that now snakes through the estate, where Cape cobras and puff adders also hunt and nest.

After establishing that there's no sign of a forced entry, no shattered glass or broken windows, I inhale deeply.

I unlock the front door. It's dark inside.

I fumble for the light switch and then, one by one, I open each shutter and let the day in.

My heart is pulsing. First coffee. Then tobacco. I go outside and sit on the deck. Before Friday night, this had felt like the safest place on the planet. Fuck. Just as I feared. In my heart, everything has changed. Everything.

The air is thick with dark deeds of blood and murder. Where I once momentarily languished in a cocoon of safety, I am now white-knuckling the edge of my seat. I stare across at the steel-grey murder house, the one I'd once jokingly called a "coffin", so out of place in this wild and wilful paradise. Now it's the scene of the crime. The huge metal monstrosity obliterates the mountain scenery, obstructs my line of vision. It stands there, planted. A memorial site to remind us that blood has been shed, that heinous deeds are indeed possible even in the most heavenly of places.

It's more than heartbreak that I feel. It's huge and violent anger. How can one night have changed everything?

✳

I need to speak to someone. I need to find out what happened and hear how the others are coping. It's only 7.30am. The estate is otherworldly silent. People are either asleep or dead. So I head across the gravel road to find out whether my opposite neighbour is awake.

He is an old Afrikaner, and hard of hearing. After I knock, he eventually comes outside. He seems strangely relaxed. Of course he is upset, he says, but life goes on.

There is nothing that can undo what has happened.

That's it.

I go home and make more coffee.

Then there's a bang on my door. My heart triple-jumps.

It's my neighbour on the lower side – another one I have yet to meet. We sit on the deck overlooking the breathtaking Breedekloof valley, careful to avert our eyes from the morgue to the right.

It's bizarre that he and I connect under these circumstances. We do not swap the usual trivia that might emerge when meeting a stranger for the first time. We cut straight to death.

"I think I'm going to get a gun," he says.

"Do you know how to shoot?" I ask.

"No, but I can learn."

"I think I'm going to get a dog," I say. "Yesterday, I did consider a gun, but I don't think I could live with one. I will always be aware of it. It will be with me all the time; it will drive me mad even if I learn how to use it. It will cause me so much stress. I will be constantly shrouded in the possibility of violence all the fucking time. I don't think I can live with that."

We sit and stare into the valley, silently contemplating our options to ward off future violence. The beauty of the scenery that unfolds before us cannot penetrate our wall of fear. How did it all come to this? A single night, one tightening of a rope, and everything is blood-soiled.

He eventually leaves.

The caretaker who discovered The Woman's body arrives a few hours later. Years ago, he fought in Angola in the Border War. He has seen a lot. He's a tough Afrikaner. A man who confesses to not normally being shaken by violence.

"I have seen many dead bodies in my life, but never anything like this." He takes a deep drag on his Rothmans Red. "I went with her to the nursery that morning ... We bought plants. She was so happy and excited. And then I had to see her lying dead like that. This country is fucked."

Words escape me. I should reach over and touch his weathered hand. But I don't. We sit in silence. I wonder what flowers she liked.

Later in the day, a friend from a nearby small town pops by with biscuits. I make coffee. She cuts to the chase. She believes there are many things that don't make sense about the two crimes. For example, after they murder The Woman and rob my neighbours, the men ditch some of the stolen goods in a cemetery and abandon the car a little further on. So was this even a robbery?

She tells me of a growing suspicion around town that The Woman's murder is looking more and more like a hit. *A hit?* Who would want to kill this beautiful and successful woman? I can't wrap my head around it. Perhaps she angered one of the builders who constructed the grey, metal-clad house? Maybe she had enemies at work?

My friend decides to call one of the top cops in the area. She puts him on speaker phone and motions me to keep quiet.

"*Hoe gaan dit met die ondersoek?*"

I hear the crackle of a man's voice. "*Alles 'n bietjie stil vandag, my ou ding. Maar jy weet niks maak sin nie.*"

"*Wat bedoel jy?*" She looks at me knowingly. I move in closer.

"*Kyk, oor die jare het ons al baie misdade in hierdie deel van die land ondersoek, maar hierdie twee ... Hierdie twee maak geen sin nie.*"

My Afrikaans isn't great, but I manage to get the gist of what he is saying. That they've investigated many crimes in the area over the years, but these two – the murder and the robbery – don't make any sense.

"*Ons is nou besig om deur die man se selfoon rekords te gaan.*"

Jesus. That much I understand. That's hectic ... "*Die man*"? They are going through The Husband's cellphone records. *The Husband?*

Of course in any murder, it's quite normal to look at the people closest to the victim, but now my mind races with dark and twisted imaginings. I channel my trauma into curiosity. I force myself to focus on trying to solve the crime. I am ashamed that I am perversely intrigued to discover more gory details. I tell myself it's better than allowing myself to contort my head into a knot of panic accompanied by triple-terror heartbeats.

If this was indeed a hit, then it would remove the arbitrariness of this unexpected and senseless crime that has, overnight, torn apart the peace and tranquillity of this estate.

After my friend leaves, I search The Woman on Instagram. Her account is still live. Her profile is filled with love and laughter. She looks so happy, so successful, so rich, so elegant and so in love with her husband.

But then we all know that we only post happy pics on Insta. The rose-tinted-glasses ones. I try to clear my brain of dark thoughts. The entire situation seems too unreal.

I don't even know this woman. What I do know, though, is that my "playing detective" is a coping mechanism, a form of bargaining with reality, as in Kübler-Ross's five stages of grief. I'm trapped between "denial" and "bargaining". I know I am trying to avoid grieving for my safety, for my dream that's been shattered overnight, by pretending I'm Lieutenant Fucking Columbo.

Why am I not aching for The Woman who's been bludgeoned to death?

How can I be so callous and simultaneously intrigued by sensationalist theories?

But I can't stop myself wondering: "What if?"

Chapter 5

HOME ALONE

The night draws in. The entire day has been spent dredging up details of The Woman's murder. All the talk of hits and motives and scaled-up security measures, of guns and cameras, walkie-talkies, farm-patrol groups, panic buttons, alarms and tasers has done my head in.

It's just me now. Home. Alone. Oh God, I need a stiff one – or at least something that will quell this panic. I don't drink. I don't take nerve calmers. My anxiety tightens like that rope pulled taut around the neck of The Woman.

I get into my pyjamas.

I pace up and down my wooden floors, directionless.

I move outside to my deck. I try to focus on the majestic sunset, the six-foot Buddha statue that keeps watch over my unfenced property. My racing heart erases the panoramic views. The sinking sun, the rising moon.

As the estate darkens, I begin to notice that the only lights that I see are from my own home. The house next door, belonging to the robbed Dutch couple, usually brightly lit and familiar, is now pitch-black except for a tiny, sinister blue light that shows that the alarm is active.

The big grey house of murder is blotted out, ink-black. Higher up on the hill there's no sign of life. The lights at my opposite neighbour are out too. He's gone to sleep.

Further down I see that the caretaker's lights are still on. So, apart from him, I am all on my own here. Fuck. Every creak, every whisper of wind stabs fear into my heart.

I decide to barricade myself in.

The previous owner spent a small fortune on American shutters on every window and door and so I check each slat, each lock, and seal myself in. Now I am caged up in a wooden, steel-fortified box.

I could be anywhere. Tokyo, Joburg, Melbourne, Louisville.

But I'm not. I am all alone on a huge, empty, unfenced plot of land in the middle of nowhere, where just three nights ago a woman was brutally murdered. What happened to my "escape from The Pandemic" plan? What happened to my purchase of Joy and Freedom? All that remains is me, here, trapped in my fortress of fear.

I climb into bed. It's not even 8pm. I start googling: *Are American shutters really safe?*

And *Can you break through American shutters?*

A Vimeo pops up showing the set-up of an attempted break-in. The "robber", who looks like a harmless stoner, hauls a hammer and crowbar from his grimy rucksack. Despite his rather wimpy attempts to break through the metal, for the sake of the advert, he is unable to penetrate the aluminium.

Jesus, I am going mad.

Now I begin playing through scenarios of a break-in, of an attack on my cabin. What would I actually do if I heard someone trying to get in?

I know there's a large, blunt meat cleaver in the kitchen. That's about the closest I have to a weapon. I have a set of steak knives, but they too are dull-edged. I've been told that squirting Spray & Cook into an attacker's eyes can temporarily blind him. I don't use the stuff. Too many GMOs.

I eye the panic button to the right of my bedroom door. I know there's another one beneath the kitchen counter. I climb out of bed and retrieve my house keys, which have both a panic and an alarm button, and take them back to bed with me, placing them within reach right next to my pillow.

This is not the way it's supposed to be, I keep muttering to myself.

I need to put an end to this paranoia, this mad-mad mind of mine. I download an episode of *Love Island UK*. Season 6. Episode 1. I recognise the scenery. It's been filmed in Cape Town.

The first thing I notice is that the bubbly blonde presenter, Caroline Flack, has been replaced with a frothy, flaxen-haired doppelgänger. That's weird. Why would they ditch The Flack? She was pretty much the one constant, the heart and soul of the series.

I start googling.

"Caroline Flack was found dead in her flat in Stoke Newington, London, on 15 February 2020, aged 40. The lawyer acting for her family stated that her death was a suicide."

What the actual fuck! *The Flack*? The pretty presenter who looked so together and bouncy in every single episode of *Love Island UK* I'd been glued to since the start of lockdown? I'd only recently finished Season 5.

On 15 February 2020? This was unbelievable. So all the while I'd watched back seasons, she'd been dead? She'd seemed so alive. And how did I not know that she'd killed herself over a year ago, just before we went into lockdown?

I scramble to read more.

Apparently, on the night of 12 December 2019, Caroline had discovered a text from another woman on the phone of her athlete boyfriend, Lewis Burton. She'd lost her shit and ended up hitting him with a lamp, allegedly while he was asleep, leaving him with a cut on his head. He'd called the police to report that his girlfriend was "trying to kill me". She would maintain that it was an accident.

While waiting for the cops to arrive, a highly emotional and distraught Caroline grabbed a glass, smashed it and cut herself, leaving blood all over the bed. When the police arrived, the apartment was in disarray and looked as if there'd indeed been an attempted murder. Most of the blood was Caroline's. The police took her into custody, and the following day, a Sunday, charged her with assault.

Four days later, following the scandal that inevitably erupted, management of *Love Island UK*, the series that had made her a global sensation, terminated her contract for Season 6. Caroline had lived and breathed the series. According to friends, her dismissal sent her into a deep spiral of depression, an affliction she had suffered from since childhood but had managed to keep out of the public eye by adopting a bright, upbeat social persona.

On 23 December, she appeared in court and lodged a not-guilty plea. At this stage, Lewis tried to withdraw the charges but the state opted to go ahead with its case. According to friends and family, Caroline was petrified she would end up in prison if found guilty of assault. She was also highly stressed that the public would find out about her mental-health and self-harming issues if the police's video footage of the night of the assault, showing her bleeding, half-undressed and threatening to kill herself, was used against her in court. The hearing was scheduled for 4 March 2020.

The media and public had always been obsessed with The Flack but, with the assault case pending, things hit an all-time low. She was suddenly labelled "the most hated woman in Britain", and the trolls and clickbait-obsessed social media had a field day, delivering one cruel blow after another.

On Valentine's Day, her good friend Lou stayed the night

because she was "not in a good way". The following morning Caroline sent Lou home, insisting that she was "fine". She then hanged herself.

First Sophie Gradon. Then Caroline Flack. Two beautiful, intelligent but emotionally fragile women on *Love Island* who had been hunted down by the tabloids, crucified by social media, and had snuffed out their own lives, unable to cope with the venom. And now, of course, there's The Woman, who had every intention of living, who had just bought plants at a nursery, who didn't want to die, whose life was literally strangled right out of her.

I sit cross-legged in bed in my Hello Kitty pyjamas, in my barricaded room, clutching my panic button. I contemplate these three women and the ghosts of other women who are no longer with us. Dead by their own hand or by the hand of another. I remember my own sad past self who for so many years wanted to die.

I start to sob, big hulking gasps of sorrow. But when I am spent and there are no more tears left to shed, I realise that my ache is not just for the cruelty, the violence and the arbitrariness of life and death; it is also for my dream of safety, the implosion of the notion that I had finally found a room of my own – for the dream that had just been slaughtered.

Chapter 6

TO ESCAPE OR NOT TO ESCAPE

"He who jumps into the void owes no explanation to those who stand and watch."
– Jean-Luc Godard

By the time I found the new house in January 2021, my craving for freedom, for a new vista to settle my brain, contorted in anxiety, was palpable. For decades, long before the virus came along, I had dreamt of some kind of "escape house". But back then, in my naivety, I hadn't fully understood how much I would need it one day or what "freedom" even really meant. Just as Joni Mitchell sings in "Big Yellow Taxi": we don't know what we've got till it's gone …

And so, too, especially when it comes to the concept of freedom, we only realise what we had once we've lost it.

✳

Like so many woman writers, I'd carried Virginia Woolf's "every woman needs a room of her own" in a secret compartment of my heart ever since I decided I wanted to write, age 12. Like me, Caroline, Sophie and countless other women, Virginia also suffered from suicidal ideation; the only difference was that they'd managed to do it and I hadn't.

After twice attempting suicide by taking an apparent overdose of her husband's medication, the barbiturate Veronal, Virginia, finally managed to shake off her mortal coil by filling her overcoat pockets with stones, walking into the River Ouse, and drowning herself.

Probably my favourite writer of all time, Sylvia Plath, had also managed to take the plunge. By the time I found the house, apart from a brief flare-up at the start of The Pandemic, I had long set aside the desire to kill myself, but suicide still fascinated me.

I'd often wondered about the house in which Sylvia, at the age of 30, died by her own hand. I even knew off by heart the address where her self-determined exit took place on 11 February 1963: 23 Fitzroy Road, Primrose Hill, London. I'd visited it on my first trip to that city.

Sylvia had chosen this house carefully two months before she ended it, after her marriage to her Welsh husband, the poet laureate Ted Hughes, collapsed like a sad sandcastle crushed by a nonchalant wave. Like me when I first set eyes on the "escape from The Pandemic" house, Sylvia had been overjoyed when she had found the place. The bronze plaque on the maisonette in Fitzroy Road, signifying where one of her hero poets, William Butler Yeats, had spent his childhood, had thrilled her. Believing she had finally found "a room of her own", she'd signed a five-year lease on the apartment, to finally "write, write, write".

At that point, Sylvia had not earned the kind of recognition male poets like Yeats or her husband enjoyed, but it would be in that house that Sylvia, in a frenzied outburst of creative genius, would go on to pen some of the finest lines in English literature.

I'd love nothing more than to shower glory on Sylvia and fill the narrative here with quotes from her poems. Like the first line from "Morning Song", where she writes how love sets us going like a fat gold watch. Or the opener in "Stopped Dead" in which she compares a squeal of brakes to a birth cry. Oh, don't get me started on my Sylvia … But apparently, it's a real bitch trying to secure publishing rights from the Hughes estate, so my enthusiasm here must be cauterised.

Talking of rights … After Sylvia's brutal death, Ted got to pick and choose what would be included in his wife's posthumously published *Ariel* collection. In the first edition, in 1965, a trove of her genius verse that referred to her six-foot philandering husband in an unflattering light, got the executioner's treatment: "The Rabbit Catcher", "Thalidomide", "Barren Woman", "A Secret", "The Jailor", "The Detective", "Magi", "The Other", "The Courage of Shutting Up", "Purdah" and "Amnesiac".

While I am not a Ted-hater – in fact, I love his poetry, especially "The Thought Fox" and his play *Prometheus on Crag* – I find it sad that the very one who had driven her to such desperation was the one who got to decide what to include in her book. I also find it hard to get my head around the fact that on the night that Sylvia took her life, Ted was in bed with another woman – not Assia Wevill for whom he had left Sylvia in July 1962, but a new one, Susan Alliston, whom he was seeing behind both Assia's and Sylvia's backs.

According to a number of biographers, Sylvia had been compulsively calling Ted the entire weekend prior to her death, striding in the freezing sleet and London snow to a call box on the corner to spit her venom. To escape the incessant ringing that crackled and cackled outbursts of Sylvia's rage of betrayal, Ted allegedly left the apartment to stay at a friend's in order to get "some space" with Susan, his secret new lover.

On the night in February 1963 that Sylvia decided to shove her head into the gas oven, the UK was in the midst of an especially harsh winter. Known as the "Big Freeze of 1963", it was one of the bitterest on record, with only those of 1683–1684 and 1739–1740 apparently colder.

After Ted had upped and left their marital home in Devon, in

July 1962, where they'd lived as a happy and successful poet couple, and birthed two young children, Sylvia tried hard to navigate a new life as a single mother and poet in the sprawling country house. But by October of that year she had had enough. She wrote to her mother, Aurelia in the United States: "I miss brains, hate this cow life, am dying to surround myself with intelligent, good people."

So it was that Sylvia arrived in London in the December of 1962 and quickly fell in love with Yeats' old house in Primrose Hill. A single mother to their daughter Frieda, who was just three, and son Nicholas, who had not yet turned one, she hoped to find her footing again in the intellectually stimulating life of the city. She also, more than likely, wanted to be in closer proximity to Ted, perhaps hoping to win him back.

But during that freezing December, London was not exactly the social buzz she'd yearned for. Although Ted did visit to see the children, he was clearly involved with not one, but two other women. Most days, it was too cold to set foot outside. Snow fell heavily. The air hung thick across the city, dense with the smoke from coal fires as households tried to ward off the icy freeze. Christmas must have been a dismal affair, the first without her husband.

In between trying to take care of her two needy young children, she did, however, make progress with the collection of poetry she'd started in October 1962, the month in which she had turned 30. In a frenzy of words exploding like a newly discovered oil well spurting black gold, inspired by her marital betrayal, she produced the *Ariel* collection, which on its publication in 1965, two years after her death, would make her one of the world's most celebrated poets.

Deeply depressed, struggling to sleep and keep it together, in January, Sylvia finally reached out for help and consulted Dr John Horder, who'd become her GP in London. She revealed to him that the debilitating depression she'd suffered earlier in life had reared its surly head again after she discovered Ted's affair back in Devon seven months earlier. In his notes, Dr Horder recorded her state of mind as "marked by constant agitation, suicidal thoughts and inability to cope with daily life".

Sylvia had by now lost a lot of weight, although a friend noted that she continued to make an effort with her appearance. From what his patient told him, Dr Horder clearly deduced that Sylvia, alone with her two children, was someone at risk and so he prescribed an antidepressant and visited the Fitzroy Road house daily. He recommended, too, that she be admitted to hospital but Sylvia refused. He then arranged that she employ a carer, which she did.

The shocking weather in London continued. For Sylvia there must have been no sign of thaw or hope. In early February 1963, a 36-hour blizzard swept across England and Wales, causing snow drifts of up to six metres in places, blocking roads and obstructing rail lines. Stuck in the London house with two toddlers, Sylvia must have been losing her mind. Trying to write while attempting to be a mother, while her heart raged and bled for Ted, must have been brutal. I'd been there once.

There was no respite.

On 9 February, she sent an emotional letter to Ted, a kind of blackmail rant of sorts, telling him she planned to leave the UK with the children and would never see him again. I suspect she hoped her words would force his hand and lure him back. Like so many men, Ted probably retreated even further. Nobody loves a crazy woman. I can vouch for that.

When Ted arrived at the Fitzroy Road house with her letter on Saturday, Sylvia apparently snatched it out of his hands and burnt it. The following night, on 10 February 1963, a Sunday, Sylvia executed her plan. She tucked little Frieda and baby Nicholas into their cots in their bedroom upstairs. Then she poured two cups of milk and placed them alongside two slices of buttered bread, which she left beside her children. Despite sub-freezing temperatures, she opened the window of the bedroom and, closing the door on her sleeping babies, sealed the doorframe with tape and shoved tea towels into the gaps. Such sad consideration.

I imagine she must have done this robotically. Clinically, in fact. She'd thought it through. A considerate suicide. Her mind was set. Like a fat gold watch.

Although I understand her thinking – I had been in the deepest pit of my dark days in my early thirties, trying to find a gun, contemplating rat poison, or imagining drowning like Virginia and the poet, Ingrid Jonker – the part where Sylvia decides to leave her children upstairs is the detail that still haunts me.

I had been at my most suicidal when my boys were tiny, but despite me being smacked out and cracked up during those stifling days of their early childhood, their existence put the brakes on my plans. To be able to carry out her mission, Sylvia must have been in such a no-hope cul de sac that not even the knowledge of her defenceless babies in the room upstairs could have deterred her.

Perhaps, on that freezing night, she believed that everyone was better off without her. Depression makes one feel that way – deeply, despairingly useless. But I always wondered how, having actually thought it through, she had been so certain. Was she without any doubt that her nurse/carer would arrive that Monday morning to discover Frieda and Nicholas? The transport system had all but shut down due to the deep snow and dangerous ice across London. Did she know with absolute certainty that the gas with which she planned to kill herself would not find a way to seep and swirl from the kitchen and make its way upstairs? It seemed like a risky plan.

Downstairs, in the tiny kitchen, she mechanically folded a

little cloth as a type of pillow for her head. She arranged it on the open oven door. She knelt down. She lit the gas. She placed her head on the square of cloth, her final resting place, and allowed the noxious fumes to drift and carry her away.

I often think about those precise actions and the method she chose. I wonder whether it was when she first saw Yeats' house back in December 1962, when she noticed the gas oven, that the notion, her plan of escape, first flashed in her head. Probably not. After all, she'd signed a five-year lease. But her choice of place … It was surely some kind of statement to kill herself in the kitchen? I guess she needed a weapon and the gas oven was at hand, but on a deeper level, I understood how powerfully symbolic that functional room was, a reminder of the cage of motherhood in which she found herself.

The round-the-clock preparation of meals for dependants can be a noose around the neck for a mother, but it must have been especially brutal for Sylvia, now man-less, money-less and audience-less, as yet unrecognised for her genius as a poet. All while her soulmate, her nemesis and now her betrayer, Ted, the toast of the literary scene in Britain, held new women in his arms.

When the carer Dr Horder had arranged, arrived at 9am that Monday morning of 11 February, the house was locked. Despite the woman's persistent knocking, no one answered the door. Perhaps she heard the wailing of the children inside? Surely Nicholas and Frieda must have woken by now? Perhaps the nurse became aware of their plaintive cries through the locked front door? We might never know. Something told the nurse not to turn back home, and she finally gained entry with the help of a workman. On entering, they found the lifeless Plath with her head deep in the oven, the gas still leaking.

Sylvia left us her poems. And me with a death wish and a love of the dark.

Chapter 7

THE KITCHEN WON'T DO

In the years when I contemplated ending it, often hourly, the kitchen – perhaps like for Sylvia – was the room that most reminded me of my failings. It symbolised all the societal and pseudo-expectations forced on mothers, that just because I had a slit between my legs that bled and birthed, I was the one expected to prepare meals, three times a day, seven times a week, 365 days of the year. Biology was my executioner. Time, in all its predictability, stretched ahead – a gaping, mocking yawn.

Shopping for food while depressed was torture. Aisles and aisles of indecision. I could not choose between a carrot and a bean. The muddle of a mind consumed by a death wish can prevent one from making even the most rudimentary choices. But, unlike Plath's freezing London in 1963, Klerksdorp, South Africa, in late 1998, was boiling. Too hot to even properly kill myself.

The one time I did seriously try to end it, I chose to do so outside on the veranda, so as not to spill blood on the kitchen tiles in the home given to us by my husband's mother. Like bait at the end of a rod, she had hoped that her "gift" would lure us to that godforsaken town and get clean. Perhaps it would be some incentive to transform ourselves from two lost and useless junkies into stable and productive parents. A house can be a great pretender. A facade that hides the weeping rot and deceit behind the curtains and carefully grouted tiles.

On the day I decided to stop breathing, I had made sure that my three-month-old baby and almost two-year-old son were with her, their grandmother. I think it was a Wednesday. I know it was 34 degrees and sweltering. My husband had invited me to accompany him to an 11am showing of *Titanic* in an air-conditioned cinema in town, a movie that had already won Best Picture at the Oscars in February that year. I declined. I watched his car roll down the driveway.

Finally. Home alone. At last.

That day was not one grasped at impulsively. To kill yourself needs careful planning. In principle, you have to be on your own. An audience will only disrupt the mission.

I have no recollection what month it was, but I clearly remember the glassy heat of the day. So it was definitely summer. I had been planning to do this for a while, long before my red-faced youngest, my colicky second son, made his way through my unwilling birth canal in August 1998. I have a strong feeling it must have been November. Around my mother's birthday.

By that point, I had stopped reading and watching the news. When all one can think of is dying or scoring, what point is there knowing what is unfolding in the world outside the head? Years later, now clean, when I was trying to piece my shattered life back together, I would realise that in 1998 I wasn't the only one having a shit time. The year was also a shocker for Bill Clinton.

Although he wasn't a junkie, he definitely had serious compulsive issues. This was the same year that he went on US television and denied ever having had "sexual relations" with *that* woman. Very few believed him. I didn't care enough to have an opinion. His wife, Hillary (who I'm almost sure didn't believe him either), kept up a poker Hamptons face in public. A day after her husband publicly blanked Monica, Hillary went on *The Today Show* and defended Bill, claiming that the accusations were part of a "vast right-wing conspiracy". By the end of 1998, Bill had been impeached.

I do have some vague recollection of watching CNN that year and seeing blood-stained shoppers flee a shopping centre in Kenya's capital. The footage flickered in the background while I scraped the dregs of a crack pipe. Years later, when I googled the incident, I discovered that a bomb had been detonated at the US embassies in Dar es Salaam in Tanzania and Nairobi, Kenya, in August 1998, which would explain the blood-spattered people I recall seeing. I would subsequently learn that 224 people died, with 4 500 injured in the blasts. The name Osama bin Laden meant nothing to most of us back then, but the US Secret Service linked him to the terror attack.

Bin Laden would ultimately be held responsible for master-minding the implosion of the Twin Towers in 2001 – which, by the way, is something I do remember. By then I had been clean for two years and I vividly recall watching the incident intently as I left a yoga class.

While my world back in 1998 had shrunk – becoming tightly insular, my only thoughts on scoring, using and killing myself – in the same month (August) that I turned 32, a birthday that passed me by like a powdery dust cloud, two guys who were definitely getting their shit together were Larry Page and Sergey Brin. The duo were given $100,000 by another guy, Andy Bechtolsheim, to fund their start-up and, 14 days after my entirely forgettable birthday, on 4 September 1998, Google Inc. was born.

I, of course, was also completely oblivious that, in the weeks leading up to my botched "goodbye-cruel-world, fuck-you-cruel-world" attempt, while I was reading the list of ingredients on the box of rat poison, and conjuring plans to steal my brother-in-law's gun, a young college student from Wyoming was tied to a fence, tortured and beaten to a pulp by two gay bashers

50

who also robbed him. A cyclist, who at first thought that he had spotted a scarecrow, found a torn-up, bloodied young man hanging from a fence. He was still breathing, but only barely. He died a few days later from massive head trauma. His name was Matthew Shepard.

So, while Google was being birthed, Bill was being impeached, Matthew was bleeding out, skewered to a fence, I was scraping pipes and trying to conjure ways to die. I do, however, clearly remember listening to "Bittersweet Symphony" by The Verve for most of that year. The epitome of a 90s junkie rock god, lead singer Richard Ashcroft was skeletal and elegantly wasted. His hollow face, bulging eyes and gaping mouth evoked Munch's *The Scream*. Unsurprisingly, Richard's lyrics pick-axed my soul. His words drew me in, telling of how we were slaves to "the money" and then we died. He made me want to end it all as he sung about life – that bittersweet symphony.

But, in trying to recall the bigger world against which I attempt to snuff out my tiny inconsequential life, I digress ... Not having a gas stove, access to pills, a gun or a sea in which to drown myself, once I was certain my husband was not going to return unexpectedly from the cinema, once all alone, I took a large glass Coke bottle, smashed it against a stone and sliced it hard across my wrist in the desperate hope that I would bleed out before the credits rolled for *Titanic*. I knew it was a three-hour-14-minute movie. I'd checked.

However, I made a rookie mistake by cutting horizontally across, instead of vertically down. This is a common error that many people make when trying to kill themselves, and so it's perhaps unfairly labelled as a "cry for attention" rather than a genuine attempt to die. At the time, I felt as though I meant it, but who knows ... Maybe it was indeed a desperate holler across the callous dust bowls of AWB-infested Klerksdorp.

As I stared at the red blood seeping through the strange fold of skin now opened like a tin of tuna, I knew it hadn't worked. Dripping in shame – there was now hard evidence of my insanity and failures – I wrapped a tea towel, like the one Sylvia had used to stop the noxious gas from seeping into her babies' room, around my weeping wrist. I then made my way across the road to the neighbour and asked if I could borrow a phone to call my husband to take me to the doctor.

My wound was bleeding profusely. He was not impressed having to leave before Jack and Rose took their curtain call to Celine Dion's "My Heart Will Go On". On that day, I wished mine had stopped.

Chapter 8

THE PRISONS I'VE LIVED IN

"Get out! Get out of this house, you motherfucker! Leave. Go!"

It was a few months later. My sliced-wrist scab had by now slowly turned into a sad white scar reminder.

The man who snarled from across the living room was my husband. His words cut deeper than my wrist-slit. Ever since my botched attempt at death, my fellow drug lover and life partner, the one I'd dragged out of *Titanic*, had given up on the idea that I was ever coming back. So had I.

✳

I am crumpled into the couch in a corner of the Klerksdorp house. If I don't make a sound, I might disappear between the cracks where the cushions meet the sofa.

My husband sits across the room in the olive-green, brushed velvet armchair. His mother has gifted it to us along with the rest of the furniture that now inhabits this house after we are dragged from our wedding-present home in Westdene to Klerksdorp. There's been a family intervention – by both my family and his – to try to kill our appetites for heroin and crack cocaine. They've discovered that we are still in deep addiction despite the arrival of our firstborn. They've been praying that if we are spirited away from the lure of drugs in Joburg that we will stop. We don't.

The house they move us into is perched on the outskirts of the dusty mining hellhole that is Klerksdorp, far enough away from the rest of the conservative town to hide the evidence of shame that we have brought on his well-heeled family. The following year we have another baby.

"What are you still doing here?" he growls. His pupils are black. He's just hit the crack pipe and offered me nothing. Diddly fucking squat.

I stare at a cigarette burn hole in the beige wall-to-wall carpet. I am totally still except for my heart. It's jittering. Yearning. Desperately craving.

He cradles both our small sons in his arms, but still finds a way to hold the glass pipe in his mouth as he lights the tiny white rock and takes his next hit to oblivion. To me, he looks like a caring father, while I ... I can't hold a thing.

I eye the sizzling crack pipe. I fight the urge to leap from the couch and kill this motherfucker who won't share the spoils, scored just hours ago in Joburg. After all, I was the one who lifted two purple notes from his mother's crocodile-leather wallet when she came by to check on us this morning. These days, whenever she visits – which is every day – I wear long sleeves to hide the shame of my botched suicide.

My expulsion from the Klerksdorp house, my dry bosom of enablement, occurs a few months later, one afternoon in April 1999. My boys are ripped from me by his mother. He goes to rehab. I go to hell.

✳

The rooms in which I find myself during the last months of my using, before I get clean in September 1999, are crowded with hookers and dealers and junkies. The smell of bicarbonate of soda mixed with cocaine sizzles off glass crack pipes. The sickly sweet reek of heroin cut with strychnine, sliding down scraps of tinfoil, invades my nostrils. Each Hillbrow hotel room resembles the next. Bodies strewn across floors. Are they dead or high? Narcotic narcolepsy.

I feel perfectly at home here, where I will slip seamlessly from the life of a fucked-up junkie housewife with a coffee percolator, two babies, a full-time maid and a worrisome drug problem, to one of a cracked-out, skeletal whore.

How fast it happens, that demise, that decline from "unmanageable" to "unredeemable". How quickly I forget the life from which I have been expelled.

As I travel from one hotel to the next, kicked out of one room after another, I keep an eye on Ponte, the 54-storeyed, 173-metre-high conical building on the edge of Hillbrow nicknamed "Suicide Central". I'm strangely comforted by its entirely hollow core. When I have had enough of the drug hell in which I now find myself, when these dark and dingy rooms no longer feel like home, I plan to plunge into its moonless vortex.

I'm ripped off the streets by my family before I can jump.

⁜

Two decades later, in the early days of The Pandemic, when we are forced to stay inside, I am reminded of those dark days before I got a life.

Sometimes rooms can be prisons.

My childhood one in Roosevelt Park, Johannesburg, feels like a cage in which captured lions mark the passing of days, dull eyes listlessly dreaming of springbok bounding across endless savanna. In that room, I lie on my bed, glassy-eyed, after our father suddenly drops dead at the age of 40. I am four. It's a Wednesday afternoon. Dates are weird. They seem to mean something, have significance.

I stop using drugs on 1 September 1999, and his heart stops beating on 2 September 1970 as he bends to turn up the volume on the old gramophone in the dining room. Then: Bang. Crash. Dead.

"Close to You", one of the big hits of that year, by The Carpenters, could have been playing. The one in which Karen croons, wondering why birds suddenly appear, every time "you are near".

I have always hated The Carpenters and their sickly, goody-two-shoes vibe, with their toothy smiley faces and perfect pageboy haircuts. Meanwhile, behind the scenes, Karen was crumbling. Starving herself to death. Like my dad, she too would die from heart failure. She was only 32.

Back in 1970, before he hits the floor with a thud, my father works at a bank. I am not sure why on this day, midweek, he is at home. The year is a weird one in South Africa, but for the majority of whites, this is a time of heavenly Aryan domination. BJ Vorster is prime minister. It's the decade in which gold is king. In 1970, the rand is double the worth of the pound. It's the calm before the storm.

I will spend most of my life trying to imagine who my father really was. I know that he loved rugby. I know that he had one glass eye. When he was a young man, he'd had the left one gouged out in a vicious scrum. Because he loved the game so much, I imagine he must have spent the last few months of his life glued to the radio, listening to the All Blacks' tour of South Africa. This was the one for which three Māori players from New Zealand were given "honorary white status" so that they could play in whites-only South Africa. I am sure he must have been overjoyed that South Africa won the series 3–1. I am not sure whether my dad had any opinion about the Māori players or whether he was racist. I know my mother was. I really hope he wasn't.

Outside the country, Charles Manson releases his album *Lie: The Love and Terror Cult*. The Concorde makes its first supersonic flight at a speed of 700 miles per hour. The *Apollo 13* mission launches and "Houston, we have a problem" is broadcast across the world.

The Vietnam war rages on in East Asia, the North Tower of the World Trade Center in New York is completed, and the Methodist Church allows women to become full-time ministers, while the Miss World pageant is disrupted by Women's Liberation Movement protests. South Africa doesn't yet have television, but I am sure my dad knows these things by listening to the news on the wooden radio.

Sixteen days after Dad dies, Jimi Hendrix is found dead in Kensington, London. Janis Joplin is found deceased (also from a drug overdose) a few weeks later.

I will only learn about these individuals and events much later because, at four years old, in 1970, I have no idea what is happening in the world, in my country, in the suburbs, or even in the rooms of our house. I will only learn how to read actual words the following year.

Everything is covered up with a shroud of silence, including my father's death.

After that black day when he leaves us, and for many years to come, I will lie on my bed, staring at the ceiling that stretches upwards, the walls narrowing, closing in.

It is in this room-cage that I am catapulted overnight into the realisation that life holds no guarantees, that death awaits us all like some bald vulture hovering on the periphery. It is a harrowing, watershed moment.

Although I will not have the words to express this at the time, after my father's sudden death, I will realise my powerlessness, and that this thing called "life" is destined to end in a thing called "death". Which means *I will die*. The horror of it is a shocking awakening. If my father can disappear just like that, then so can my mother – and so can I.

The realisation hurtles me out of my naive sense of safety into full-blown neurosis. At the age of four, I meet existential terror for the first time. It is my entrance into the theatre of absurdity, otherwise known as human existence. My introduction to vulnerability. It aches deep within and terrifies me. I make a subconscious vow that, going forward, I will do everything I can to *not* experience loss and pain. I will consider sadness and weakness my enemies. And I will expect death at every intersection.

After my dad's evaporation, I soon notice that my mother enjoys drinking. Glasses of wine hidden around the house tell me that it is her secret. I will start drinking by the time I'm nine. For close to a decade, before I leave "home", I will conjure up plans of escape while I gulp stolen brandy at every opportunity. I will have recurring nightmares of my dad, dead on the floor. I'll think about dying a lot, but I will be most tormented by the notion of my own passing. I will come to the realisation that, if we are all to die, what is the point of living? And so I will begin my journey of glorious self-immolation.

That death urge shadows me and follows me to Cape Town in 1985, after matric, during the first year of the State of Emergency in South Africa, where I register at the University of Cape Town as a drama student.

My first "digs" is a dank, grimy room above a bottle store in Kloof Street where the bergies congregate, shrieking alcohol-infused obscenities deep into the night. The reek of booze seeping through the floorboards is familiar. It feels like home. The Cape wind's tentacles screech through cracks in the windowpanes.

When I am not acting, getting drunk or stoned, I'm eating.

Over the next three years, I'll move in and out of rooms a dozen times. While the addresses and shapes and sizes of the boxes I inhabit change, my hunger for erasure doesn't.

Most days I find myself cross-legged on the mattress that I drag along from one room to the next. Piles of junk food comfort me. I shove marshmallows, chips, biscuits, doughnuts down my throat. I am a chewing wind-up doll. Only once my belly is distended, resembling that of some Somali famine victim, unable to squeeze in another morsel, will I head for the room to which I am most beholden of all the rooms I move through: the bathroom.

I will clutch the cistern as if it is my marble Greek lover, heave up the binge, and destroy all evidence with a flush to destroy my shame. Post-vomit, the death urge will return – it is only the sweetness of junk food that can distract me from my obsession with obliteration.

By the time I graduate, I've disposed of enough food, by hurling it up into the drains that run like veins beneath the city, to feed the entire homeless population on Kloof Street. I am, however, devoid of any conscience when it comes to the waste I have executed.

It is my retch of rage against life, against death, against the State of Emergency, against the racist government, against my father's passing, against my slurring mother, collected in a sick bag containing all my privileged whiteness.

Years later, when I end up on a homeless farm in the Magaliesberg, post my Hillbrow drug wreckage, I'll rub shoulders with "outies" like the ones I passed by on Kloof Street as a 19-year-old student. Tramps, beggars, bergies. Except this time I've left that oblivious teenaged self far behind. I'm now one of them. An outcast. I'm 32 years old.

I've been delivered from the dark side, the ghetto of vampires, rescued by my brother and sister who find my soulless, skeletal body roaming the sordid streets of the Brow, screeching for a hit. Against my will, they bundle me into a car. Like an unwanted parcel with no return-to-sender details, they hand me over to a bearded man who leers at me before dropping me on this dump. A Christian outreach for the mad and dispossessed.

At the homeless farm, I'm given a small, stone-walled room upstairs while the rest of the wrecked and ravaged are relegated to rusty caravans, filled with Bibles and hoarded, broken relics of the life outside. From my tower, I sneer down at my subjects. Rapunzel of the Rubbish Dump. I'm the only one who's been to university, worn a prefect badge at school. My pride tells me I am better than them. In truth, I am much worse. Delusion is an ugly thing.

For the first two weeks on the farm, I flit around, day and night. I am a manic firefly gone berserk.

I find no sleep.

I am well and truly wired. After the shit's kicked out of me, and I'm forced to give my life to Jesus, the farm is where I will find my sobriety.

Chapter 9

IN MY MOTHER'S PENITENTIARY

"There is but one truly serious philosophical problem and that is suicide."
– Albert Camus, *The Myth of Sisyphus*

At three months clean, I leave the farm. I travel full circle and find myself back in the spare room in my mother's home, now a townhouse on the edge of Montgomery Park, Joburg. It's a stone's throw from Westpark Cemetery. How convenient. Living next door to the fields of the dead. They won't even have to hire a hearse to bury me.

It's November 1999. I've just turned 33. On the farm I learned that Jesus was the same age when he died. Unlike me, he had at least done something with his life by the time they nailed him to that cross. All I have are taunting reminders of how I've fucked mine up monumentally with drugs, fraud and deceit. Against the stench of my mother's box wine, I white-knuckle through days that stretch like Dalí clocks. Now back in the umbilical room that has birthed my delinquency, this ghost house has the power to kill me.

It is during those endless days of nothing that the voice whispering, *Kill yourself*, the one that first appeared in incomprehensible form when I was four and followed me to the many rooms of my life, settles in and gets serious. Every morning I wake up when the world is still dark and my first thought is: "Die." On rare occasions, I manage to find my way back to sleep, perchance to dream. But always, when I wake, my mind is centred on it. Suicide. *Soo-i-cide.*

Suicide: Noun: self-murder, self-slaughter, *felo de se*; self-immolation; *Hinduism, historical* suttee; *Japanese, historical* hara-kiri, seppuku; *informal* topping oneself, ending it all.

In Albert Camus's *The Myth of Sisyphus,* a philosophical meditation on the theme of suicide, the central figure of Sisyphus has to push a heavy rock to the top of a hill, only for it to roll back down again. Every day he performs the same meaningless task. He, however, has an even bigger obstacle to deal with: the gods have decreed that suicide is no option for him.

My days are Sisyphean. There seems no point. My children are gone. My drugs are gone. My husband has shacked up with a new blonde lover who, overnight, has become mother to our two little boys. I have no home. I have no job. I have no life.

Sob-sob-sob. Victim-victim-victim.

As light breaks every morning, my gunky eyelids struggle to part, glued shut from tears shed in my sleep. I can barely lift my head from the saline-sodden cushion when I need to navigate the bathroom to alleviate my night-swollen bladder.

In the daytime, I cannot read. I cannot think.

Like Sisyphus, condemned by the gods to perform his meaningless task, for me the effort to draw breath into my lungs between sunrise and sunset is gargantuan. The pointlessness of pushing the rock up the hill of life, only for it to roll back down, thuds heavily. I am suffocated by the absurdity of forced existence, trapped in this life, while the world seems oblivious and keeps on turning.

However, unlike poor Sisyphus, who is forbidden to bail out, suicide *is* an option for me. I see no point in continuing to push that rock up the mountain against the torture of time's cruel ticking.

"A man devoid of hope and conscious of being so has ceased to belong to the future," says Camus.

Without hope, we are nothing.

✳

After nine months in my mother's penitentiary, from November 1999 into most of 2000, the first year of the new millennium, I finally find a job as a zombie waitress. To escape the frowning disapproval, carved in every line of my mother's wine-hardened face, of having an adult drug addict for a daughter, I finally find a two-bedroom flat to rent. I have spent almost a year trying to rewire my mind into a new existence.

Perched above an intersection where cars brake and hoot at all hours of the night, where drunken drivers sometimes lose control and veer into sidewalks and shop windows, the three-roomed box sans garden is where I finally reunite with my two toddler sons.

The boys share a room with a bunk bed. I count the coins that I make from waitressing to pay the rent and feed their rosebud mouths. Somehow, in the act of moving between tables and shifting my scant belongings to my new abode, the voice to die becomes a little quieter. One day it is a whisper. And then it's silent.

But the craving to find a room of my own accelerates.

Along the way, my mother dies. Pancreatic cancer. Her last breath is accompanied by a river of black bile that seeps into the white sheets. From the woman who gave me life, I inherit (against my siblings' wishes) enough to put down a deposit and purchase my first piece of real estate. I'm working at a real job now, as a features writer for a magazine, so I'm deemed bondable by a bank.

It is the first time, at the age of 38, that I experience both the freedom and bondage of property ownership. The art deco flat in Killarney, with its gleaming parquet floors, is proof that I have finally become a productive and responsible member of the human race. The real world. I am acutely aware of my privilege. If my mother hadn't died, having squirrelled away her money, I'd not be part of the landed gentry. In death, she has given me a leg up. I am deeply ashamed that in life I treated her so badly.

Eventually, one room begets another. Three years later, I sell the Killarney apartment for triple its purchase price and become the owner of a renovated pressed-ceiling house in the "good part" of Orange Grove. I squirrel away like my mother taught me and pay the bond off over the next five years.

When, after meeting Soul-Mat on Tinder, I sell the Grove house, I have accumulated enough to pay my half in cash when he and I decide to purchase our Cape Town home: three bedrooms, two bathrooms, a swimming pool and a garden. I'm now an owner of half a fully paid-for home. But soon after the narcotic rush of new love calms down, I find myself longing for that "room of my own", one to which I can retreat like a hermit and write.

Soul-Mat is the first man I've ever been involved with who gives me endless latitude, who has no issue with my gypsy lifestyle, who loves his own space as much as I love mine. We are indeed a perfect match, just as Tinder told us.

The lounge in the Cape Town house is steeple-tall. My wandering mind begins to imagine a loft, a crow's nest in the rafters. I manifest my lofty dream a year later with stairs that double as a bookshelf. I christen them with the growing pile of books I'm publishing. It is my monument dedicated to that screeching junkie girl who once so badly wanted to die. It is an ode to poor Sisyphus who couldn't escape his meaningless existence. It is a gift to my healing self, to celebrate everything that I have conquered against all odds.

I lug many of my books to the magic house in the mountains before the sale even goes through. And then The Woman is killed. The number of mourners at after-death events is limited during lockdown, so I watch her memorial on my iPad.

Chapter 10

A ZOOM MEMORIAL

In René Magritte's iconic painting, *The Lovers*, a man and a woman are entwined, shrouded in a white cloth. We do not see their faces. Are they in love or are they trapped? Claustrophobic in their embrace?

Created in 1928 by the artist who became famous for his surrealistic style of painting, Magritte's work often included veiled faces. Many art experts have linked his fascination with shrouds to the death of his mother, who committed suicide when he was 13 years old. Her body was dragged from the Sambre River, close to his birthplace in Lessines, Belgium, with her nightgown wrapped around her face. Magritte would later say that he was never sure whether "she had covered her eyes with it so as not to see the death she had chosen, or whether she had been veiled in that way by the swirling currents".

When masks are mandated and become a part of our everyday lives at the end of March 2020, I am reminded of *The Lovers*. Overnight we become biohazardous, apparently harmful to each other's existence. Overnight half our faces, which consist of 43 tiny muscles, allowing us to express the emotions of joy, fear, sadness and confusion that make us human, are erased. It becomes impossible to see what people are feeling. It becomes hard to hear what people are saying.

At first, we are told that these face coverings will only be necessary for three weeks. Twenty-one days. That seems doable. Then we'll all unmask ourselves and go back to "normal", to a time when we breathed and heaved and sneezed on each other. When we kissed long and slow and tender. I stare at *The Lovers* a lot in the first year of The Pandemic. Shrouded. De-expressioned. Silenced. I fear that when we cannot move our faces, we cease to exist as individuals, as human beings.

During the time of The Plague, millions of souls take leave of this plane alone, without families and friends to hold their departing hands or stroke their brows. Sometimes people are only allowed to observe their suffering loved ones through hospital windows. Others don't get a chance to see them at all, restricted from travel by Covid lockdown law.

I think often of our mother on the day she left back in 2004, how we gathered around her bed at intervals, held her withered, age-pocked hands, and how I am now grateful that she did not have to live through and die in the isolation of The Pandemic.

Grief takes on a whole new meaning during these strange and unprecedented times. For many, the traditional ways of mourning are arrested. Numbers at funerals are severely restricted, depending on the lockdown level decreed at the time. "After-tears" gatherings are banned during hardcore levels.

What happens to a world where tears are shed alone? Where touch is outlawed? Where communal mourning is paralysed by isolation? Where virtual funerals and memorials replace the real-life expressions of loss? Where grief becomes dis-enfranchised?

Long before The Pandemic, in 1993, a group of doctors come up with the term "Prolonged Grief Disorder", or PGD, which refers to a person who has lost a loved one and experiences intense or pervasive yearning for the departed soul. For the bereaved, struggling to accept the loss, there is an emotional numbness, a sense of being "trapped in grief".

As days pass, I become increasingly convinced that the world is suffering from chronic PGD.

✳

On 31 March 2021, less than a week after The Woman is murdered, her friends and family hold a live-streamed memorial service. I belong in neither of these groups, but I am curious. Death can be a magnet for voyeurs.

It's a Wednesday. I log on to the Zoom link from the new cabin. The Woman's coffin house lurks in the background. It all feels so surreal. I have learned more about her in the last five days than I would probably ever have found out about her if she were still breathing, living her life just across the way. It's clear from the size of the online crowd of more than 500 that she was loved by many who feel the loss deeply. I sit behind my screen like an unidentified intruder, watching this intimate affair from the outside.

The Husband delivers his tribute to his wife. He appears controlled and unemotional. He does, however, break down at the end, gasping back a sob.

After he speaks, The Husband pulls his mask back on, so it's hard to tell what he is feeling. He then returns to his place alongside The Woman's mother. She comforts him in an embrace.

It has become increasingly strange that the three men who killed The Woman found their way onto our secluded estate by pure coincidence … It's complicated to find the estate; it doesn't even reliably appear on Google Maps. Did someone tell them how to get here? The details that have emerged tick many boxes that may point to this murder being "a hit". But "a hit" needs a motive. Who would want to kill The Woman?

I now know that The Woman was dropped off at the couple's

home by The Husband earlier in the week. He had reportedly felt ill and left her there alone without a car. Perhaps I will discover something while watching this digital memorial. I wish the people would take off their masks.

The following day, on 1 April 2021, exactly six days after The Woman is murdered, I get a bright and happy text from the transferring attorneys: *Congratulations! Your house has been registered. You are the official new owner.*

Fucking hell. How's that for timing? Just when I thought I'd found my piece of heaven, my room of my own, my Place of Joy and Freedom. My ownership of the new house is now a noose of terror around my neck, leaving me gasping for air like Magritte's mother, as her nightgown dragged her under.

The following week my good friend Monica comes to visit. Unmasked.

PART TWO

MAGIC

"The moment you doubt whether you can fly, you cease forever to be able to do it."
– JM Barrie, *Peter Pan*

Chapter 11

MEETING MONICA

When I meet her for the first time in early 2015, I am intrinsically drawn to Monica Cromhout. I've been commissioned to write a story for *City Press* about this "Somerset West grandmother" recently arrested for the possession of a large amount of magic mushrooms. This elderly woman, who is 69 at the time of her incarceration in late 2014, subsequently faced serious criminal drug charges. I was intrigued. I mean, what kind of granny becomes a drug dealer?

It's 42 degrees in Cape Town. My weather app tells me it's the hottest city in the world today as I drive east to Somerset West to meet Monica.

In researching the story I am to write, I've discovered that she was arrested on 20 December 2014, after a battalion of police officers raided her home at 3am, while something called a "sacred mushroom ceremony" was taking place. She was subsequently charged with "dealing in an illegal substance" – in this case, containing the active ingredient psilocybin. On 23 March 2015, Monica was hauled in front of a Somerset West court on a charge that carries a maximum prison sentence of 15 years. Luckily for this granny, the case was struck off the roll and subsequently postponed because, according to the judge, it appeared that the prosecution had taken too long to attain the lab results for the seized mushrooms.

As I pull into the quiet suburban street, I notice Monica's home is the only property without a fence or walls. The "Healing House", the name by which it is known, nestles in lush greenery. A tangle of wild, unruly bushes and trees knits together to create an almost otherworldly fairy playground. A concrete angel near the front door rests alongside a rockery of succulents, watched over by a sentinel of 12-foot San Pedro cacti. Surely a house where these "secret magic mushroom ceremonies" are conducted should have some type of security – a proper gate at the front door at the very least?

Monica welcomes me in, garbed in black trousers and a brightly coloured kaftan top, open-faced and radiating warmth – she looks more like a fairy-tale gingerbread lady than some dodgy drug dealer. She ushers me past floor-to-ceiling bookshelves, to the front room on the left, lined with cushions, mattresses and comfy couches.

"This is where the mushroom ceremonies take place," she announces proudly. I'm taken aback by her soft-spoken openness. Aren't drug merchants supposed to be more secretive? But Monica is no ordinary Escobar. I soon discover that she trained as a nurse and was the director of LifeLine in the Eastern and Western Cape between 1974 and 1987.

As we share a cup of coffee, she explains how her "spiritual growth" sessions (known as "Soma ceremonies") are quiet, deep and peaceful affairs. Mushrooms are handed out to the participants – usually around 5 grams dried, which are taken along with honey tea and a square of dark chocolate. "Calm, atmospheric music plays gently in the background," she tells me. "During the sessions, people often move to the outside area in the wild garden and settle in around a fire."

All very hippy and lovey-dovey, I think to myself.

But what started out as a serene Soma ceremony in late December 2014 took a dramatic turn when a 77-year-old professor, who'd arrived to "journey" for the first time, became restless and fled, running straight to the cop shop three blocks away.

"It was most unusual for someone to react this way. He was extremely agitated and began crawling out of the room, pushing all help away," says Monica. "I was terribly worried about him and sent my helpers out on the streets to find him."

A little while later, there was a loud banging on the back door. "I was so relieved when I saw two policemen in the shadows, I could have kissed them! I said, 'You've got John!' and they said, 'Yes.' I said, 'Come in, come in.' It was only later that I found out that this gave the police permission to legally search the house. I inadvertently let them in."

Soon the two policemen transmogrified into eight as another six armed officers, who'd been crouching in the darkness, burst in.

"They were convinced there was something like a sex orgy going on," chuckles Monica. "They stormed into the house, probably expecting crazy partying. Now you can imagine how the poor people who were deep in this calm, gentle spiritual experience must have felt when all these armed police marched in, shining flashlights into their faces."

I'm furiously taking notes. I'm riveted.

The cops, led by a belligerent constable, searched the house and eventually found Monica's carefully packaged mushrooms, stored in airtight containers in a small freezer in her bedroom. "They also seized 10 dagga cookies and a box of dried sage," she smiles.

While the police hurtled off back to the station to test the "drugs", Monica was instructed to stay put – she was not to leave her home under any circumstances.

"I felt calm and confident. I had a clear conscience; I knew I'd done nothing wrong. You see, mushrooms that contain psilocybin have been used for thousands of years, playing a significant role in the development of philosophy and religious thought in many earlier cultures. Early man used psilocybin and other psychedelic plants in shamanic rituals, especially in South and Central America."

She then tells me that the Ancient Greeks consumed *mykes* (from where we get the word *mycology*). These ancient, sacred psychedelic rituals would take place in the city of Eleusis, the site of the Eleusinian Mysteries. I found it fascinating that these ceremonies involved visions of the afterlife and everyone who was initiated via a psychedelic experience brought on by taking the mushrooms was given the hope of life after death.

"Unlike other drugs, like cocaine, heroin and tik," explains Monica, as we imbibe a second cup of coffee, "psilocybin does not cause addiction and therefore does not belong in the same class as dangerous and dependence-producing narcotics. Plus, there are no recorded deaths resulting from magic mushrooms. One can't say the same about some 'legal' substances like nicotine and alcohol."

But, according to Monica, the Somerset West cops who arrested her that night were clearly of a different opinion. Some 30 minutes after they left the Healing House, a cacophony of sirens screeched back – two police vans, containing an army of cops, had returned with evidence that the mushrooms were indeed of the "illegal kind".

How they in fact established this in the small hours of the morning remains a mystery. The police had told Monica that the only way to ascertain whether the mushrooms were illegal would be to send them to a special lab in Europe. "One has to wonder whether the cops didn't perhaps test it on themselves," she grins impishly.

Monica was subsequently arrested in the early hours of 21 December. At the police station, unable to establish how much the mushrooms weighed, a somewhat comedic hunt for a scale ensued. The Somerset West cop shop was clearly not kitted out to deal with kingpin dealers like Mrs Cromhout. Finally, a small flour-dusted scale was found in the bakery section of a local supermarket. She was duly informed that her stash weighed two kilograms. Oops.

"I didn't realise I had been able to accumulate such a large amount."

Back at the police station, Monica had to sign several documents that she could barely read as she'd left her prescription glasses at home. When she requested to use the toilet, a full body search ensued, "including a hand in my crotch".

Then it was cell time.

"It felt like I was in some hardcore American gangster prison movie. They led me to the holding cells through one gate after another. It was so noisy with all these gates and keys clanging and banging. It really felt quite unreal."

Finally, Monica found herself in her cell. A woman's voice, thick with the ravages of years of coughing from Mandrax pipes, broke the silence.

"What you in for?" croaked Nina.

"I told her 'mushrooms' and then she sighed deeply and said: 'With mushrooms you touch God.'"

Nina had been in Pollsmoor Prison three times on drug-related charges, and that night, in the Somerset West holding cells, she spent most of the time trying to push her teeth back into her drug-damaged gums.

Instead of crumbling during the two nights she spent in prison, Monica saw it as a learning experience. Her fascination for expanding her consciousness had been strong all her life. After her beloved husband passed away from pancreatic cancer in 2005, a deep grief engulfed her. Having just turned 60, she suddenly found herself forced to face life without him. So when she stumbled upon information about ayahuasca, a psychedelic South American brew, she was determined to try it. Up until then, she'd been a devoted teetotaller and non-smoker.

When she received a chance email alerting her to an ayahuasca ceremony in the Cederberg mountains, she decided to join the pilgrimage. "I'd reached a point in my life where I was simply waiting to die. I didn't want to face life without my husband. But this offered some incentive."

Monica tells me how, after imbibing the foul-tasting potion, she underwent a deep and profound life-changing experience. By now we've been chatting for more than three hours.

Her first experience with psilocybin mushrooms came about a year later, when in October 2009, inspired by the Beatles hit "When I'm 64", Monica decided to throw a huge birthday celebration. More than 300 people from all walks of life attended, and one of the late arrivals, a psychologist friend, brought a little gift of magic mushrooms.

"I took them on my own a few days later, and I've never quite had an experience like that again. I just remember hearing the birds singing and never wanting to ever come back to earth. I also got a very clear instruction: 'Your home must become a school for mushrooms.'"

We both burst out laughing, fully aware of how absurd the statement sounds.

"I said out loud: 'But I don't know anything about mushrooms,' and the voice said: *You don't need to know anything. All you need to do is open the door and hold it open.*"

There was, however, one major obstacle: she had no mushrooms. Her psychologist friend soon came to the rescue and posted a package to Somerset West.

"On the day the mushrooms arrived, a young guy was in my study fixing my computer. I was so excited I asked him if he wanted to use some with me."

The following night, the unlikely couple headed into the back garden, lit candles, took mushrooms and listened to music on their iPods. "That's how the mushroom school was born."

The second mushroom ceremony, attended by four women, took place four weeks later, and within three months, by January 2010, the ceremonies were hosting up to 18 individuals. By the time Monica was arrested, she was being asked to facilitate ceremonies every Saturday night, with larger and larger groups attending.

"I have never turned anyone away from a mushroom ceremony. I always try to leave the front door open."

If Monica had been found guilty back in 2015, she could have been sentenced, alongside hardened and dangerous criminals, to up to 15 years in Pollsmoor Prison, a jail built for 4 500 prisoners, but which at any given time, houses no fewer than 8 000 inmates sardined inside.

Back then, at our first meeting, she seems at peace about the fact that this remains a very real possibility.

"If I land up going to jail, at least we'll have brought attention to this issue. Sometimes we need to go through discomfort in order for things to change. Ultimately, I feel that it's my constitutional right to take psilocybin in the privacy of my home. I know it causes no harm and, in fact, its prohibition infringes upon my right to human dignity, my religious and cultural rights, and my individual sovereignty."

✳

A few years after our first meeting, Monica will apply to have certain parts of the Drugs and Drug Trafficking Act 140 of 1992 declared unconstitutional. In fact, like those ancient people throughout history, so strongly does Monica believe in her right to take psilocybin for spiritual healing and enlightenment that the cornerstone of her Constitutional Court argument will be a challenge to the law that criminalises and prohibits its use by asserting her right of spiritual freedom.

I leave my meeting with Monica back in 2015 deeply intrigued. Despite having only spent a couple of hours with her, I sense that I've made a special soul connection with this unusual woman.

A few weeks later I find myself back at the Healing House.

Chapter 12

SOMA

It's a sweltering summer's evening in Somerset West, back in late March 2015.

We're in the far corner of a candlelit room among 30 strangers. I sit on a mattress beside Soul-Mat. It had been four months of heady bliss since I'd met him on that online dating app in a fortuitous swipe right. Although we still glisten in the aura of all-consuming new love, my chest is tight, my breathing ragged, as I cling to his warm hand.

I don't think I've been as petrified since back in 1999 when, high on crack, I'd been pistol-whipped and gang-raped by three drugged-up gangsters in Soper Road, Hillbrow. That was almost 16 years ago, a lifetime really. Back then I danced with death on my ravenous seven-year smack and crack binge, culminating in a brutal rock bottom. I'd sought oblivion in a bid to forget the life I'd once had – my husband, my home, my two babies, my career as an actress and filmmaker – all slipping away like the smoke that snaked from my toxin-laced crack pipe.

Although there is nothing in this room now to remind me of that dark time, my heart thuds the same beat as it did the night I'd lost all my power to three scummy rapists.

Memory is a strange thing. It can be an unwelcome intruder. In this dimly lit space with shadows leering on the walls, I had not expected to be reminded of that night. I thought I'd boxed it away and dealt with it. I'm feeling fucking vulnerable and, boy, do I hate it when I'm not in charge.

Perhaps it's because I haven't felt as out of control since that night in Hillbrow, now forever etched into my life's chequered journey. The unknown of what I am about to embark on has me by the throat.

I had first heard of "the ceremonies" – or "Soma" as they have become known to me – from Soul-Mat, during one of our initial online conversations in November the previous year. Distance has been our obstacle from the very start – I live in Joburg, he in Cape Town. Our love story was birthed on the Internet, with a simple swipe right on my iPad when I happened to log on to Tinder late one night on an overnight car launch in Hout Bay, Cape Town. He'd made the same swipe right-hand gesture seconds before my fingers moved across my screen. Just minutes earlier, I'd set my geographical distance for "men" within a "50 km radius". He was 48 kilometres away. Just 2 001 metres could have changed everything.

You've got a match flashed simultaneously on both our screens, heralding what would develop into a long-distance spiral of passion. From the moment our data collided, we were connected; a double-helix strand of DNA.

Three days after our lives intersected, he had written to me about a "mushroom ceremony" he was attending the following Saturday night. The word "Soma" popped up in our WhatsApp convo. He also used big words like "prosopagnosia", which I had to google to find that it meant "face blindness – a brain disorder characterised by the inability to recognise faces". It was rare to encounter a man who knew more words than I did, especially in an online world where conversation was scarce and "Hie how r u?" was often the deepest Tinder exchange on offer.

Googling "Soma" after "prosopagnosia", I discovered its meaning:

soma

ˈsəʊmə/

noun HINDUISM

noun: soma

an intoxicating drink prepared from a plant and used in Vedic ritual, believed to be the drink of the gods.

- a plant used to make soma. plural noun: somas; noun: soma plant; plural noun: soma plants
- (in Aldous Huxley's novel *Brave New World*) a narcotic drug which produces euphoria and hallucination, distributed by the state in order to promote content and social harmony.

Four letters. One word. Soma. It clung to my brain like a barnacle. It heralded terror. There was no way I could ever even *consider* venturing back into a realm swimming with words like: "intoxicating", "euphoric", "narcotic" and "hallucination".

I had already danced too close to drugs and death. For seven years, between 1992 and 1999, I'd had front-row seats to the car wreck that would be my life. Seatbelt-less. I'd lost the plot, a mad King Lear blinded to all reality. Drugs had rendered me homeless – not just down and out and cash-strapped. Home-fucking-less. I'd finally managed to get clean and sober on 1 September 1999, on that Christian farm near Hekpoort, surrounded by drunks, tramps and beggars. Drugs had broken me. When I eventually left the farm back in late 1999, just after my 33rd birthday, I was faced with the catastrophic realisation that I was a total useless loser. Perhaps the only way forward was to snuff myself out. Permanently.

I had crept into the rooms of Narcotics Anonymous meetings after leaving the Bible-punching, work-for-your-bread mission with my back up against the wall and Death calling me. Like a wounded dog, I slowly began to lick my self-inflicted welts, trying to get to the root and rot of my seeping discharge – my deranged denial – and start what appeared to be an entirely impossible journey to get my life back on track. Sobriety was not a salve – it was a cruel reminder of just how low I'd sunk. Time taunted me with the nauseating realisation that seven years of my life had gone up in crack and smack smoke. And that I had absolutely nothing to show for it but loss.

For most of my first year of being clean and sober, I woke up each morning frozen in the knowledge that I could never retrieve the years I'd smouldered away. But the NA meetings I dragged myself off to – sometimes nightly – began to stitch my brokenness together, knitting a tapestry that would, one day at a time, slowly meld to form an intricate, miraculous motif – one that saved my life.

In the early days, I met others who, just like me, had lost everything and were finding ways to rebuild their shattered existences. For the next 16 years of my recovery, I faithfully attended 12-Step programmes. NA: Narcotics Anonymous. AA: Alcoholics Anonymous. CA: Cocaine Anonymous. SLA: Sex and Love Addicts Anonymous. ACOA: Adult Children of Alcoholics.

There is absolutely no doubt that these 12-Step meetings helped save my life. I was a dedicated member of what may have appeared to an outsider like a "fellowship" that resembled a recovery cult. But I didn't care whether people thought we were being brainwashed and limited by a reductionist philosophy, repeatedly chanting, "I am an addict". It had worked for me. It gave me a life when I had nothing. My fellow recovering addicts taught me to bury my junkie pride and ask for help. And, even after my life slowly morphed into some kind of miraculous order, over the years, I continued to attend these meetings.

I had a cupboard full of keyrings and medals marking my sobriety birthdays. Just as most people had passports and ID books, these little mementos *were* me. In those raw, early days when I had nothing to hold on to, I was advised to stick around and wait for the miracles. And, like a good faithful service dog for the blind, I did.

Of course, me being me, always the rebel, I often bent the rules. Like the one relating to "anonymity" – a cornerstone of the stringent 12-Step programme. I totally bust that one when I wrote my first book, *Smacked*. The same happened with the follow-up, *Hooked,* and then *Crashed*. But, having collected a heap of keyrings and clean time, I had found a way to mould the programme to suit me, just as I had learned that the only way to get real clean time was to take it one day at a time. I firmly believed that coming out and identifying myself in public spaces was part of my healing, part of neutralising the debilitating shame often felt by addicts hiding away in the shadows.

Standing up and owning my shit paid off. After *Smacked* came out in 2005, my life sprung into action and the rewards rained down. My first book sold tens of thousands of copies. I was told by many that I had become their inspiration, their poster child for recovery. Over the following years, I shared my story of narcotic horror at packed-out corporate captains-of-industry events. I was a sought-after speaker at schools, at NGOs, and regularly attended and shared my testimony of strength and hope at NA meetings and conventions.

In 2011, I went back to university and, for the next two years, studied part-time and finally walked out proudly with an Honours degree in Publishing with distinction. By the time I met Soul-Mat in late 2014, I was a successful publisher, author and journalist. I had not waited for the miracles. I had gone out there and created a life – a huge one, compared with the broken existence I'd left behind. In all senses of the NA mantra, I was "living life on life's terms".

But something profound was missing. On the outside, I looked as if I'd made a miraculous recovery, that I was successful in the eyes of "society", but inside I didn't believe that at all. I still carried lead-heavy baggage. I didn't *feel* connected. I didn't even really *like*, never mind love, myself.

And now this word "Soma", with its narcotic, mind-altering associations, had entered my consciousness.

The 12-Step programmes, specifically that of NA, were very clear that we, as addicts, were to stay away from "all drugs, all mood-altering, mind-changing chemicals", including alcohol. (Strangely – and what I believe to be somewhat hypocritical – caffeine, nicotine and psychotropic, mind-numbing and often highly addictive meds like Zoloft, Prozac, Urbanol, Ritalin and Suboxone were all A-OK.) At every meeting, glazed-eyed pharmaceutically induced "recovering" addicts, often zombified by their *Walking Dead* prescriptions, put their hands up for clean time. At the end of every meeting, stacks of ciggie butts were cleared and umpteen caffeine-dredged mugs were washed and packed away. I found these inconsistencies strange, but remained silent about these supposedly "sober" incongruences.

A few days after Soul-Mat and I met online, he attended his mushroom event in Somerset West while I, now back in Joburg, trawled the internet on a Saturday night. My mind whirled in obsessive loops as I imagined my yet-to-be boyfriend at his "Soma" ceremony. What did the room in which they held this secret ritual look like? Silk sheets? Diaphanous curtains? A candlelit, incense-infused cave? Sensual, naked women swaying to sultry Eastern rhythms? I had been too embarrassed to ask him if these "ceremonies" entailed sex. My mind kept spinning. Who was the leader? He'd mentioned this woman "Monica" who appeared to run the show … Was she a carnal goddess?

A Modesty Blaise of mushrooms? Some steamy Kama Sutra wench?

The following day I found the secret Facebook page, Soma Ceremonies, and asked to become a member. Permission was granted by this Monica woman, clearly the one in charge.

Her profile pic looked nothing like I'd imagined; instead, she looked decidedly elderly, really quite grandmotherly and kind – very jolly, in fact.

Within the first week of meeting Soul-Mat online, I booked a ticket to Cape Town to meet my Tinderella. The weekend turned into real-life bliss. I left Cape Town certain that he, like that Nick Cave song, was the one I'd been waiting for.

By mid-December I was back in Cape Town to spend the festive season with my new love. On Christmas Eve, as we lay entwined, Soul-Mat received a late-night WhatsApp alerting him that Monica had been arrested. It was just a few weeks later that I met her to write that story for *City Press*. And now, here I am in her Healing House, on the brink of taking psilocybin mushrooms. I am truly petrified.

As we sit in the huge circle, the participants introduce themselves one by one. There's burly farmer Paul, medical doctor Costa, psychologist Fawzia, PhD student Henry, journalist Marcia and teacher Carina; there's also Sue, who has suffered from depression, and who says, "I'd been in a bad mood for 45 years until I started using mushrooms."

As we make our way around the circle, each person explains how Soma has changed their lives. My mounting fear as my turn approaches is off the charts. What if someone from my "other life", the "real world", is under this roof, among us? Maybe someone here has read *Smacked* and recognises me! What if word gets out and people start claiming that I've relapsed? Me, who pretends not to give a damn about the outside world's opinions, clearly gives far too much of a fuck about what "the people" think of me.

I pull my hoodie lower.

I reach for Soul-Mat's hand. I intrinsically trust him, deeply. He's a psychiatrist by profession, one who's turned his back on the pharmaceutical approach to address mental "disorders". He's disgusted by many in his own profession and fraternity – the "pharmawhores" he likes to call them. Rather than prescribing pharmaceuticals, his maverick approach is to help patients by giving counsel based on a gut-health nutritional and lifestyle-based approach. Among many things he believes in are the healing powers of psilocybin.

But, despite reassurances from both Soul-Mat and Monica that psilocybin is not addictive, that mushrooms have no reason to be on the chart of scheduled drugs – where it's listed at number seven in South Africa, tucked ominously between heroin and tik – I can't shake the fear that perhaps I am about to totally jeopardise my hard-fought 16 years of sobriety, my status as the poster child of recovery. My brand, my reputation, my credibility.

Who the fuck do you think you are? No one actually cares …

I ignore the voice.

My hard-wired fears, cultured over almost two decades of I-am-an-addict mantras in 12-Step programmes, are telling me to run. What if I just grab the car keys, without telling Soul-Mat that I am leaving?

The circle is closing in on me.

And then, suddenly, it's my turn to speak. I take a slow, deep breath. My voice is uncharacteristically quivery.

"Hi, my name's Melinda, I'm a recovering addict. I've been clean for 16 years and I am terrified that by doing this I will feel as if I have relapsed."

There … I've said it. Now I want to cry.

Chapter 13

WAITING FOR THE DOORS TO OPEN

The room is inky black. Only candlelit shadows dance on the walls. Thirty people lie alongside each other like overgrown babies on mattresses spread out across the floor. The March evening is still warm, no need for blankets yet. My head aches against my memory-foam cushion. Only my heartbeat seems to thunder through the silence. I've just swallowed a cup of warm tea containing honey and 5 grams of cubensis. The mushroom mixture tastes weirdly loamy, almost musty. It's neither inviting nor unpleasant, although the dregs at the bottom of the cup take some effort to swallow.

Why am I doing this?

Lying here, waiting for the psilocybin mushrooms to kick in, I'm not really sure of anything. What I can't deny is that something's been missing in my apparently "inspirational" life. Despite having religiously attended so many 12-Step meetings – hundreds and hundreds over 16 years – there's still a hole in my soul. Some might refer to the dull ache as a lack of "spiritual meaning". I am not a religious person, although over the years I've convinced myself I believe in a higher power. Kind of. Some people call it "God". But I find it hard to bring myself to name mine using those three letters: G.O.D. I think that's mainly to do with the fact that, in my opinion, so many people on the planet who chant the word "God" are fuckwits.

Like many others who had come before, and those who would surely come after me, I struggled with that "God versus ego" concept throughout my recovery. Somewhere along the line I gave up on seeking "God" outside of myself and settled on the idea that "God" was within, a force that lived inside me like some magic genie.

As my life improved, I came to the convenient conclusion that "God" was in fact *me*. The notion suited me perfectly. It nourished my ego and completely validated my need to practise self-will. It was much easier to trust myself, flaws and all, than hand my life and free will to some unknown power greater than myself, a power that was vague and non-relatable. A power with which I simply could not connect.

But the problem with believing that "God" *is* you, is that the ego thrives on that notion. At some point, I came to the sad conclusion that, no matter how hard I tried to work on myself, how many meetings I attended, how many shrink sessions I booked, how many crystals I rubbed or how many empowering self-help books I read, something unnameable was still missing. Deep down inside, I didn't feel "godly" or spiritually connected. I often felt alone, disconnected and anxious. I hardly ever acknowledged this – my inner panic, my secret awkwardness, my faithlessness – to the outside world; I covered my dis-ease well with outward layers of brash confidence and an extroverted persona.

After the Ferrari accident in 2013, which I write about in my book *Crashed*, I developed extreme PTSD that forced me to check myself into a mental-health clinic for three weeks and walk out with a bag of psychotropic meds I was told I would need to take for the rest of my life to address my "Bipolar 2" diagnosis. By the time I met Soul-Mat in late 2014, I was desperate to chuck out the pills that had begun to insidiously alter my energy levels and dull my old zest for life. Being a maverick psychiatrist, Soul-Mat soon helped me to taper off and become "meds free". By the time I find myself on the mattress in Monica's Healing House, I am off the pills but the PTSD from the car crash is still alive and kicking.

✳

Before that evening in Somerset West, I armed myself with knowledge. I read studies on psilocybin and watched a string of documentaries. There was an overriding opinion, especially when it came to addiction, anxiety and depression, that this strange psilocybin substance had the power to work miracles. But what had probably finally tipped my decision to go on my first Soma journey was stumbling across an article about the father of all 12-Step programmes, Bill W, aka Bill Wilson.

He started AA with another alcoholic known as "Dr Bob" back in 1935, and the duo soon grew into a fellowship of thousands who all suffered from the same disease: alcoholism. In 1939, Bill W penned *The Big Book*, which subsequently became "the Bible" of the AA programme. Today there are millions of AA members worldwide, with more than 200 000 groups across the globe.

I knew all that historical stuff about Bill and the 12 Steps – after all, I was one of the programme's most faithful "unanonymous" converts, but what I had only recently discovered, almost as part of some synchronised script, was that Bill W had, over time, also become a vocal proponent of psychedelics.

Always controversial and curious to explore a spiritual path, legend has it that in the 1950s, he hooked up with Aldous Huxley, American psychologist Betty Eisner and consciousness guru Gerald Heard to take part in medically supervised psychedelic experiments using LSD to achieve altered states. Bill's world was rocked after he imbibed the psychedelic, and experienced "a profound spiritual reawakening". Having endured a lifetime struggle with his ego, just as I had, he believed that LSD eliminated the restrictive stubbornness of the self and enabled a mystical connection to the cosmos and God.

When he tried to explain to other recovering alcoholics how spiritual enlightenment might be assisted by the controlled use of psychedelics, he chose his words carefully: "It is a generally acknowledged fact in spiritual development that ego reduction makes the influx of God's grace possible. If, therefore, under LSD we can have a temporary reduction, so that we can better see what we are and where we are going — well, that might be of some help. The goal might become clearer. So I consider LSD to be of some value to some people, and practically no damage to anyone."

As I read his statement, I noticed how carefully he'd worded his observations.

In the weeks before my Soma journey, I found myself reading his words over and over again. Just as it had for Bill W, the term "God" that flowed freely at NA and AA meetings and was a fundamental element of all 12-Step literature, had been a barrier to me from the start.

In fact, the constant referral to "God" or "higher power" on the night I stumbled into my first NA meeting back in July 1999, cracked to my eyeballs, had sent me screaming out of the room – a vampire blinded by the light. I couldn't stomach all the religious referrals: "We made a decision to turn our will and our lives over to the care of God as we understood Him." Or: "I came to believe in a higher power that could restore me to sanity."

Who were these people? What was this cult that chanted the word "God" and a serenity prayer at the close of every meeting? The very notion catapulted me right back into my negative experiences of religion – the forced Methodist Sunday-school classes from the age of two; the mournful organ pipes that cast shadows over my Sundays; me stealing coins from the collection plate when no one was looking; the heated arguments with my mother as I entered my teen years over my refusal to complete my Methodist confirmation classes at the age of 16.

Turning my back on God and everything associated with religion became my way of asserting my independence. I did not want to have anything to do with those hypocritical Christians who put on their Sunday best once a week, and beat their wives and children on other days. By the time I dragged my drug-ravaged soul into my first NA meeting, like Nietzsche, God was dead to me. At my first meeting, I vaguely recall someone saying that "if the word 'God' chases you out of the rooms, the drugs will chase you back".

Before the session was over, I had hurtled out, back to the comfortable numbness of my heroin and crack lovers, back to the freezing streets of the Hillbrow ghetto. Back then, the word "God" had enough negative association to ricochet me straight into my Lalaland of high denial. And even when I did eventually crawl back into an NA meeting a few months later, to embark on my journey into recovery, I continued to wrestle with that three-letter word for the next 16 years.

But now, stumbling across the literature tracking Bill's spiritual struggle gave me a deep sense of comfort, knowing that the same battle I had fought for most of my life, my disdain for organised religion and my abhorrence of puritanical "God squadders", was what Bill had experienced too. Despite my fears about what people would say or think of me, I was moved by his willingness to seek an alternative solution, to experiment with psychedelics.

It placated me somewhat to read in my research that, after his first LSD journey, Bill W claimed to feel "absolutely no guilt".

In 1957, soon after his first "trip", he wrote a letter to Gerald

Heard, saying: "I am certain that the LSD experiment has helped me very much. I find myself with a heightened colour perception and an appreciation of beauty, almost destroyed by my years of (alcohol-induced) depressions."

In fact, so inspired was Bill W by his psychedelic experience that he chose to share those details with the AA fellowship to suggest that others who struggled with the concept of a higher power might also benefit from regular use of LSD under structured and medically controlled guidance. He strongly believed that using psychedelics could help "melt the icy intellectual mountain in whose shadow they lived and shivered".

But, of course, most traditionally Christian people in AA back in 1950s America could not get their heads around their "leader" using psychedelics. Some were highly alarmed; others horrified. The AA gossip machine, a sad but real element of the fellowship back then – just as it is today – spewed vitriol against Bill W. This clearly hurt him deeply.

From the very start, Bill had enjoyed huge popularity among the AA fellowship, where he attained an almost cult-like messiah status. At large gatherings, followers would stand in line to touch his sleeve, try to grab a word of hope or advice from their "leader", despite the AA doctrines clearly stating that no one person was ever to control the organisation. However, along with friends and admirers came enemies who now leapt at the opportunity to bring Bill down, accusing him of betrayal, morally debased principles and power-mongering.

The conservative forces in AA, which as an organisation had by this stage grown hugely in numbers, went batshit, recoiling in horror from the idea of Bill W advocating the use of any mind-altering substances.

And so, lying in the room in the little house tucked away in a panhandle in Somerset West, almost 40 years after Bill passed on, waiting for my own doors of perception to be unlatched, I fail to calm my racing heart. As I close my eyes and try to keep them shut, I think of the man who changed the lives of millions of addicts. If he could walk through the invisible doors, seeking spiritual meaning, surely it was okay for little old me to try to open mine?

"Please help me, Father Bill," I pray.

Chapter 14

THE JOURNEY

"If the doors of perception were cleansed every thing would appear to man as it is, infinite. For man has closed himself up, till he sees all things thro' narrow chinks of his cavern."
– William Blake, *The Marriage of Heaven and Hell*

Like an impenetrable veil, khaki-green sludge hangs thick against the lids of my eyes. Nothing. I have been lying on my mattress for what feels like forever. In real time, it's probably been less than an hour, but absolutely nada has happened besides this image of a slimy, dark olive membrane that seems intent on obliterating all possibility of the "other side".

Perhaps I'm not able to go there. Perhaps I have been clean and sober and part of this real world for so long that it's impossible for me to "get altered". Maybe my mind is so tightly shut that it's unable to open. This does not make me feel relieved in any way. I have come this far. I need *something* to happen. Too terrified to open my eyes to see what is happening in the room, I long to reach out to Soul-Mat beside me and fall into the comfort of his arms.

But earlier, in Monica's study, when I'd gone to collect my carefully weighed-out mushrooms, she had specifically told me to "leave Mat alone". In fact, she had urged me to find a spot on the opposite side of the room and stay as far away from him as possible. Of course, I had defied her. There was no way in hell that I was not going to be right next to my rock on this possible journey into hell or insanity.

And then, just as I have all but given up on the idea that anything is going to happen, just as I surrender to the complete nothingness of non-expectation – *it* happens.

Like a torpedo crashing through a thick canvas, a *Pow!* in a Lichtenstein painting, a comet hurtling through an impenetrable dark sky, *it happens*.

In one crack of a split second, just when I had neglected to keep my slimy veil of vigilance intact, I burst through to the other side, through The Doors that Blake spoke about when he said: "If the doors of perception were cleansed every thing would appear to man as it is, infinite."

In that single, unguarded instant, the narrow chinks in the prison of my own making are flung open, far and wide. And what I see does not terrify. No. What I see and experience in the deepest pores of my body, my mind and my soul is a thing of such beauty, such wonder, that it will change me forever. Words are pithy symbols, weak substitutes for what happens within my being that night.

A million fragments of patterns – Aztec and Inca – dazzling colours, the splendour of a world not dreamed of beyond The Veil, are revealed to me. I twirl and whirl. I swoop across fiery deserts, jewel-like oceans and golden plains. Like Buzz Lightyear propelled by a backpack of power, I transcend the atmosphere and whoosh into the multiverse.

Time loosens her claws.

Later, I will appreciate just how powerful the melting away of the clock is. The tick-tock of the ego. For years I had been trying to capture the essence of the *now*, the present, trying to escape the dread of the future and the regret of the past. But in my maiden voyage to the Great Beyond, I find myself completely immersed in super-presence, in all its boundary-defying fullness. I am free.

After what feels like a new kind of forever, a delicious emancipation from the ticking seconds and minutes that define us in the real world, after who knows how long, I slowly open my eyes. The room that had earlier seemed so strange and alien now drips in silver threads. Everything – the clock to the left, the candles on the mantelpiece, the mobile swirling from the ceiling, the painting on the wall – all have magically become three-dimensional. The strangers from earlier now enter my newly birthed world, no longer separate, all somehow woven together by something untappable. We are all part of the magic, connected to The Source. I feel a peace that transcends all understanding. The one they talk about in the Bible.

I feel full. I experience the deep "knowingness" that everything is exactly as it should be. No longing, no fear, just … what is. There is nothing I yearn for. I sense the All Rightness of me within the whole. I feel – dare I even say it? – bliss.

The "thing" I have been seeking … for so, so long … in one single night has been revealed to me.

✳

The next morning, instead of feeling edgy and craving – as so often happens when a drug or other addictive substance is consumed – I feel whole. In the days and weeks that follow, not a single cell or fibre of my being wants the dreaded "more". I am truly amazed and mystified. Bamboozled.

Now I am intrigued to find out as much as I can about this substance that has managed to bypass my ego trip switch, open my tightly shut doors of perception and leave me with inner quiet. That has taken me on a journey into the unknown and delivered me back, all in one full, full peace. The journey leaves me inextricably changed.

Chapter 15

MY BRAIN AND PSILOCYBIN

Amid so much misunderstanding around psychedelics such as psilocybin mushrooms, ayahuasca and ibogaine, I am – after my virgin Soma journey – keen to find out more about their origins and how "the world" got to hate on them so much. I am also determined to find out what actually *happened* in my brain that Saturday night.

I soon come across a foreign-sounding term, "the DMN", which I will discover means the Default Mode Network. What the hell is that? I soon realise, as my reading deepens, that I have had issues with my DMN for as long as I can remember.

In simple terms, the Default Mode Network is the pathway in the brain that operates as a kind of control system and dominates everyday "normal" activity and consciousness.

The DMN helps us function and perform tasks in the real world. It is also deeply connected to our egos. But over-activity in the DMN can often lead to obsessive and compulsive thinking and behaviour, and, of course, addiction. It's believed that people suffering from depression, anxiety, PTSD and substance-abuse issues have especially high activity in this area of the brain. I am the unfortunate vessel of all these afflictions.

I'm fascinated to discover that those tormented by chronic pain also appear to have excessively high commotion in the DMN.

I experience a true Aha! moment when I discover that, when

ingested, psilocybin has the power to *silence* the DMN – in other words, to put it to sleep. Oh my god (in lowercase), how amazing is that! Research has shown that magic mushrooms have a miraculous ability to *reset* the DMN and therefore act as an authentic antidepressant!

Professor David Nutt, director of the Neuropsychopharmacology Unit at Imperial College in London, has spent many years studying images of the brain and its response to psilocybin mushrooms. The Prof has discovered that when the substance is used in therapeutic doses (around 5 grams of dried mushrooms), it changes the actual cortical functions of the brain, "making them more fluid and less rigid" – in other words, slowing down activity in the DMN.

These neuroimaging studies correlate exactly with what I experienced first-hand on my psilocybin journey. He described it as "ego-dissolution". I experienced it as a shedding of the controlling and critical part of my mind.

I am riveted by what I am unearthing. Once these restrictive boundaries between the self and the world are dissolved, the temporary loss of the ego can do miraculous things in the release of neurosis, obsession, addiction or depression. According to the Prof, this is considered one of the most profound effects of psilocybin, one that can induce powerful personal and even spiritual transformations. My brain tingles with excitement.

It also amazes me to read about studies that show that in the weeks following a psilocybin journey, the DMN reactivates and, in this resetting of its pathways, depression is reduced, allowing users to experience even further deep healing and transformation.

Aldous Huxley believed that "normal consciousness" – our everyday existence – acts like a "reducing valve", which, rather than expanding, is a constraint to the world we experience and the information we process, because "normal consciousness" cannot handle too much uncontrollable or chaotic stimuli.

I realise that the psilocybin I ingested had literally expanded my mind because the part of my brain that always insisted on being in charge and controlling my thoughts had been silenced. This is what allowed me through The Doors, to move to "the other side" and experience a whole new world of consciousness. That's how I was able to transcend the constraints of "normal" time and mundane, obsessive thoughts. Oh. My. God!

Now I can't stop reading as much as my newly awakened brain can ingest. I devour it all. I come across an eccentric-sounding Brit, Amanda Feilding, also known as the Countess of Wemyss and March. She sounds like someone I would really get on with. Not only is she well known globally as a drug-policy reformer and lobbyist, but in 1998 she also established The Foundation to Further Consciousness, which later became known as The Beckley Foundation.

In a world facing an epidemic of mental illness, where one in five individuals are classified as depressed, the Foundation is doing ground-breaking work in the research on the effects of psychoactive substances on the brain and how they can be used to help treat depression, anxiety and addiction, and enhance well-being and creativity.

"The psychedelic experience can shake the brain out of its mal-adaptive patterns," says Feilding. "It is like heating up metal – it becomes more flexible, allowing new thoughts and behavioural patterns to take root. It is like pressing the restart button on a computer. In one session one can achieve what would normally take years of 'talking' therapy. Whereas SSRIs (psychiatric drugs) need to be taken daily, a single psychedelic experience can bring about a change at the root of the personality. Combined with psycho-therapy, it can bring about a paradigm shift in psychiatry."

As I read, I keep asking myself why *more* people are not using psychedelics like psilocybin or plant medicines like ibogaine and ayahuasca in order to heal? Why had I felt such shame before embarking on my first journey? Such fear of recrimination?

It appears that there is an overwhelming conspiracy of silence around the miraculous benefits of psychoactive medicines, where ignorance and denialism have defeated benefits and logic.

Gabor Maté, the Hungarian-Canadian physician and world-renowned expert in addiction, has an interesting take on denialism in research. Despite mountains of evidence pertaining to, say, the connection between childhood trauma and addiction, many so-called academic experts in the psychiatric and medical fields insist on making statements like: "Childhood trauma *may* be connected to addiction, but more research is required."

"What planet are these people living on?" asks Maté in a clip I discover on YouTube. "Are they not familiar with the hundreds of studies on the relationship between childhood trauma and addiction? Are they not aware of the studies of brain development and trauma? What intellectual labyrinth have they been lost in for them to come up with these statements? What I am saying is the over-intellectualisation, the very need for research, is a factor of denialism."

So, if it's that hard to convince the medical science world of the obvious relationship between childhood trauma and addiction, imagine how difficult it is to convince the greater world of the therapeutic benefits of a substance like psilocybin?

In my reading, I am relieved to discover that there has at least been some progress in the past 10 or so years, with highly reputable institutions, including the Johns Hopkins University, publishing astounding evidence of the therapeutic benefits of psilocybin for cancer patients and people suffering from anxiety, depression and addiction. But still, these studies are on the periphery of Big Pharma, which maintains an iron grip on the mental-health industry, peddling often addictive and side-effect-riddled drugs like Adderall, Suboxone, Zoloft and

Wellbutrin as ways of plastering over depression and anxiety.

"More research is required" appears to be the mantra of denialism. But I believe the problem lies even deeper.

We do not live in a society that aims to empower and nurture the individual. We live in a world that's divided into consumers and producers, and one of the most significant results of this is that it leads directly to enrichment of the few and the exploitation of the many. Whether it's sending men down mines to sweat in the hunt for gold, paying them a pittance for their back-breaking toil; exploiting children in sweatshops where the average age is 11 years; workers trapped in factories, supermarkets, call centres, office blocks and banks, the ants in the production machine that is our world all work the cogs for the benefit of the few. I don't believe that ours is a society that seeks to address *holistic* development by way of the spiritual and mental enlightenment of its people.

And so the denialism grows.

I'm not surprised when I discover that Gabor Maté is an ardent advocate of the use of psychedelics like ayahuasca, MDMA and psilocybin to address and heal addiction. He believes that their beneficial use far outweighs the misconceived recreational one, primarily ingested for escapist purposes.

"In its proper ceremonial setting, under compassionate and experienced guidance, the plant – or, as tradition has it, the spirit of the plant – puts people in touch with their repressed pain and trauma, the very factors that drive all dysfunctional behaviours. Consciously experiencing our primal pain loosens its hold on us. Thus may they achieve in a few sittings what many years of psychotherapy can only aspire to. It may also allow people to re-experience inner qualities long missing in action, such as wholeness, trust, love and a sense of possibility. People quite literally remember themselves."

Despite all the substantial evidence that psilocybin and plants like ayahuasca have the miraculous ability to assist in the healing of the broken, the addicted, the traumatised, the mentally ill and the suffering – which is most of us, actually – the mantra of denialism chanted by those who will not benefit financially, deafens the evidence. The hollow roar of "more research is required" stamps on the truth and cultivates ignorance.

Because of this denialism conspiracy, substances like psilocybin and ayahuasca are all illegal "drugs", shunted into the highest class of "danger", right alongside real demons like smack, crack and meth. So the chances of broad research and funding deemed "acceptable" to the big players in the pharmaceutical industry are almost zero.

But I do believe that there is light at the end of this dark tunnel. Exciting pockets of hope, like Amanda Feilding's Beckley Foundation, the research at the Johns Hopkins University and work by Professor David Nutt, have all produced astounding evidence of the healing power and efficacy of these substances.

At this moment in time, however, both psilocybin and ayahuasca are still conveniently criminalised in most countries, and so the mental-health industry remains largely in the iron grip of Big Pharma. And here's the rub … If people were to be enlightened and "cured", I believe an entire "mental pill" industry that peddles highly addictive drugs, riddled with damaging side-effects, would be severely compromised, maybe even eventually shut down.

I don't believe it's in the wider interest of the medical, psychiatric and mental-health industries to actually cure people.

Chapter 16

JOURNEY TWO

I embark on my second Soma journey on 3 September 2015. I've just celebrated 16 years clean and sober at an NA meeting. Six months have passed since my first psilocybin experience in which my brain was set on fire. I know deep in my bones that I am still clean and sober and that my profound experience has not meant a relapse of any kind. In fact, it is intrinsically connected to my new vista into a far deeper recovery.

While I have continued attending NA meetings, unlike my usual transparent self, I have not been able to share a single word about my recent awakening. I sense that the majority of people in these rooms will instantly see me in a fallen light, as many saw our father of recovery, Bill W.

Back in 1958, a year or so after he'd experienced his psychedelic spiritual awakening, in an attempt to "clear" himself, Bill wrote a long letter to the AA fellowship explaining reasons for using LSD. It fell mainly on deaf ears. He subsequently resigned from the AA governing body. He was now free to continue exploring his spiritual journey, but the negativity from some of his fellow alcoholics struck him deeply.

I too, over the years, experienced the damaging effects of toxic gossip in NA, especially in my first few years after joining the fellowship, at a time when I was at my most vulnerable. I had entered the rooms of NA back in 1999 a deranged and very ill individual. My descent into hell had entailed losing my babies, my home, my marriage, as well as a violent gang rape. Drug-frazzled and shattered from PTSD, my erratic behaviour had been all over the place, bordering on psychotic. Often, I was not able to be contained in the strictly formulated 12-Step meetings.

When I was about 60 days clean, word got to me that certain NA members were campaigning to have me thrown out. I was devastated. Highly vulnerable to a relapse during those early days, I craved love and acceptance. I seriously contemplated going back into Hillbrow, scoring heaps of crack, getting totally wasted and then OD-ing on heroin. It didn't help that my husband had taken up with a pretty blonde he'd met at an NA meeting. It felt as if the rooms were literally abuzz with whispers every time I made an appearance. Somehow, I managed to turn the other cheek and glue myself to my chair in the circle and listen to those who said, "Keep coming back." But, in all honesty, thoughtless cruelty and toxic gossip nearly killed me.

Later, in 2005, when *Smacked* came out, word again got back to me that certain people, including the then chairperson of NA, were furious that I had broken the tradition of anonymity. Fortunately, by that stage I had developed a thick skin and could shake off the slings and arrows of my detractors. But still it wounded me, and I often wonder how many less tough-minded addicts have relapsed and possibly died because of gossip in a fellowship that is touted as "loving and supportive".

And now, with 16 years of sobriety behind me, although I wholly embrace the notion that "the truth will set you free", I cannot open myself to the probability of attack. The thought of once again being subjected to the NA gossip machine convinces me to keep my psychedelic experience to myself. I suspect some of the less spiritually inclined members would wring their hands in glee at the news that I had "fallen".

Yet still, my encounter with psilocybin weighs heavily on my NA conscience.

I have had a number of arguments with Soul-Mat, who believes I should publicly own my new experience. He does not seem to understand the hold that NA has over me. He continues, rightfully, to point out that psilocybin is not a drug, that it is not addictive, that it is a "teaching" and "healing" agent. He also regularly mentions the hypocrisy in the rooms – that many of the recovering addicts at meetings are buzzed out on caffeine and nicotine or under the influence of a medicine cabinet full of mind-numbing antidepressants and side-effect-laden mood stabilisers. Yet still I lack the courage to speak about my profound and spiritually charged experience at meetings. I am in no way ready to risk transparency in exchange for the judgment of others.

Of course this reluctance all has to do with my ego. I thrive on being respected and loved at NA. I have worked so damn hard to get where I am. I need these people to admire me. I still give "too many fucks" about what "they" think of me.

The truth is that in the past few years before I embarked on my first journey, I'd hit a locked door in my recovery. I had stopped exploring. After so many years of hearing the same preambles over and over again at meetings, I had stopped feeling excited. There was no unknown for me in these rooms. In all honesty, I was bored – primarily with myself.

And although the wisdom of the 12 Steps can never be doubted – the programme literally saved my life – after my first Soma journey, feeling as spiritually ignited as I did, I know I am now forever changed. I will never forget that gunky, dark green sludge so prevalent on that first night. It seems symbolic of my inability to access "God" during my past 16 years in 12-Step recovery.

Of course, that's not to say that a spirit-filled journey is not possible in 12-Step programmes. Many others before me have accessed it, and many others will do so after me; I am acutely aware that this has been *my* experience, due to my own "god-doubting" limitations.

I also now know that for me to attain ongoing transformation, I need to step into the unknown. I need to accept that there will be overwhelming fear and many soul-destroying doubts to work through regardless, before I am able to make it to the other side, all the while without a fucking clue where I am going. But venturing into mysterious realms has always appealed to me …

✳

It's not yet summer in the Western Cape. There's a chill to the evening air. Back for the second time in the Healing House, this time round I am far less anxiety-stricken. In fact, I am calmly excited. The memory of my first journey is still stored as *the* most meaningful, joy-filled and perception-shifting experiences of my life. I am not the same person I was six months ago. And because my first voyage was so exhilarating, I fully expect number two to be an extension of that. But I will soon come to understand that Soma has other plans.

I'm flushed and ready to party in the cosmos. Soul-Mat is by my side. This time, I'm not clutching his hand, although I still can't bear the idea of not having him right next to me.

Just a few days earlier, on 28 August, I arrive for good in Cape Town, having resigned from my job and sold my house in Joburg. I've moved my entire existence to set up a new home with Soul-Mat. I land at CT International with the last few objects of my life checked into the plane's stowage. For some strange reason, I have the landline telephone in my handbag. A huge truck carrying all my worldly belongings arrives at our new rental later that afternoon. It's Soul-Mat's birthday.

"Happy birthday, darling," I say as we jam-pack my life into his garage. "I am your present."

Now, as the psilocybin kicks in, there is no lethargic, sludgy green veil as before. I move swiftly into a brilliant world of patterns and colours.

And then, suddenly, all that changes. This time I am taken into a much darker place.

Tonight is a journey of tears. A deep, hard and choking ache in which I am shown the pain I have caused others in my life. They say an addict negatively affects, on average, 40 people. I have definitely filled my quota. As the night runs its course, it is revealed to me how deeply I have hurt my family: my brother, my sisters, my sons and my mother.

I see my brother weeping as he begs my skeletal drug-addled body to get clean. I watch through his eyes. I feel the deep pain in the hearts of my sisters as I turn from them and run off with my narcotic demons. My firstborn strapped into a baby car seat as we head off on desperate drug runs to score. I see his little brown eyes watching as we bend over tin foil, to imbibe our fix and chase the dragon. I watch my pregnant body carrying my youngest son, me aching to die, as my body grows heavier, his foetal soul screaming to get out.

The pain is relentless; it seems to have no end. My mother stands before me. Her heart is broken; her eyes stream sorrow as she watches her daughter destroy herself. She is shattered, and I brought that on her.

Somewhere, during the course of this long night of knives, I am back in the womb. I taste the tears of the woman who bore me. She is in grief as she carries me. I see my sister Marianne, the baby my mother lost before conceiving me. I am delivered into this world in heartache. I am birthed into pain. I see my father fall, stricken by heart failure, when the ticking of his own life source comes to an abrupt halt. I watch my mother broken. I see us all – me, my sisters and brother – abandoned in the widowed, weeping house. I observe how I embark on my journey of sorrow, how my little confused self is drawn to a death urge. She knows no better.

My journey of self-destruction unfolds. I turn the powerlessness of inherited pain on myself. Running-running-searching for that which is familiar: Death. I become my own supreme punisher. And, as I hurt myself, I destroy everyone who crosses my path.

After what feels like hours, all images fade. Now I only *feel*. There are no pictures; my entire body reverberates with a gazillion aching neurons. I have been transported, taken beyond my defences, deep into the source of my sorrow. It is impossible to really describe what happens on this night, but these are the remembered images of my revelations.

What I do know is that I connect to the root of the pain I have carried with me always, the pain with which I have painted my world and hurt so many others who crossed my path.

And then right at the end of the night, just when I think I can take no more, that I cannot go on, that I will die from all this heartbreak, from above, in the throes of the infinite ache, I hear a voice:

The only thing is love.

✳

Long after the rest of journeyers have left their mattresses to partake of Monica's special soup in the kitchen, to gather around the fire that sizzles and burns outside, I lie alone in the ceremony room. My pillowcase and the tissues beside me are drenched in saline. This is the salt of my soul. I lie in my rebirth space and let the images play back.

For the first time in all my years of recovery, naively believing that I had healed all these wounds, I have now been forced to confront the seas of unshed tears that I hold within me. While the pain I have caused my loved ones is immense, the suffering I have meted out to myself is as big as the world's.

I am struck by the deep realisation of why I've been hurting myself and others my entire life. Why pain has been such a familiar place for me to gravitate to. The light finally goes on! While, intellectually, I have understood the concept that "hurt people hurt people", I have never truly embraced it. All the years and years of my using – the heroin, the crack, the dagga, the booze, the toxic love affairs, my torturous relationship with my mother, my attempts at trying to die over and over again – all have been hollow efforts to self-medicate. To stop the pain that's been ripping at my forever soul. To unravel from a life muddled by death.

Tonight is a breakthrough. I have gone into the heart of my own darkness. In a single session, I have had a revelation of self so deep that it is beyond anything I have ever known. I have seen the pit of my pain. There are no plasters left to hide it.

I stare at the ceiling. Leonard Cohen is singing just to me. Of gathering up the brokenness … New tears roll down my cheeks. That voice of his. It echoes in my soul. He sings of gates of mercy, how none of us are deserving of "the cruelty or the grace". He speaks of the darkness yielding and draws me in to believe that my spirit and "limbs" can indeed be healed.

This is the church I have been looking for all my life.

What I now know as I lie on my tear-soaked sheets, listening to Father Leonard's deep comforting words, is that I want to mend, deeply, and that the road that stretches before me is long.

Strangely, I am comforted. I feel a sense relief. It's as though all my carefully constructed veils of denial, those mummy-like bandages that didn't serve me, and instead strangled me, have now been torn asunder.

Am I Lazarus, who has risen from the dead?

No therapist, no 12-Step meeting, no self-help book, nothing of this conscious world has been able to show me what I have seen and felt tonight – the unassailable gift of truth.

And yet, in all the suffering, that of my family, my sons and my own, the message is one of release and comfort: *The only thing is love.*

As I step outside the ceremony room, I turn to look at the clock in the kitchen. It's 3am. I have been deep in journey since 9pm. Six long hours in the real world, a lifetime in the one beyond The Veil.

Outside, under the sky's umbrella hood of stars, the night world looks shiny and new. I sit around the fire, beside my fellow psychonauts. Each of us radiates infant rawness.

On a bench across from the gathering, I see my mushroom mother Monica smiling at me, shadows of the flames dancing across her beautiful face. She doesn't need to say it; I see it in her eyes. *You've worked so hard. Now your real journey has begun.*

I am bone tired, yet fully energised. I have been to hell and back. But it's a wondrous feeling and, for the first time, I think I finally understand that much overused word – "catharsis". The Greeks called it *katharos* – pure. Cleansing through drama.

Chapter 17

THE PRICE OF FORGIVENESS

The following day, as the real world re-emerges and I revisit the night's events, the weight of my past wrongdoings has me slouching around our home in Cape Town in deep contemplation.

In the first few years of my recovery, I did Step Four in NA a number of times, an exercise in which I was asked to do a "searching and fearless moral inventory" of myself. I wrote hundreds of pages. Then I admitted all my wrongdoings to my sponsor by completing Step Five and later made a list of those I had harmed. I tried to make amends wherever possible, as the 12-Step programme instructed me to. Some people accepted my pleas for forgiveness, others didn't.

But now I ask myself: Have I really? Made amends?

My previous night's journey tells me there is still much pain in the ether, that all the ache has not been resolved. I know that shame is not the most productive of emotions, but now it seems appropriate. I feel knocked out, cauterised by it. How am I to fix the hurt I have caused others, especially those in my family? Clearly, my "sorrys" have not been enough.

In the weeks that follow, I find myself able to dwell on the things I have done in my past without beating myself up. For the first time since I got sober, I can truly place myself in the shoes of those I've hurt, without resorting to my usual line of defences. I am able to take a step back and fully accept that

I have hurt my two sons, as well as their father. I've hurt my brother. I've hurt my two sisters and my mother deeply. I have hurt the rest of the extended family.

Before this journey, I'd tried to convince myself that I'd done as much as I could to fix things – the letters, the WhatsApps, the attempts of shame-filled real-life conversations – all genuine efforts on my part to say "sorry". But have any of those pleas actually made a difference? My Soma journey has shown me how the damage of addiction is ground like grout into the grooves of our relationships.

In those first few years of recovery, when I didn't receive the blessing of absolution from some of my loved ones, I experienced enormous rejection and pain. Unable to change their hearts, I switched focus and tried to transform my life.in the hope that I could restore pride and dignity to the family. I had worked incredibly hard to become self-sufficient, to not be a financial burden or embarrassment to them. I had saved money, bought property. I had tried to care for my boys in the best way my broken self could. I wrote books, went back to university to get an Honours degree.

But now I see that I may well have deluded myself in thinking that the successes I accumulated have made them proud. Perhaps my achievements are salt in their wounds because in their eyes I have "gotten away with it" without paying the full penance. Perhaps, for them, it would have been easier if I had died …

"What is the price of forgiveness?" I ask myself.

I know that my mother – the one person I probably harmed more than anyone else in my life because I was her shining star who crashed into a black hole of self-destruction – was proud of me in the last months of her life. This gives me some comfort. At that time, I had been clean and sober for almost five years.

In mid-2004, we find ourselves in a hospital room in the Linksfield Clinic after she has undergone a brutal Whipple procedure, performed on pancreatic cancer sufferers where the head of the pancreas, a portion of the bile duct, the gall bladder and the duodenum are removed. In my mother's case, with the cancer so far advanced, a portion of her stomach is also cut away. I will come to believe later that it is the trauma of this operation that quickly kills her.

Still woozy from the morphine, my mother has an otherworldly serenity shrouding her as I sit holding her hand in the golden afternoon sunlight. It is here that I say my deep-felt "sorrys" and she receives them in her heart. And so we find our way back home, to our root of love.

In my Soma journey I had experienced my mother's gaping dark pain, as I shifted right into her being to experience what I had done to her during the years of my addiction. And what her addiction had done to mine. At some point in the night I connect to her soul as she leaves this earth. My mother departs this world as a bird. My heart is filled with love for the woman who toiled for me, gave me life and finally flies free.

✳

Weeks go by. I keep experiencing flashbacks of the journey. There are days that I am dogged by self-doubt. Am I really getting better? Maybe I am getting worse. With all this knowledge, this achingly hard and brutal work, why am I not "recovered" yet?

I think this is a question that plagues many of us fallen souls seeking redemption and enlightenment. I now see how ludicrous it is for me to dwell on some misguided notion that "it" should somehow be easier. Life is hard. We carry the wounds of our ancestors deep within our bones.

The more one searches, the more difficult it becomes, because to go deeper is always to touch the bottomless well of pain. And once that journey starts, there is only a mirage of an end point.

The end can feel like the beginning, and the beginning the end. There is no end to what we will discover.

Any notion that taking psilocybin will offer some kind of miraculous quick-fix that will solve all of life's problems has been shattered by my second journey. The thing with psychedelic medicines like ayahuasca and psilocybin is that they are *temporary* ego obliterators. For a few magical hours, a shining light is cast that allows one to see the "other side", when the all-controlling "I" steps aside. For a few hours, one gets to experience the possibility of a better and freer self, but once back in the real world, hard-wired defects and old habits return. Sometimes they hit back even harder. But because we touch the truth as we journey deeper, each time we come away armed with a little more insight. This soul search may eventually lead to expanded wisdom and enlightenment, depending on what we do with that awareness.

What Soma gives us is the magic switch to confront our hidden, fist-clenched lies and face our delusions and denials. Then, in stark daylight, we must summon the courage to embark on the hard path into the unknown real world of change, forging a trail towards the long and brutal process of creating a new and ever-evolving self.

To search the soul is a lifelong and arduous journey. It is hard, *hard* work unpeeling the layers of the past, our pain, our wrongdoings, our denials and all the pretty lies we sell ourselves. And, just as a wound throbs and aches as it is healing, there may be times when we feel we are even more injured, that we are getting worse, not better.

Once again, I am not the same person after my *See the pain you have caused others* journey. Something deep has shifted. And then, quite unexpectedly, by acknowledging and accepting the hurt I have caused those I love, I find an unexpected release from my shame.

I now realise that maybe I've been going about this forgiveness journey the wrong way. For how can they forgive me when I haven't even come close to forgiving myself? I am powerless over how they perceive me. I cannot force them to love or even exonerate me.

Finally, the road has opened for me to embark on my journey of becoming gentler, kinder and more loving to "me", to unburden myself from guilt. It is the only way. This path will slowly lead me to feel compassion for others, to love those who are yet to find a way back home, who cannot love me. Or themselves.

The only thing is love.

Over the next months I have no need or desire to return to journey. I am sated by this deep feeling that has shaken me out of the coma of what I thought I knew and understood about myself. My entire framework of recovery has changed. My brash ego, the one that tried to tell me I was "better", has grown a little quieter. There has been a chink cut in my pride, a humbling of self that whispers gently: *You still have so much to learn. You have so much brokenness that still needs to be healed.*

I am finally beginning to clear my inner debris, connecting millions of chaotic dots in the hope of becoming a better me.

A baby crawls, then walks. One tiny step at a time.

Chapter 18

RAT PARK AND HILLBILLY HEROIN

"Love binds, and it binds forever. Good binds while evil unravels. Separation is another word for evil; it is also another word for deceit."
– Michel Houellebecq, *The Elementary Particles*

In my long and troubled experience of narcotics and alcohol, the cavernous black hole of emptiness inside was the driving force that screeched for more. Just as Carl Jung had described addiction as a "spiritual thirst", I too had this "hole in the soul" that drove me to search dark and dangerous alleyways to get my "fix". So I truly believe that the opposite of addiction is connection.

Connected. Definition: awaken meaningful emotions, establish rapport, bring together or into contact so that a real or notional link is established.

In more than 20 years sobriety, I have never met an addict who didn't suffer from "disconnect" – a feeling of not belonging in this world. Among the thousands of addicts I've encountered over the last three decades, both when I was using and after I got clean, this schism often has its roots in some kind of childhood trauma. It's usually connected to dark abuse, a deep pain that lingers behind the feelings of being "lesser than", resulting in a sense of feeling isolated from one's self and the rest of the world.

A few years ago, you might remember a post that did the

rounds on Facebook about rats and addiction. I assumed that these were recent, breaking-news findings but, on digging deeper, I was surprised to discover that the "Rat Park study" referred to an experiment conducted way back in the 70s by Canadian psychologist, Bruce K Alexander.

Alexander basically set out to prove that it wasn't drugs that, in fact, caused addiction but rather living conditions and *disconnection*. To prove his theory, he established a huge rat colony in which he made the rats' living space 200 times larger than a normal rat cage, resembling a kind of five-star Rat Hilton Hotel. The place was fully equipped with entertainment, including wheels and balls, plenty of food and ample space for mating and frolicking. Alexander then placed two liquid dispensers on either side of the cage – one filled with water, the other with a morphine-based solution.

He then placed single rats in small cages that were cramped and held no distractions. The rats here were essentially in solitary confinement, their only choice being between a dispenser of "straight" water and one laced with morphine.

In his findings, Alexander discovered that the Hilton rats consistently resisted the morphine-laced water, preferring to drink the plain tap water. Next door, however, the lonely single-cell rats were 19 times more likely to hit the smack-infused water.

But when, after 57 days of drinking nothing but morphine water, he placed the cramped rats into the larger Hilton community, the addicted rats all went through voluntary opiate withdrawal. It wasn't long before they were playing and frolicking with one another – and gravitating towards the plain water.

Based on Rat Park, Alexander had his revolutionary evidence: that rather than drugs driving addiction, feelings such as loneliness, isolation, hopelessness, boredom and shitty living conditions were the real catalysts to becoming substance dependent. Just as the rodents in Rat Park indicated, people are more likely to resist drugs and alcohol under pleasant and connected conditions.

One might argue that rats and people are not the same, but rats by nature are in fact pretty close to human beings: they are social, industrious creatures who thrive on contact and activity. A rat in solitary confinement, with no diversions, is driven to use drugs, much like humans are, when deprived of any stimulation.

We need only look at the extraordinarily high levels of substance abuse in overcrowded prisons. The Rat Park experiment made me realise that, in many ways, addiction has so much to do with the cage in which you find yourself.

However, rather than Alexander's findings being embraced and used to address the scourge of addiction in new and effective ways, the Simon Fraser University, where Alexander had conducted Rat Park, inexplicably shut down the experiment. It appears that his discovery threatened the "stamp out and punish the addict" approach. The concept that drugs may not be the actual problem and that at the root of the scourge is, in fact, the way we *mistreat* addicts, was simply too revolutionary for people to handle at the time – and still is, actually. Acknowledging Alexander's results would mean that we would have to treat those suffering from addiction with compassion.

If we, as a society, are compelled to own up to the responsibility we have towards the broken, abused and dispossessed, then we will have to actually *do* something: spend money on recovery, create safe spaces and actually *care* for people. Gabor Maté famously said: "All you have to do is treat a child well. And addiction problems will all but disappear."

Since the 1970s' Rat Park experiment, very little has changed in the way that most governments and society as a whole choose to deal with addiction.

In fact, over time, the battlefield has become a lot more

dangerous, with Big Pharma sometimes actively going out of its way to *create* addicts.

Nowhere is this more evident than in the OxyContin epidemic that Purdue Pharma unleashed on American consumers in 1996 under the guise of "safe", "non-addictive pain alleviation" medication. Driven by profit and greed, the Sackler family-owned pharmaceutical empire made outrageous claims, endorsed by the corrupted FDA, that only one per cent of users could become addicted to their miracle slow-release opioid.

Oxy soon became particularly popular in rural Appalachian communities, in places like West Virginia, hence the nickname "Hillbilly Heroin".

Between 1996 and 2020, Purdue reaped $35 billion in revenue as it peddled America's bestselling painkiller. Since its appearance on the market, overdose by Oxy has killed at least 400 000 addicts, significantly contributing to the US opioid crisis that's claimed more than a million lives since 1999.

Ironically, while the medical establishment endorses "respect-able", but potentially lethal drugs, the world is still steeped in a "War on Drugs" mentality. This war demands that certain sub-stances are criminalised while others remain legit. However, the real losers are always the addicts who are regarded as degener-ate misfits who need to be punished, isolated and incarcerated.

Chapter 19

THE IRRATIONAL WAR ON DRUGS

"Psychedelics are illegal not because a loving government is concerned that you may jump out of a third-storey window. Psychedelics are illegal because they dissolve opinion structures and culturally laid down models of behaviour and information processing. They open you up to the possibility that everything you know is wrong."
– Terence McKenna, *The New Science of Psychedelics* (2013)

I began to read whatever I could to find out how the War on Drugs had come about and how it had landed the world in this misinformed and highly regressive mess.

The guns were drawn when American president Richard Nixon made a speech from the White House Briefing Room on 17 June 1971 announcing that "[P]ublic enemy No. 1 in the United States is drug abuse. In order to fight and defeat this enemy, it is necessary to wage a new, all-out offensive."

The back story to this statement was far more sinister than I could have imagined. In the last two decades, there was growing evidence that Nixon's War on Drugs had never actually been about drugs, but rather a thinly veiled excuse to declare war on black people, uncontrollable anti-Vietnam War "rebels" and unruly, pot smoking, LSD-infused hippies.

In 1996, in his book, *Smoke and Mirrors: The War on Drugs*

and the Politics of Failure, Dan Baum quoted John Ehrlichman, Nixon's domestic policy advisor and Watergate co-conspirator at the time: "The Nixon campaign began in 1968, and the Nixon White House after that, had two enemies: the anti-war left and black people. You understand what I'm saying? We knew we couldn't make it illegal to be either against the war or blacks, but by getting the public to associate the hippies with marijuana and blacks with heroin, and then criminalising both heavily, we could disrupt those communities. We could arrest their leaders, raid their homes, break up their meetings and vilify them night after night on the evening news. Did we know we were lying about the drugs? Of course we did."

Although the War on Drugs lost at least some of its momentum when Jimmy Carter came to power in 1977 – his election campaign included decriminalising marijuana – by the early 1980s the gains Carter had made in bringing America to its senses were lost when the War on Drugs gained new energy with Hollywood actor-turned-president Ronald Reagan winning the US presidency.

I was in matric in 1984 when Reagan's wife, Nancy, launched her "Just Say No" campaign to educate America's children on the dangers of drugs. That same year, a small group of anti-druggers representing a similar campaign, "Say Yes to Life", visited our school.

The nerdy woman who stood on stage in the hall, hyping the dangers of dagga, only exacerbated my desire to get stoned. I'd already experienced the heady joys of being high the previous year. Her impassioned pleas for us to abstain from all drugs did not, however, include alcohol.

I longed for the lengthy, yawn-inducing session to be over, for the second-break bell to ring so I could scurry off to take a swig of the bottle of wine hidden in the rose garden, light up a Camel filter, toke up a joint and forget about her anachronistic incantations. Thinking back on my rebellious teenaged self back then, if anything, the badly dressed woman with her thick specs and equally thick ankles made me want to get even more voraciously drunk and high.

It was in 1986, when I was in my second year at UCT Drama School, smoking copious amounts of "illicit" weed, that Reagan's Anti-Drug Abuse Act was passed in the US, establishing tougher, mandatory minimum prison sentences for certain drug offences. And this was where the ugly head of racism really drove the new laws. Longer prison sentences were handed out to crack cocaine offenders (a drug mainly used by black people) than to cocaine powder offenders (more popular among white drug users). Never mind that today there is irrefutable evidence that crack was shipped in and planted in black communities across America to wreak havoc and vicariously create a perfect excuse for black men and women to be incarcerated for supposed "serious" drug offences.

It turns out that the "lie" on which the War on Drugs was based proved to be highly effective. There is no doubt that people of colour – black people and Hispanics – were targeted and arrested on suspicion of drug use at much higher rates than their white counterparts. American jails subsequently began filling up with a disproportionately higher number of black "offenders". Human Rights Watch estimates that more than 40 million "drug arrests" have been made over the last four decades in the US. And for every one white drug incarceration, 10 black people are imprisoned.

※

In early August 2017, Cape Town hosts a week-long conference on substance abuse. One of the keynote speakers is Ethan Nadelmann, the American founder of the Drug Policy Alliance.

Although I am not in attendance, I hear about the fired-up speech Nadelmann makes at a delegate dinner on the eve of the conference, castigating America's War on Drugs for its total failure. I google his name and come across a similar-themed TED talk he made at a drug-policy conference in Rio de Janeiro in 2014: *Why We Need To End The War On Drugs*. I am transfixed. I find his email address and mail him on the off chance that he will give me permission to quote him in this book. A week later I receive a response. He happily agrees, pointing me to his 15-minute powerhouse TED talk. Here is an edited transcript:

I'll tell you something else I learned, that the reason some drugs are legal and others not, has almost nothing to do with science or health or the relative risk of drugs, and almost everything to do with who uses and who is perceived to use particular drugs.

In the late 19th century, when most of the drugs that are now illegal were legal, the principal consumers of opiates in my country and others were middle-aged white women, using them to alleviate aches and pains when few other analgesics were available. And nobody thought about criminalising it back then because nobody wanted to put Grandma behind bars. But when hundreds of thousands of Chinese started showing up in my country, working hard on the railroads and the mines and then kicking back in the evening just like they had in the old country with a few puffs on that opium pipe, that's when you saw the first drug prohibition laws in California and Nevada, driven by racist fears of Chinese transforming white women into opium-addicted sex slaves.

The first cocaine prohibition laws were similarly prompted by racist fears of black men sniffing that white powder and forgetting their proper place in Southern society. And the first marijuana prohibition laws, were all about fears of Mexican migrants in the West and the Southwest. And what was true in my country, is true in so many others as well, with both the origins of these laws and their implementation.

Put it this way, and I exaggerate only slightly: If the principal smokers of cocaine (crack) were affluent older white men and the principal consumers of Viagra were poor young black men, then smokable cocaine would be easy to get with a prescription from your doctor and selling Viagra would get you five to 10 years behind bars.[1]

✳

The "War on Psychedelics" was declared even earlier than the War on Drugs. During the turbulent, anarchic sixties, dominated by hippie flower-power counterculture, these psychedelically altered "druggies" posed a grave threat to conservative American society – far more so, apparently, than cocaine snorters and heroin spikers. People were outraged by these "degenerates" who were travelling through The Doors and, on returning from their "trips", protesting against the violent and corrupt worlds of American politics and society. But perhaps even more importantly – and why psychedelics really needed to be stamped out – was research showing that they had the potential to revolutionise the billion-dollar mental-health industry by addressing in a holistic way widespread issues such as depression, anxiety and addiction.

So what did good ol' President Nixon do? He decided to curtail all federal funding for psychedelic research and placed all psychedelics on Schedule 1 of the Controlled Substances Act. By 1968, the fear-mongering had become contagious and all psychedelic research was banned across the globe. An article,

---

1 Ethan Nadelmann, TED talk, Rio de Janeiro (2014):
https://ted.com/talks/ethan_nadelmann_why_we_need_to_end_the_war_on_drugs?utm_source=sms&utm_medium=social&utm_campaign=tedspread-b]

"The Trip Treatment", published in 2015 in *The New Yorker*, noted: "Research soon came to a halt, and what had been learned was all but erased from the field of psychiatry."

Much later, in 2016, a year after I experienced my first psilocybin journey, despite a revival of research sparking serious interest in the healing powers of psychedelics in the field of mental health, the UK passed the excessively prohibitive Psychoactive Substances Act, making the production, supply, importation or exportation of a psychoactive substance entirely illegal.

And so, absurdly, we still find ourselves in a world where certain "drugs" – let's call them "teacher plants and fungi" – are vilified and scheduled alongside highly addictive and dangerous drugs while the devastating harms of alcohol are, for instance, repeatedly ignored.

On Professor David Nutt's "drug harm" ranking table – remember, he's the guy who has been researching the effects of psilocybin (magic mushrooms) on the brain – he places alcohol right on top as the most harmful addictive substance, just above heroin and crack cocaine. Interestingly, on the Prof's table, psilocybin is right at the bottom, with no determinable harm to the user or society *at all*.

But alcohol at the top? "What the fuck!" you may protest, as you sip on your martini, or take a slug of your seventh beer. But tarry here a moment … Professor Nutt stipulates that to get your head around this claim, it's important to separate harm to individuals from harm to society. While heroin, crack and crystal meth are ranked as the worst drugs because of the harm they cause to individuals, alcohol, heroin and crack cocaine (in that order) are assessed as the *most* damaging to society.

When he published this research back in 2009, his suggestion caused a frenzied outcry in medical circles, embarrassment to the Tory government, outrage in the alcohol industry and sensational headlines in the media.

The Prof, who at the time was the UK government's chief drug adviser, was sacked a day after his findings were made public. Most people simply could not digest that supposedly harmless beer, wine, brandy or whiskey could possibly outscore deadly heroin and terrifyingly addictive crack cocaine on a harm table.

In an interview in 2010, the Prof told the BBC: "Overall, alcohol is the most harmful drug because it's so widely used. Crack cocaine is more addictive than alcohol, but because alcohol is so widely used there are hundreds of thousands of people who crave alcohol every day, and those people will go to extraordinary lengths to get it."

It's old news that we, as an alcohol-reliant society, are in denial when it comes to the potential harm of booze. It's a huge part of our lives – it's advertised and available almost everywhere, and is consumed and revered by most global communities as part of most celebrations and social encounters. Think weddings, bar mitzvahs, wakes, after-tears, engagement parties, birthday celebrations, after-work drinks, Friday-night bar crawls, clubs, corporate functions, launches and so on and so on.

✳

It's hardly groundbreaking news that the mental-health industry is in a mess. In a world in which one in five people are depressed, and with 50 per cent of those not responding to traditional antidepressants (such as SSRIs, or selective serotonin reuptake inhibitors) and where research in the UK has shown that one in six people for whom psychiatric meds fail attempt to take their lives, a new, holistic approach is desperately needed.

The crazy thing is that there is mounting and deeply compelling evidence that a viable alternative to traditional psychiatric meds *does* exist. There's one that offers users the tools to understand the roots of their mental illness through controlled journeys, and then, afterwards, with therapeutic guidance, the opportunity to create conscious connections to self-heal. Its name is psilocybin. And it's illegal.

I think of Monica Cromhout, who was criminally charged with possessing magic mushrooms, a charge that could have landed her in prison with hardened criminals and serious drug dealers. Monica, who has taken the plunge and stood by her deep convictions, who is taking the fight all the way to the Constitutional Court – the highest court in the land – to assert her right to practise spiritual freedom, to heal herself and provide a safe space for many others who wish to do the same. Monica, who has tirelessly opened the door of her home to allow people to "touch God".

I think of all those broken souls who have journeyed and been restored to health and sanity at Monica's Healing House and other "illegal" places all over the planet. I think of myself, who could be arrested if I was to be found with psilocybin in my system, incarcerated for having a deeply spiritual and enlightening experience. I would be arrested for trying to heal myself. Yet if I were found with 10 000 bottles of tequila, I would be waved along.

Something is very wrong with this picture.

Chapter 20

THE INHERITANCE OF "NEVER ENOUGH"

My childhood was steeped in alcohol. After my father died, my mother took to the bottle. Who could really blame her? Everyday she woke up to four headstrong, hungry children and a litany of financial worries. Brandy and coke and boxed white wine became "mother's little helper".

When I took my first sip of brandy at the age of nine, I was simply mirroring my mother's behaviour; my mother, who transformed daily from being a capable, organised housewife into a woman who would pass out in front of the television or in the bath at night. Her habitual drinking was, however, only part of the harm that wrapped its languid, liquid tentacles around those of us left behind.

Growing up in an alcohol-infused home had far-reaching and infinitely damaging effects on our lives. From a young age, I noticed how booze affected my mother's moods and speech. But it was only much later that I realised how the consequences of having an inconsistent parent played out in my life, as I continually abandoned myself in exactly the same way my mother had abandoned herself. Alcohol was my gateway drug to heroin and crack cocaine. I believe it was alcohol that killed our mother.

For much of my life, I blamed her paranoia around money for my own fears of not ever having enough. After our father died and left her with four kids to feed, clothe and school, her tight-clenched fist of lack permeated our childhood. It's only in the last few years that I've been able to see that her "not enough" financial mentality was directly linked to the fact that she was an addict, just as I am, who could not help control her fear of deprivation and her ache for needing "more", rather than some moral failing on her part.

By the time I learn to feel empathy for her, by the time I really stare down the barrel of my own financial fuck-ups, my mother had been dead for almost 14 years. Now I have to face my own shortcomings.

✳

My hang-up with money explodes, threatening my relationship with Soul-Mat. Money moves in and drives an ugly wedge between us. Much to my horror, I find it impossible to share the ordinary things that couples are supposed to. I am a financial cripple.

Up until I relocate to Cape Town and start cohabitating with my new love, I have run my own money ship for all of my recovery. After moving out of my mother's home in early 2000, I go on an all-out solo mission to attempt to right the financial devastation caused by my seven years of using narcotics – by working. Working. Working. Working. Saving. Scrimping. Saving. Scrimping. Trying to play catch-up on all the years I smoked away, trying to put distance between me and my deepest fear – that of being homeless – which manifested in all its wretchedness back in 1999.

As a child, I was deeply disturbed by the tramps I saw on park benches, by beggars on the street. The sight of the vulnerable triggered a dark chasm of fear within. And finding myself homeless on that farm was as if my script of deprivation had been written long ago.

My mother's preoccupation with having no money after our father dies spreads across our childhood in a blanket of terror. The shame of not having enough sets in. My mother's fear of life is contagious. Thrown out of the safety of marriage, of the illusion that "love lasts forever" and with no real qualifications to go out and work, my mother becomes a bean counter, frozen by her financial fears.

On the nights when she hasn't consumed enough to pass out in order to escape her fear-stricken thoughts, her eyes remain glued to the ceiling, computing endless sums of how she will provide for her four children. In the room down the passage, my eyes are just as focused on the unresponsive ceiling, recalling my father's lifeless body and imagining my own death.

Going to "big school", I feel my "differentness" like a niacin-induced flush. When asked to draw a picture of our parents and ourselves, I watch my six-year-old classmates sketch bright and colourful sketches of "Mommy, Daddy and Me". The space beside my crude stick figures of my mother and me remains empty. When the teacher barks, "Melinda, draw your father!" my eyes burn with hot tears. A haphazard squiggle of a man with a moustache appears on my page. I cannot find my voice to say: "My daddy is dead."

Fatherless and filled with shame, my lies to myself and the world multiply.

As children, we are made aware on a daily basis that there is no room for indulgences. Clothes are passed down from sister to sister – I am the youngest girl – so by the time I get mine, they are often faded and a little threadbare, worn and worn out by the two ahead of me. One packet of biscuits must last the month.

By age 11, I am so crippled by worry that I start planning to find part-time work. I lie about my age and, just after my 12th birthday, I find a Saturday-morning job in Cresta shopping centre, manning the cash point at the clothing section at OK Bazaars. I feel all grown up as I ring up items, cash up the till at the end of the day, and stand in a queue with the grown-ups to get paid once the doors are locked at 1pm. I open a bank account and start saving. It feels like a giant step forward. I am at the start of my first journey to financial freedom. I watch entranced as my bank balance grows weekly.

By the time I turn 13, I'm embarrassed by the idea of working at the rather tacky and uncool OK. I'm already aware of what's hip and trendy. I've recently been exposed to punk via the British Top 10 broadcast on Radio 5 every Sunday night. The Sex Pistols, The Clash and The Stranglers have blown apart my colonised-by-ABBA world. My wardrobe is fast becoming all black.

The following year I land a job at the local cinema. I sell tickets in the downstairs ticket office and man the customer query landline. I'm 14 years old and saving every cent. The exact moment is murky, but at some point down the line, perhaps the following year, I start stealing. The turn coincides with my descent into bulimia, the ultimate master of the more-more, never-enough diseases.

As I'm selling tickets one Saturday afternoon, it dawns on me that there are few checks and balances at the cinema. In no time, I'm skimming cash during my three-nights-a-week shifts. I stash the notes in a jacket pocket at the back of my cupboard at home. It grows in bulges.

Stealing becomes addictive: the fear, the accelerated heartbeat, the moment just before the decision, the actual take, the thrill of not being discovered. The act of thieving fills me up for a micro moment, only to drop me into a chasm of guilt. I'm at war in my head – terrified that I'll get caught: the humiliation, the shame – yet another part of me feels victorious and can't wait to do it again. The addictive klepto cycle has started.

While I have genuine but intermittent pangs of guilt, the kick of the high always outweighs common sense. I tell myself that we have no money, that my father is dead, that I deserve the cash that I take, that they don't pay me enough anyway. I demonise my mother and her constant hand-wringing whinges and blame her for my new klepto tendencies.

My pilfering from the cinema diversifies into shoplifting to feed my hungry disease, the greedy-big-hole-in-the-stomach-need-for-food addiction. My relationship with money becomes enmeshed with lies, deceit and eating. Much of my pilfered cash is splurged on ridiculous amounts of sweets, guzzling them all in one crazy gluttonous binge, and then promptly purging the stash.

Finally, in Standard 9, I am caught shoplifting in school uniform, pockets stuffed with sugary goods. Flushed with shame, I stand in the manager's office, head hung low. My blazer is covered in accolades – badges and scrolls for academic, drama, debating and sport achievements. He looks at me, at all my emblems of excellence, as he warns, a sneer of disgust in his voice, "Next time I press charges."

Gooey pink-and-white marshmallows are a favourite. But they are hard to flush away afterwards – the stubborn fuckers float. My mother's painstakingly budgeted meals, flavoured by her bean-counting resentment, are flushed down the loo too. Peas, potatoes, stringy beef mixed with marshmallows float away in drains beneath the house. Heavy with the weight of my sick secret, I dream of the geyser heaving with puke, exploding on me as I sleep.

One night, my mother catches me hugging the loo, freaks out and removes all keys from the bathroom door. I must now find more devious ways to practise my foxtrot of purging, so I hide the evidence in plastic packets in the far recesses of my wardrobe.

After binges, I secret down to the bottom of the garden, near where I once played with my dolls. With my fingers, I dig shallow graves in loose soil to hide the sloppy packets of my sickness.

Like the earthen graves where I try to bury my shame, the hole inside me, which has all but enveloped me, keeps growing bigger.

By the time I meet heroin and crack in my mid-20s in the early 1990s, my cunning brain, adept in deviousness, is never short of plans to steal, commit fraud and, finally, beg for the next fix. I have been wiring my deviant self since I was young. By 1995, I am a walking, talking con artist.

I find my niche in life. I am an ace forger. I can copy signatures, photograph them in my mind and then reproduce each curve, each squiggle, each line to perfection. But the cheques are never enough; they run dry like ghosts down drainpipes. The cash is smoked up – the need for more yawns bigger, screaming and clawing to fill its yowling belly.

By 1996, the year of the birth of my first son, heroin and crack have devoured my soul and consciousness. I feel nothing when I approach friends, colleagues and strangers with concocted lies to skim R50 … for "nappies", for "formula", for "the paediatrician". The money I con is always for a hit of crack and smack.

I am the walking dead.

After a near-arrest for fraud, my heroin-addict husband and I are packed up overnight and exiled to the scintillating mining town of Klerksdorp. There I collapse into a well of inertia. After all these years of lying and cheating and working so hard to keep it all together, I slump into a heap of dependency. I will not earn a cent for my own upkeep for the next four years. I am no more than an old, outdated floppy-disc computer that's gone on the blink. I simply can't operate any more and no one, least of all me, knows how to repair me.

It's that sense of abject uselessness that very nearly kills me.

Most of my husband's family abhor me. I feel it in their glares and avoidances. I am a mouth that eats their food, a body bag living in a fully paid-for house, a lump of nothing who turns on lights and runs full-to-the-brim baths at will. All the bills that I don't pay are the evidence of my failures. My husband doesn't work either, but somehow that's okay – he's flesh and blood, he has their support by means of his birthright. I, on the other hand, am an intruder, the incubator who birthed a son who carries their name, but still an unnecessary oxygen thief.

"Why don't you go and get a job at the local Spar?" my mother in-law asks me weekly. She who's all made up to the nines can hardly look at my dishevelled, glassy-eyed gaze as she reverses her massive BMW 7 Series out of our driveway, an icy glare behind her Ralph Lauren sunglasses.

I rage inside with junkie pride. Work as a checkout girl? Pack bags at a till? Who, I? I who have been to university, I who have a degree, I who have an Einstein-like IQ? Even when I was 12, I worked a till and now she expects me to be the packer?

I seethe in entitled silence. I slump down on the couch, switch on the lights in every room in the house, turn on heaters, run overflowing baths and take food out the fridge in a house I don't pay for. I have lost all ability to generate any other thought besides where I can get my next fix; I am a gaping hole of financial and chemical dependence.

Finally, in 1999, after my babies are taken away and I plummet, burrowing my way into Hillbrow, seeking drug amnesia, I steal, I beg, I whore. I am penniless. I need a fix.

Then, eventually – reluctantly – after being rescued from the gutter by my family, I find myself on that homeless farm, surrounded by money-less ghosts. Swollen, purple-fingered alcoholics, tramps and junkies. The Robot People.

The farm is called Enoch's Walk. Named after Enoch from

Genesis, a direct ancestor of Adam, he was one of God's beloved and one of the only two men in the Good Book – the other was Elijah – to biblically escape death. According to Hebrews 11:5, "By faith Enoch was taken from this life, so that he did not experience actual death: He could not be found, because God had taken him away."

Back then, I do not give a flying fuck about Enoch, Elijah, the Bible or the church services I am forced to attend daily. All I can think of are plans to escape this hillbilly-hellhole, this cult Christian camp and get another hit. To find oblivion, I down quarts of Black Label, which I score by manipulating the farm workers. But, as each long day without my smack fix and crack pipe passes, I become increasingly aware that my glorious armour of denial and pretension is slipping.

I wake up one morning to a deathly cold clod of reality: I have nothing. I *am* nothing. I have completely slipped off and fallen from the wheel of life.

Now clothed in church-donated rags, as I try to dig my way out of each waking morning, I am faced with the harsh truth that I have lost everything. Song lyrics whir through my mind to taunt me: echoes of Leonard Cohen's "If It Be Your Will". I am one of the children in those "rags of light" … I am the girl in the Bob Dylan song who once upon a time dressed so fine … and now I am nothing more than a stray dog, a pavement special.

It's hard to explain so that anyone will understand – *really* understand – what happens to your psyche when you lose all earthly belongings. I imagine that only those who have endured natural disasters like fires, floods and wars can relate to this state of material nothingness.

What makes it an even more bitter pill for me to choke down is that all of this devastation is of my own making … I am no victim of an accidental inferno or an unexpected tornado; I am the junkie whore who sold her soul for a hit and exchanged "a walk-on part in the war" for Pink Floyd's "lead role in a cage". I am the one who had a sole hand in designing her own spectacular unnatural disaster.

But – although I am oblivious to this at the time – there is an unexpected gift waiting. For it is the rock-bottom realisation that *I am nothing* that ultimately forces me to surrender, to stop using and lying to myself. It is this awareness that finally saves my life. *You have caused this – it is only you who can get yourself out. Swallow that bitter pill, baby ...*

Without anything to numb the reality of my sodden life, I reluctantly begin to remove the scales of denial. I see myself clearly for the first time in years. I am fucked. Well and truly fucked. I have messed up all my chances and everything good that has ever been offered me. I have led myself to the brink of self-destruction. I have dragged everyone down with me. I am empty and devastated by this newfound self-awareness. Like a ground-shattering earthquake, the traumatic aftershocks of what I have done tremor through my synapses.

While my deepest childhood fears of being homeless and bereft of the material have manifested, and I can just about die from the shame that I feel, I will later see the power in that homeless farm, how it kicked all my pretensions and denials right out of my sorry, skinny ass and empty solar plexus.

Finally, after three months of digging trenches on the farm in exchange for food, I – now clean and sober – stuff my few belongings into plastic packets (just like those I used to puke into when I was 16) and slouch my way back to Joburg.

It is November 1999. I have lost all those I love: my sons, my husband, my siblings and, worst of all, my drugs. My new name is Disgrace. The only door that stands slightly ajar is the home of my mother. I have no choice but to worm my way back into the inhospitable womb of my deepest lack.

Chapter 21

CRAWLING BACK

I arrive at my mother's house with empty pockets. I come with nothing but a dark depression. I have nothing to transact with. Not a coin. I am 33 years old. I am a body bag.

Each day I stare, numbed, at *The Star* classifieds. I know I need to work, to find a job, to start addressing the state of my uselessness. But where do I begin?

I am nothing. I can do nothing. Who will have me?

After scouring the columns for work, any work, my eyes fix on the ads for escorts, sex workers, exotic dancers. I can't even do that. I can't even whore. I am gnarled in stasis. I can hardly lift my hand to brush my hair.

My fears swell bigger.

If you can't even get a job as a hooker, then you really should just kill yourself.

I long to use, to get lost, to get high, to die.

Instead, every night I drag myself to 12-Step meetings. I beg lifts, I catch minibus taxis, I get there somehow. Meetings are all I have to look forward to in the long, taunting daylight hours.

Shame travels with me, my eyes cast downwards. My poverty screams at me. I am surrounded by Nike, Puma and Converse. My sole pair of shoes, donated by the pastor at the homeless farm, are sad and scuffed. People arrive at the meetings in souped-up GTIs, Mercedes-Benzes, BMWs. I beg for lifts back home. Ignominy is my cloak for all to see.

My tongue has gone numb and my brain is no longer functional. How will I ever land employment if I can't even utter a sentence?

I watch in envy as the rest of the world works: street sweepers, bank tellers, even the beggars at robots seem to be part of the cycle of earning. I do nothing. Not a single thing.

Even when I try to read a book, the words I see running in meaningless black lines on white pages stutter and remain incomprehensible. I can't hold on to them. I have become lost in the mire of no meaning. So, I just stare at the clock as it tick-ticks by, snail-slow seconds, mountainous minutes dragging themselves in circles to display hours, days, weeks … The rest of my life.

While my body is slowly healing, day by day, my mind becomes increasingly obsessed with the realisation that I am unable to join the world and work, that I am entirely useless. Oh God. Does anyone know how long a day can be when you are doing nothing, paralysed by Time?

Finally, after almost a year of stasis, I manage to break out of my labourless prison and find a job as a waitress. I, who have a university degree, who was once an award-winning filmmaker, who in another life was the girl who looked so fine, who was a somebody, now becomes a table cleaner and a food and drinks server.

But I have lost my life force to resist. I have given in to the fact that I have fucked up my past and my present, and if I have any hope in hell of making a semblance of a future, if I am ever to be a mother to my two small sons again, if I am ever to take a guiltless breath on this planet, I need to bury this sack of sick pride and join the pack of those who work for a living. Some might call this humility. It feels like shame to me. But I need to start doing *something*. It's life or death, baby.

I know I must accumulate dirty cash and gather little piles of coins. I need to start from the destruction Ground Zero and slowly eke out some kind of validation of my existence. Otherwise, I will die. I know that for sure.

Money is a brutal master. Without it, you are a rabid exile, a leper crawling and clawing at the gates. In a city like Joburg, it's the passport to everything. Having none renders you a ghost, identity-less.

Moving between tables has its pay-off. After many months of mindless waitressing, I manage to accumulate enough to secure a deposit and rent a dingy flat in Melville. To me it's a palace. Leaving my mother's house behind has become a choice between staying alive and blowing my brains out.

Pots, pans, plates and furniture are donated by new friends I have made in the NA fellowship. At the time, I don't realise how significant my path to action has been. I can now cook simple meals and have my sons sleep over. It's the first time I have looked after myself in years. It's the first time I am taking care of my children on my own. I get divorced. I now have the boys three days and nights a week.

I give notice at the smelly fish restaurant and land a job at a demurer coffee shop. I begin to write features for magazines. Just as I used to stash my money from my cinema klepto spoils as a teenager, I now save my tips in my big jacket pocket and bank what I make from journalism.

After a year of slaving and saving, I have enough to buy a cheap Honda Ballade with those winking lights. Up until now I have been terrified of driving; I finally teach myself by practising going forward and backward in a parking lot. I can now transport myself to work. I can now drive myself to NA meetings. I give others lifts. I try to practise gratitude. Saying "thank you" becomes a pathway to seeing the world in a new light. Although my life is only inching along, at least it's moving.

And then one day I wake up and the "Kill yourself" voice is gone.

I am offered a job as a copy editor at the magazine, the one that published my very first story, "Six Weeks in Hell". I progress to features writer, then senior writer, then features editor. I confront my tax disaster. I make amends with SARS. I try again to say sorry to the people I have hurt. I write letters, many letters, begging for forgiveness.

Things are slowly changing. By taking one small step at a time, I have somehow managed to become part of the functional world again, simply by shrugging off the victim cloak of ignominy and pitching up for life.

My eyeline is no longer directed at the pavement. I sometimes even momentarily notice the sky, the stars, the birds and the trees. Life begins to thread itself into a fragile tapestry of meaningfulness and manageability.

I sporadically find myself experiencing feelings that have long been buried: a pinprick of self-love, a pinch of pride. If you water it, love is a garden that grows. Love is an elixir that heals.

But, despite feeling rare surges of a sense of abundance, my mother's ferret-like money mentality is deeply cast in my DNA. When it comes to managing my finances, it is the only way I know: to stash, hoard and worry. It is what both saves and strangles me.

Chapter 22

MEETING MY MONEY FEAR HEAD-ON

By the time I meet Soul-Mat, I am completely unrecognisable from the ragged, homeless junkie I once was. I have written a number of books. I've recently graduated with an honours degree in publishing. I head up a successful imprint. My financial issues seem to be in the distant past. My outsides look miraculously intact. The veneer of success is, however, often deceptive. Some of the apparently most "together" people in the material world are the saddest and most broken inside.

In my deepest bones it still feels as if I have been birthed in lack, and no matter how many times I have said the Serenity Prayer in recovery, no matter how many gratitude lists I've drawn up over the years, deep down, when no one is looking, I am unable to escape from the precipice of scarcity. I am in a furious race against the clock to make up for lost time.

Redeem yourself in the material! the voice yells at me.

So I ride bareback my horse of recovery, whipping myself to go faster, work harder, make more-more-more. The finishing line is always elusive. Just as I close in on it, like a mirage it disappears, only to appear again on the next hazy horizon. Like poor old Sisyphus, I must keep toiling that rock up the hill.

My achievements in the greater world swaddle me in denial about just how broken I still am when it comes to the fear of abundance. I try to distract myself from the hole in my soul by publishing more and more books and test-driving fancier and more expensive cars.

✳

After just six months of living together, to kick-start our new life in Cape Town, Soul-Mat and I decide to buy a house. But being in partnership is a sure way to expose one's deepest fears and rot. He and I come from polar-opposite financial worlds. He grew up in a safe and well-off family in a First World European country. His mind works in euros and abundance; mine in rands and lack.

Our pink-tinted, loved-up world is eventually rocked by these differences when we finally make an offer on a property. Whereas I am crunched over endless calculations, both on paper and in my head, in order to manage the purchase, he clearly comes from a much less neurotic space. It all seems so easy for him, while I crouch over my pained and panicked sums.

He's shocked by what appears to be my financial pettiness. I am frustrated that he can't see my logic, that he doesn't appear to understand my historical financial terror. I mean, in the name of disclosure, I gave him *Smacked* after our first weekend together. Doesn't he fucking get it?

I have been in denial about how deep my disease of lack lies, but now I'm forced to confront it through another's eyes. I thought things were relatively fine and dandy between us, but during this house-hunting process, we fight, we argue, we sulk, we accuse, we stand on opposite islands waving our respective banners.

I am thrown back into a world of shame. I deny. I bargain. I blame. I revolt. After each argument that plays out in a mighty battle zone of wills, I am forced to look at my stuff. I hate what I see. Why can't I share?

I want to run, leave, get away, be on my own again. Live in the solitary confinement of sweet denial where it's just *me*: *my* money, *my* space, *my* decisions, no one else to please and appease.

But I can't. I love this man. I have upped and moved my entire life in Joburg to be with him. And deep down, in clear moments, I know that what he keeps pointing out to me is true. But how do I change it?

I want to laser-cut the steel ropes that umbilical me to my past, to my childhood, to my mother. The mother I have resented all my life for her churchmouse approach to everything; the mother I once rejected in bitter anger, but whom I have now come to resemble. My fear that I should turn into her is manifesting. I, who screeched hatred at her for the way she saw the world in terror and lack, *am* my mother! I feel sick.

In Soul-Mat I have met my mirror, my hooter who blares each time I act without integrity. Which appears to be often. I twist, I turn, I scream denials. I'm a demented banshee, but deep down I know he is right. There are days that I hate-hate-hate this man.

When we first meet at the airport in real life, the world slows down as I make my through Arrivals and angels chorus from the heavens. Never mind that we are literal strangers – we gently touch each other's faces. We drink each other in. Time stops and, like two magnets, our souls meet. It's every cheesy, romantic movie ever made.

Our first weekend is the stuff dreams are made of. We talk, we laugh, we make love over and over again. It's as though we have walked a million miles in other lifetimes, only to have finally found each other.

So when we start bickering, it feels like a brutal betrayal of that loved-up "soulmate" dream. I struggle to reconcile the man I met at the airport with the one who is now breaking down all my illusions of self.

I remember reading Elizabeth Gilbert's *Eat Pray Love* back in 2007, particularly what she'd said about soulmates, but back then I didn't have the faintest clue what she was on about. Now I find my dog-eared copy in one of the boxes accumulating dust in the garage of our new house. In her book, which went on to sell a gazillion copies, she suggests that a soulmate's purpose is to "shake up" and tear apart one's ego. That a soulmate is there to "show you your obstacles and addictions". She suggests that, to break one's heart open to let the light in, one has to be driven to a point of desperation and lose control of the old illusion of self so that one can transform one's life. In Gilbert's world, your soulmate is therefore your spiritual teacher and master.

As I read these words, I know without a doubt that this man, whom I hate-love-hate-love, who at times drives me to the brink of insanity, who pushes all my buttons like a lift that refuses to budge when you desperately need it to, is indeed my fucking soul mate. If I have to break up with him, I will literally be abandoning the possibility of my better self. And, it appears, I do the same to him. Punch his buttons, drive him bonkers. If I have to trust Elizabeth G on this, Soul-Mat and I have been brought together to help each other transcend into a higher state of consciousness. Damn!

Whereas I am a talker, with far too many unprocessed words often tumbling from my supersonic-speed mouth, Soul-Mat's approach to conflict is silence. He wants to be left alone, to regroup his emotions. He withdraws into what I perceive as passive-aggressive pockets of cemetery-silent sulks. It feels like I am being stonewalled. And this drives me beyond demented. His non-communication catapults me back into all my abject terrors of abandonment.

I experience his pleas of "leave me alone" as rejection, while he experiences my desperate need to "talk", to fix, to lay it all out, as an onslaught, being caged in, stalked and attacked. We are total opposites in the way we argue. Words of anger, accusations and cheap shots tear from my lips in rage. I always end up regretting my bombs of verbal annihilation, but when my Uzi mouth gets going, there is no end to what it can destroy.

And, as I get louder, his silence deepens. My uncontrollable explosions force him further into retreat mode. Like a drowning man gasping for air, he recoils into his cave as he desperately scrambles for a lifeboat that will bring him equilibrium. I am the tidal wave that crashes down. The more my shouts gather momentum, like a growing swarm of demented bees, the more he needs to escape me. Finally, my unbridled words cause him to pop and then he roars. Soon, it's a cacophony of two mad lovers-turned-enemies, raging – the seed of the argument now long forgotten. We're all over the place.

To calm down and disengage from the heat of emotion, he sometimes storms off to the adjoining room, slams the door and shuts me out. Bang! The aftermath of that slam, the silence that ensues, throws me into a mad panic. I question my move to Cape Town, our loved-up rush to buy a house. I am filled with a debilitating sense of shame, of regret and terror. I am back in my loveless land. I am four years old. My dad has just died and I am paralysed in solitary confinement. Our fights feel like the end of the world, the implosion of Planet Love.

Of course, on a greater soul-journey level, he is teaching me about abandonment, forcing me to deal with my deep child-hood terror of facing the idea of "the end" – of mortality. Of sharing my life with another. He is also training me to be alone. I am teaching him about communication, trust and forgiveness. But that only becomes evident much later. After a number of painful Soma experiences.

✳

In 2017, I summon up the courage to do another mushroom journey about a half-year after the "the pain I have caused my

147

people" expedition. To process things, I seem to need about six months between these deep, psychedelic voyages. By now I have learned not to expect anything. Not to try to steer my own ship. I am amazed that I'm intimately discovering the essence of a key tenet in the 12-Step programme: surrender and let go. I find it profound that the teachings I've been processing over the past 18 years in recovery are now being shown to me in Soma ceremonies. The wisdom I have gained in NA and AA has given me the foundation, but now I am going deeper, embarking on what is referred to, so often flippantly, as a "spiritual journey". And while it's achingly hard and painful, it's also deeply rewarding and enlightening.

While I still encounter moments of beauty and "multiverse travelling" as I did the first time, the crux of each of my experiences has been much more about unravelling deep layers of pain and what on the surface appeared to be immovable fears, buried deep in my body, in the cells that make up "me".

There have been nights when the tears take hold and I cry buckets of salt water. Digging deeper, getting closer to the source of my sadness, mistrust and fear. Releasing the ache. And always there's the Aha! moment where I go, "Aah, that's why I am the way I am!" Then, in the days, the weeks and the months that follow, the mulling over of the experience, the threading together of realisations, all leads to the big questions: *How do I change this? How do I become a better version of myself?*

Between Soul-Mat and Soma, I am having a turbulent ride.

✳

In this journey I am forced to confront my deep distress in the sphere of "not enough". It's about a year after we've moved into our new house. On the way to Monica's, we argue in the car. It's something to do with money. About me not sharing. Again.

The drive to Somerset West is steeped in stewed-up silence.

Tonight, the journey with psilocybin is strange. There are no patterns, no otherworldly colours, no bliss-filled hurtling to the stars. Instead, my mind seems trapped in a huge calculating machine, endless lists and mazes of numbers. It's hell. It's as though I am being shown my Default Mode Network in spastic overdrive.

It feels never-ending as I am drawn deep into my inner workings, my pettiness, my need to control, my financial fears, my facile preoccupations with the material. The till slips that spew from my subconscious twist like deranged vipers. Forced to watch, I find no escape.

And what I see I abhor. But, beyond the repulsion, far deeper than the loathing, in the darkest chambers of my soul, I stumble across a pearl of connection. I am witnessing a primary wound, my inherited mother trauma. I now see how I am part of the bigger, deeper wound, the vampire ache of a gluttonous world that tells us that there is never enough, there will never be, that we will always need more-more-more. Of everything. That there is not enough to share.

As painful and dark as the experience is, when I emerge back into the real world, I feel unexpectedly stronger. Enlightened. I have felt my fuck-ups deep in my cells. I have been given a front-row ticket to self-awareness, a clue to self-knowledge. A confirmation of my human flaws. Over the years, as part of Step 8 in NA, I have written reams and reams about my defects, but I have never encountered them so full frontal. And I have never had the tools to actually *change* any of them.

Is this not what I have been looking for all my life? Is this not why I took all those drugs – smoked that first joint, swallowed that first cap of acid, schnarfed that line of coke, chased the heroin dragon, burned my lungs on that crack pipe? All in the search for "enlightenment".

Enlightenment: to discover insight into a transcendental truth or reality.

✳

We drive back to Cape Town in the morning. I quietly describe my journey to Soul-Mat. I tell him I am sorry that I am so screwed up about money. I tell him that I know that I have much work still to do on myself. He nods. He has his own issues and much work to do too. We have work to do together.

I am exhausted. It seems so endless. I vacillate between realisations and, just as quickly, just when I think I know myself, I've slid back into that well-trodden territory of old habits. How long this rocky path towards elusive self-knowledge and authentic healing is.

Now that I've opened The Doors, my Pandora's Box, the hard stuff keeps crashing. And almost all of it has to do with the past and the fuck-ups I've made in terms of hurting others.

And myself.

But little cracks of light are finding their way in. I can feel it.

Chapter 23

INTO THE HEART OF DARKNESS

"He cried in a whisper at some image, at some vision – he cried out twice, a cry that was no more than a breath:
The horror! The horror!"
– Joseph Conrad, *Heart of Darkness*

Winter is fading as we head off to Somerset West in late August 2019.

Despite arriving early to secure good spots in the ceremony room, I'm annoyed to see a long line of cars already parked outside Monica's house. Fuck. I hate not being able to choose my space.

The room is seething, packed full of people who, like us, are all trying to find their way back home. Soul-Mat is forced to find a vacant spot on the opposite side of the lounge. I settle for one in a faraway corner. It's the first time I have journeyed without him at my side. To my left I spot a familiar face – a golden, long-haired Peter Pan boy I met a couple of months earlier on his first journey. He looks a bit like a spaced-out Jesus. He's clearly delighted to see me. At least I have someone beside me who I kind of know.

There are 25 journeyers in the candlelit room tonight. There are seven watchers. I feel the imminent promise of a meaning-filled night.

After house rules are announced and introductions made, one by one we head into Monica's study where the mushrooms are weighed and handed out. As I receive my sacrament, it doesn't escape me that my little cup of ground-up cubensis resembles the parchment given out by the priest in the Catholic Church as part of the Sacrament of Communion.

Tonight I'm feeling adventurous. Usually, I take five grams, but this time I decide on seven. Seven is a holy number. Peter Pan Jesus has decided that it's his lucky number too. We giggle as we wait for the rest of the room to settle down.

Once everyone has their cups of ground mushrooms, we sit in the large circle along the edges of the room and wait for warm, honey-sweetened tea to be added to the dry psilocybin powder. I block my nose, gag a little as the loamy mushrooms travel down my throat. I shudder. It's not exactly a culinary delight.

The lights are dimmed, only the candles now lick the blue hologram-painted walls. The mobiles hanging from the ceiling turn slowly in the winter breeze.

I sink into my corner. Eyes closed, I wait. The day, the week, random images like some foreign movie begin to roll through my mind. I wait. I let it flow. I curl deeper into the corner, the place where the two walls meet. I tug the duvet over my head and cocoon myself. I am a dusty moth as I wait for the psilocin to attach to my serotonin receptors.

Who knows how much time passes because here, in this place of the other dimension, time distends. It's a Dalí clock. More images flow in. It's as though my mind is unravelling, peeling its way through layers, a computer expelling data, the psilocybin like some mental hygiene agent, cleaning away the overload, deleting the debris to take me to the other side. Stilling my Default Mode Network. Clearing musty pathways for The Doors to be unlatched.

Finally, after what could be minutes, hours, days or weeks,

I open my eyes. The room has changed dimension. Everything is hyper-real. More 3D than I have ever seen it. I watch the watchers watching. The one in front of me is a creature straight from another planet. The blue girl from Avatar. I turn slowly to look at Soul-Mat across the room. He is perched; my solid eagle, a wise old Chinese sage.

I stare ahead. I am completely content. Full.

And then it starts.

A deep moaning beside me. The low groan becomes a pant becomes a grunt becomes a sexual snarl. I recoil. There's a knife in my brain. What is this? The sound grows deeper and louder.

My eyes move to the lump to my left. The groans emanate from beneath the brown mink blanket that covers the long-haired Peter Pan Jesus. My eyes fix on the watchers. I wait for them to quieten him. Avatar stares beatifically ahead. She does nothing.

The sighs get louder; they've become grunts – sexual snarls. I feel it coming, a rush of darkness, a tremble of panic.

Somehow, I inch out from my corner, crawl towards Avatar. I find a whisper. "You need to get him out of here."

Every fibre of my being knows that his removal is vital. She smiles at me. Benign. She does not move.

I manoeuvre back to my corner. The lump beneath the blanket is now in the throes of sexual ecstasy. Each writhing groan drives daggers of terror into me.

It's 24 July 1999. I am back in that room in Hillbrow, the room of my gang rape. Later, when I look at a calendar, I will realise that what I am about to revisit is two days short of 18 years to the night.

I have a gun in my mouth. I don't know much about guns, but the taste of metal makes me want to gag. It's July 1999, 3am on a Saturday, Hillbrow, Johannesburg, and I've never been more terrified in my life.

There are four people in the dingy, one-roomed flat in Soper Road: a Nigerian dealer, two coloured gangstas and me.

"Open your legs," a surly-faced specimen called Baby Face instructs me. I'm huddled in a frozen ball. My hands press my knees together.

"Please don't rape me." My voice is small. My lips mercury cold. I'm a broken bird – no crying, just a crackled whimper. Oh God, this can't be happening to me. The terror. The fear gets the better of me. Hysteria rises.

"Shoot me, don't rape me, shootmedontrapemeshootme." The words are a desperate mantra. God's not listening.

The gun thuds against my temple. Pistol-whipped. Metal on skull silences me. Blank out.

Time has undone its stitches. Each grunt that comes from the heaving lump beside me drives another nail of recall into my present. Monica replaces Avatar. She moves in closer to me. Peter Pan Jesus's writhing and sexual pants permeate every cell of my hyper-realised being. I am repulsed, nauseated; my eyes implore Monica closer. "You need to get him out of here …" but my lips remain closed. I am back in that room of tongue-numb voiceless terror. Just as it was on that night in 1999, from my soul I am calling for help but no one is listening.

A surge of violence consumes me. I want to murder this heaving mass of writhing sex beside me. He is every man who has ever hurt, terrified and violated me. I want to snuff him out, suffocate him, strangle his body. My rage is blinding.

My voice finally breaks through; my cry holds years of unshed tears that unleash my long-buried terror.

Now Peter Pan Jesus, who has become my most feared torturer, is surrounded by four watchers. Monica's gentle but firm voice tells him that he needs to stop, he needs to keep what he is expressing inside, that he is ruining the space for others in the room.

Peter Pan Jesus has morphed into an unrepentant gargoyle. He repeats her words in a singsong voice. He mocks her. He cackles in her face.

A watcher shines a torch. In the thin light I see Peter Pan Jesus's grimace. He is Bob from *Twin Peaks*. He's Baby Face from Soper Road. I want to leap across and snuff him out, take my hands to his neck and strangle his life force.

Three strong male watchers try to hoist him to his feet.

Peter Pan Jesus has become dead weight. He resists with otherworldly force. I watch as his body is drag-carried out of the room. Instead of relief, no sooner is he removed than I return to my bottomless well of horror, to my rape, when my words were vacuumed away on that cold, dark night as I lost all power of choice and voice. My night of long-buried violence has come to visit in full force.

Finally, much later, I make my way into the candlelit kitchen where soup is waiting. I have not eaten for 14 hours. I am famished. But now my rage snakes out of me. Why did no one take that demon sex maniac away earlier? Why was I forced to endure his perversions and grunts and masturbatory writhing? I am raving at whoever will hear me. I am told to keep it down, that the others in the ceremony room are still deep in journey. Fuck that. I need to expel this fury! This voice that's been locked away for all these years will not be silenced.

After my venom is spent, like a fat anaconda vomiting up the remains of its rodent dinner, my tears flood in.

"Oh God, I am so angry," I sob. "Oh God, I am so fucking angry."

It's a realisation more than a statement.

Now Soul-Mat sits beside me. My trusty eagle. As he takes my hand, I am overwhelmed by the knowledge of my extraordinary damage. How often have I allowed this irrational rage – a rage that has nothing to do with him – to consume our partnership in my constant need to fight? I suddenly see how my irritability, my murderous anger, my accusations are deeply connected to the sexual violation that changed me forever back in 1999. It's threaded to all the men who have ever taken my power away and betrayed me. Including my father.

Soul-Mat strokes my hair. How has he stuck it out with me for so long?

"I'm sorry, I'm sorry, I'm sorry for being such a mess," I sob. "I never want to come here again," I weep. "I am done with this," I fume. "This has been the worst night of my life. I am *done*!"

Monica appears. She sits on the other side of me. She is her gentle and calm self. I rage at her. "Why didn't anyone *listen* to me? Why did I have to go through all this *pain*?"

She listens. She takes my other hand. I have my two guardian angels on either side, but still I rail against comfort. "Why didn't anyone take that freak away when I begged them to?" I can't contain my tears. "I feel as if I've been raped by a hundred demons tonight."

And then, suddenly, a flash. I see it. In a room of all these people, why was I the only one who responded like this? No one else seems to have been affected in the same way as I have.

"Oh my God! This has all been about me!" I gasp.

"That's a deep insight," says Monica. Her voice is calm and gentle. "You were there because you needed to be. You were meant to be there; you were even meant to be right beside him. You needed to revisit your pain and go deep tonight. None of this is a mistake."

I see it. This is my stuff, my stuff only. Old, drecky pus and wounds that have erupted from within like some dark, otherworldly tar demon. Gashes that have scarred my being for so long, my everyday persona, my entire fucking personality. I thought I was over that violation. I thought I was over my father's death.

*

Anyone who thinks that taking psilocybin mushrooms in a therapeutic setting is some kind of happy, hedonistic escapist trip needs to take a controlled journey and see for themselves. For me, as the addict who has spent much of her life high, drunk, stoned and oblivious, taking psilocybin is the complete antithesis of "getting out of it". Rather, it is everything to do with "getting *into* it". A path to "*inner*standing".

It's an opportunity to confront buried memories and deep wounds of the past that have carved welts in our hearts, our brains, our souls and our bodies, emanating from unloved child-hoods, bullies at school, incompetent parents, vicious teachers, betraying lovers, sex crimes, abuse, grief, loss, addiction, anxiety and all the other seeping sores that we gather as we stumble our way through our lives.

What do we do with all this pain? We bury and deny it, but subconsciously it doesn't leave us. It grows like determined, irrepressible weeds. Unresolved pain erodes our souls.

Unable to process, confront and allow them to authentically heal, we allow our wounds to influence all our decisions in life – the jobs we take, the friends we make, the people we choose to love who invariably are just as hurt as we are. And so the cycle of "hurt people hurt people" continues. We become both magnets for and perpetrators of pain.

*

For the next few hours, I sit close to the fire and stare into the flames. I am empty. My anger has ebbed away. I am so tired. I am broken, right to the core. I am a skinless newborn bird. I head back into the ceremony room to lie beside Soul-Mat. I fall asleep in his arms.

Four hours later, I awake. My eyes can barely open, swollen with the aftermath of the night. In the bathroom, I slowly lift my gaze to meet myself in the mirror. A broken old woman stares back. This is how I will look when I am 90 years old. Jesus, this is how I look right now. My reflection shows me that I have walked through hell, proper hell, and come face to face with a cacophony of demons. This is me in all my rawness, stripped bare and hobbling along on my journey towards the unbearable heavy-lightness of facing the self.

But what I don't know back then, on that early morning in late August 2019, as I stare at my crows' feet in the mirror, that just around the corner a momentous event is about to unfurl. One that's not only about to confuse the hell out of me and force me to wrestle with everything I've ever held dear, and indeed not only change me, but which will also transform the entire planet.

I am unaware, as I stare into my soul, that the journey I've just endured will be the last I embark on in Monica's house for a very long time. I also do not know back then how this night of darkness will profoundly prepare me for what's about to unfold.

PART THREE

BAMBOOZLED
A TALE OF FEAR AND REVELATION

"You shall know the truth and the truth shall make you mad."
– Aldous Huxley, *Limbo*

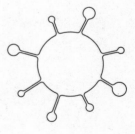

Chapter 24

LOCKDOWN

"Darling, you need to get us suicide pills. Not toilet paper."

I am sobbing. Prostrate on the carpet in our home in Cape Town. Soul-Mat is German. He's a psychiatrist, but not the pill-pushing kind. He's my rock. He never lies on the floor throwing tantrums. Instead, he slams doors.

"Just get some," I wail. "We don't have to use them right away. Just keep them somewhere safe. 'Cos if this thing is viral warfare and it all goes *Walking Dead*, at least we know we have a way out."

It's 16 March 2020, the day after the president announces that South Africa is in a National State of Disaster. I'm a disaster. A week later, Cyril will declare a nationwide, three-week lockdown that will kick off on 26 March. Lockdown. Like some B-grade prison movie. Our home is about to become Alcatraz.

At the time of his newscast, I've been clean and sober for 20 years and six months. People have often exclaimed, "Wow, you must be so strong to have kicked smack and crack." On the outside, I have a brilliant life and thriving career. Order is my middle name. Control my special gift. Although very few know, I'm well into fixing myself on my deep and difficult psychedelic Soma journey.

Now, as I lie sobbing on the carpet, the man who will soon become my only "cellmate" in this proposed incarceration strokes my forehead. My tears plop. He tells me I have beautiful eyes. But I can tell: clearly, he thinks I'm losing it.

✳

It's 4am. My mind skids awake. I've been spinning in some kind of car crash. Like that Ferrari I totalled back in 2013. PTSD. My brain flashes images of my life barrelling down the drain. Book launches, potential bestsellers fresh off the press, meetings with industry players, travel, swanky car events, my son's graduation in Joburg, the Cape Town Jazz Festival, the Kingsmead and Franschhoek book fairs – all have evaporated following our national incarceration.

How is this possible? I feel sheer, out-of-control panic. I can't keep up with this roller-coaster onslaught. Overnight, the virus has, like some psycho vacuum cleaner, sucked away all my inspiration. All motivation to wake up and fight for the light, the reasons I stopped hunting oblivion two decades ago. Gone. Yes, I am also a bit of a drama queen.

And just like that, the addict voice swoops back.

"You're fucked, it's over, what's the point? You gave up smack, you gave up crack. All that hard work, for this? The world is fucked, you are fucked. If it's all going *Zombie Apocalypse* – you may as well get trashed."

I know this voice. I'd battled her many times. But I thought she'd left the building years ago. But, no, she's back, as though she's only been hovering in the shadows, waiting in sly hibernation. I try to still my breath. My brain's bursting. I stare into a square of nothingness. I force myself out of bed. The world is still dark. I make coffee, answer emails, brush my teeth. I'm shaken. I thought I was on firm sobriety ground. WTF.

Tuesday and Wednesday drag by. I'm trying to catch up with

what's happening in our world. I google "Corona". World Corona stats. How do you get Corona? Corona symptoms. Corona conspiracy theories. Was it a bat, a snake, a pangolin? An act of bioterrorism? An evil Chinese plot? A Rockefeller-inspired brainchild of the New World Order? A masterplan by Bill Gates to get the entire planet microchipped and vaccinated? A trigger for Klaus Schwab's sinister plan aimed at a global reset? Some even say *The Simpsons* prophesied it.

The Corona virus might not yet be in me, but the dark queen's spikes are all around me. Now I am progressively frozen as I watch and read everything, unable to comprehend the enormity of what is happening in my life. My country. Our world.

✳

Four weeks after the president announces the State of Disaster, those first 21 days of lockdown have been extended. My travelling case remains unpacked in the lounge. It glares at me daily as I slipper-shuffle past. Me, unkempt, in pyjamas at noon. It had been packed for a trip to Joburg two days before the State of Disaster was announced. The launch was cancelled. I haven't had the energy to unzip it of its contents. But it's not only laziness. It has more to do with ennui. Nostalgia. The maroon Thule suitcase is a testament to that world I once inhabited, a world in which I actually left the house. It reminds me of a former life. BC. Before Corona. BL. Before Lockdown. I miss my old hometown Jozi; I miss my sons.

I haven't left the confines of these walls for 20 days. There was a time when I flew from city to city, up and down in airplanes, sometimes five times a week, on work-related travel: book events, author meetings, car launches. The sky is eerie now, empty as a disembowelled whale. Tomb silent. My life's been cancelled.

Winter is coming. How will the poor and homeless survive? I was indigent once, begging for drug money at traffic lights. I know what the months of May, June and July feel like in South Africa when you have no roof. When you are starving. But my belly has been full for more than two decades. *The Hunger Games* are now no more than a distant memory as I survey my fridge, packed full: cottage cheese, sirloin (free range), butternut, ostrich steak, anchovies, spinach, courgettes, kale, feta, halloumi, hummus. The cupboards heave. Pasta. Lentils. Rice. Tins, tins, tins. Tuna, olives, coconut cream, chickpeas, tomatoes. So many, many tins of tomatoes. I could make a soup for the world with all these fucking nightshades.

On the single occasion that I do leave the house, armed with a mask and blue surgical gloves, I wait in line outside Woolworths. These days they only let 12 people in at time. Three weeks earlier, we'd jostled, shoulder to shoulder, panicked-trolleys full. Breathing, coughing, seething. Close. Virus oblivious. Now, standing in line, masked sheep waiting to be dipped, we are suspicious, eyes downcast, appropriately socially distanced.

The virus has othered us.

Once inside, the shelves look as though they've been looted, especially the meat section. We're a bloodthirsty bunch. I'm ashamed when the masked/gloved car-park security guy offers to help load my loot into the boot. I have far too many bags. I ask him how he is. I give him a guilty R100 note for his trouble. For a micro-moment I feel better. Of course, I have bought far more food than we need, but I tell myself it's because I don't want to leave the house again in a hurry and be exposed to the virus. Back home, I grind pricey organic coffee beans to drown out the "other" noise – the incessant babble of the television delivering more bad news. The chatter of my brain screeching: *What's going on?* I sip my hot coffee, try to scald, to cauterise my white guilt and privilege.

There are days when I hate myself for all the things I have: the 12 bags of black-eyed peas, eight bottles of anchovies, six whole chickens in the freezer, three bottles of Domestos. Boxes of night cream, day cream, mascara, lipstick, lip liner and toner hoarded from the days I worked in women's magazines. Many of them are now expired, but still I keep them. I have too much. I call it "the safety of objects".

Strangely, these "things" both distract me from and remind me of my poverty within. They are sad attempts at armour against the economic mayhem I fear Corona is about to unload on our world. They insulate me against the memories of a time when I was addicted, desperate and homeless. But, even amidst the din of the coffee grinder, I can't stop thinking of the "Covid shelter" in Strandfontein, just 40 kilometres from my hoarded house, where the hungry homeless and scrawny addicts have been fenced in.

To distract me from dwelling on Africa's Dachau, I reach for my iPad to catch up on the latest scores in the World Cup of Corona – country by country, numbers crunch and body counts pile up. By 20 April 2020, the US is clearly top dog in the race. Spain's overtaken Italy. China's on the down. Or is it really? Are they cooking or crooking the books? France looks *tres* fûckin' shaky. I find myself embroiled in the macabre. I always end up on South Africa, where right now it looks as if we just might be flattening the curve. Have we finally managed to do something right? The World Health Organization congratulates our president. I feel a pinch of pride. I suffer temporary amnesia for the millions who are starving.

Like so many equally blinded South Africans, I am determined to find that silver lining. Perhaps most of our embattled people will be magically spared from The Pandemic, because we've all been immunised by the BCG (TB) shots we were forced to have as children? I can still see faint traces of the little rosette scar on my upper arm. Close to the seven dots, the burn scars I got a year ago when I did Kambo – a frog poison administered to me by a travelling Brazilian shaman on some weekend hippy retreat near Wellington.

The magic man burnt R600-worth of initiation dots into the flesh of my upper arm. On the hotspots, he then dabbed pinpricks of poison milked from the highly toxic toad, *Phyllomedusa bicolor*, also known as the Giant Monkey Frog. I joined a room of pukers retching in buckets as the toxin coursed through our bodies. White people are weird. Paying to be poisoned. The Kambo was, however, a cleanser of note. Once my yellow bile was expelled, I felt empty for days. A temporary antidote for white guilt and hoarding.

But now I grow tired of poisoning myself in the daily, never-ending labyrinth of Corona news. I hate to follow the pack. I prefer to consider myself an "idealistic anarchist". A lover of Freedom. Someone who desires to see an authentically emancipated society, where human beings connect with each other without the threat of violence – in other words, without the back-up of police, armies and prisons. Or corrupt, greedy, globalised governments. Call me a dreamer.

Before lockdown, I was planning a tattoo with this Camus quote, in tiny letters, on my right inner arm: *The only way to deal with an unfree world is to become so absolutely free that your very existence is an act of rebellion.* Now all the tattoo shops are closed.

Chapter 25

MY UNBRAVE NEW WORLD

"Our business is to be aware of what is happening, and then to use our imagination to see what might happen, how this might be abused, and then if possible, to see that the enormous powers which we now possess, thanks to these scientific and technological advances, to be used for the benefit of human beings and not for their degradation."
– Aldous Huxley, "The Ultimate Revolution" speech, University of California, Berkeley (1962)

South Africa's early lockdown regulations are some of the most stringent in the world.

From the safety of my privileged cell, I watch the bloody *Hunger Games* unfold. Reports trickle in of police and security forces using excessive violence to clear the streets: herding the homeless and addicts like sheep on Dormicum, rounding up vendors and foreigners like foot-and-mouth-diseased cattle, heavy-handedly controlling queues in shopping malls. A man is beaten to death by soldiers in Alexandra for drinking liquor on his porch. His name is Collins Khosa. He was 48 years old. He worked in a bakery. He hailed from Ga-Modjadji in Limpopo. There will be many more like Collins, and I'm left with foreboding clues of what's really going on beneath the "flattening curve".

As the months go by, lockdown is extended. And extended.

And extended. It's not so much the virus I fear as bellies growing emptier. Starvation is a much more powerful keg.

"We're a nation of protesters!" ranted bravado Twitter in late March 2020, on the eve of the first lockdown. The memes flew in: "People are never going to adhere to these shit Corona rules!" But we have. Like wind-up toys.

I keep rereading snippets of my dog-eared copy of Huxley's *Brave New World*: "If you are going to control any population for any length of time, you must have some measure of consent." And consent is what we have given. It's not like there's been a choice. It's the new law, baby. The threat of possible "death by plague" has terrorised us into submission. And, with the underlying rumble of a gung-ho military and police machine to control social isolation, overnight we become a fear-paralysed nation.

I'm reminded of a passage in Ronald Wright's *A Short History of Progress*: "In times of war or crisis, power is easily stolen from the many by the few on a promise of security. The more elusive or imaginary the foe, the better for manufacturing consent."

The promise of "security"? Is that what this is? Everyone I know is fucking terrified. In the midst of this global pandemic, across oceans and borders and continents, we've all been forced to put our lives into the hands of our "leaders". I don't trust them.

As a lover of history, I have come to believe that, throughout recorded time, those select few in power – the kings, the queens, the landed gentry, the super-rich, the bankers and the elite – have for centuries been pulling the strings of our political puppets. Those we elected and to whom we paid our taxes. Motivated by greed and a lust for power, our "leaders" have systematically betrayed us.

Time and time again, we've been shown how hard it is for

ordinary citizens to receive justice, to access basic human rights like decent medical care, for a poor man or woman to have a simple loaf of bread on the table. I am terrified that we are heading for a mega-shitshow where we have no choice but to be governed and controlled by these untrustworthy scuzzballs.

I have read much about the well-greased revolving doors between the corporates and politicians. There is an ocean of evidence detailing global corruption, greed and extraordinary deception – executed by those who rule us: the governments, the police services, the judiciary, the oil barons, the mining magnates, the bankers, the doctors, the lawyers. Blah, blah, blah. We know this shit. The world is in a fucking mess because of centralised and corrupted power.

And now it feels as though I'm watching a spectacular, but silent implosion of freedom. Where our leaders and governments have made decisions on our behalf, to "protect" us, where our rights to travel and gather in groups are constantly adjusted and revoked, where surveillance is being legislated, where protests are being silenced by force, where in certain countries, like Australia, people are herded and imprisoned in "legislated" spaces. Where I fear that hunger and depression may, over time, kill many more than the virus will. I am tormented by this mind of mine that insists on searching for clarity beyond what I read in the everyday news.

Initially I trust what I imbibe: CNN, eNCA, *The Guardian*, Al Jazeera and Sky. But, as the months drag by, I find myself wondering whether the information we are being fed is really as objective and truthful as we imagine. I discover that more and more "experts" are on the payroll of the corporation, organisation or political party to which they are performing lip service.

Later, I stumble upon information that media houses such as CNN and CBS have "close financial relationships" with companies like Pfizer. In fact, as The Pandemic rolls out, Pfizer will sponsor no fewer than 15 US news shows, including *Good Morning America*, *CBS Health Watch*, *Anderson Cooper 360°*, *ABC News Nightline*, *CNN Tonight*, *CBS Sports Update*, *Meet the Press*, *CBS This Morning* and good old *60 Minutes*.

I'm crippled in a mind-mess of doubt and confusion.

Why can't I just trust what's going on like other people appear to be doing? Why am I not able to isolate my thoughts? Why can't I just toe the line and do lockdownward-facing dog? Bake bread, stitch embroidery? Wax lyrical about the clarity of the water in the canals of Venice? The pollution-less peaks of the Himalayas? Why can't I post rapturous updates on Facebook about mindfulness and the twittering of birds? But my brain refuses. It's a tangle of thoughts wrestling with truth, proof, lies and fake.

The days drag by as I watch the Theatre of the Unreal from my hamster wheel.

During those early days, stuck in our homes – in boxes, mansions and shacks or under bridges – the fear of death is seeded into our cells. I watch the life force of what we once understood to be "freedom" trickle away. I sometimes mutter to myself: Did people not die before this pandemic? But I dare not voice this on social media lest I be thrown into Facebook Jail for spreading "fake news" or a "conspiracy theory".

In certain countries there are substantial fines, even imprisonment, for spreading "lies". In South Africa, we have sinister-sounding punishments, by way of the new Disaster Management Act regulations. The new law declares that citizens can face a prison sentence of up to six months for "spreading fake news about Coronavirus". This leaves me constantly asking myself: What *is* "fake"? And "fake" according to whom?

A lot of the time it feels as if "they" – the politicians – are making it up as they go along, that the medical fraternity is not really in charge of this pandemic and the narrated response to it. It feels like Big Tech has become the Big Brother in deciding what is "fake news" or what is "true speak". And then there are the "experts" on social media: individuals with no clue, shouting theories, statistics and cures across the virtual highway. The dumber, the louder. It's the bloody Dunning-Kruger effect. But what really does my head in is the rise of the Tattletale Brigade.

Chapter 26

THE VIRTUAL STASI

"Of all tyrannies, a tyranny sincerely exercised for the good of its victims may be the most oppressive. It would be better to live under robber barons than under omnipotent moral busybodies." – CS Lewis, *God in the Dock: Essays on Theology and Ethics (Making of Modern Theology)*

In suburbia, during the first year of South Africa's lockdown, I'm dumbstruck as citizens form "Covid watch groups". Neighbours now report neighbours for taking the dog for a walk outside curfew hours. For surfing in the ocean. For walking in a park. I'm incredulous when a car is burned because some fuckwit nosy resident is incensed that a man is feeding the homeless and "spreading the plague" in the mainly white upmarket neighbourhood of Sea Point. These are times of mass discord, uncertainty and hostility. These are dangerous days we are living in.

This sinister new trend reminds me of the bloody Stasi.

In the early 1950s, a secret police service was created in the DDR, otherwise known as East Germany. Initially, the Stasi was tasked to spy on former Nazis and gather counterintelligence on Western agents. But its powers soon seeped into keeping tabs on fellow citizens. Initially, 90 000 Stasi were employed but those in charge soon realised that, in order to be more effective, they would need mass participation.

Eventually, one in six East Germans were on their payroll. Factories, offices, schools and apartment blocks had at least one snitch spying on their neighbours or colleagues. An atmosphere of suspicion was created on the ground. East Germans grew increasingly wary of each other, terrorised by the fear that a member of your own family could rat you out. And so a climate of paranoia was created, one that proved to be an exceptionally effective tool in creating an obedient and compliant population.

✳

In 2020, social media platforms are now the new virtual battleground. People attack, censure, castigate and revile each other for not agreeing with their chosen standpoint. I watch horrified as hard-line divisions are created amongst friends, lovers, families, colleagues, husbands, wives and total strangers. In angry, impulsive swipes, people delete each other from their lives.

In this new pantomime of division and "othering", some report each other to the Facebook watchdogs. Some are banished to Facebook for "transgressions of thought", for spreading "fake news". Twitter and LinkedIn accounts are suspended. Entire archives belonging to "dissenters" against the accepted narrative are wiped out on YouTube.

In the early days, when memories of life before The Pandemic are still sharp and sweet, while I am still freshly disorientated by how quickly the world has bought into what I intrinsically feel is a narrative that needs to be questioned, I happen to load a post referring to us as "sheeple".

Fuck me blind!

Virtual mob violence breaks loose. Members of my own family attack me. People I thought were friends lambast me, and when I try to explain my reasoning, the result is an all-out war. Up until now, Facebook has been a place where I've enjoyed uncensored freedom to just be me. Now it begins to feel as if the virtual Stasi are waiting in the wings to report me.

I am horrified when I am called a "Trumpist", "right wing", a "Nazi" and a "fascist". These words carry deep insult. They cut into my heart, and I am incensed. I feel desperately misunderstood. I find myself second-guessing myself. I, who always had such an unguarded big mouth, now carefully deliberate before expressing myself, lest I am murdered by an onslaught of damning diatribe.

Then I am accused of belonging to QAnon.

QAnon? Fuck, I don't even know who or what QAnon is! I do some googling. Turns out that QAnon is this fast-growing quasi-religious cult of the supposed far right. Many are militant. Basically, they believe that American politics, business and media are being controlled behind the scenes by a group of "Satan-worshipping elites who run a child-sex ring" and "baby-eating paedophiles". And I am one of *them*?

I read more. It appears that QAnon first emerged in October 2017, when an unidentified user on 4chan, an unregulated, anonymous image-board website, uploaded a series of posts signed off as "Q". He or she claimed to have high-level connections and "Q clearance" in US security. The first Q message ever posted claimed that Hillary Clinton was about to be arrested, which would cause massive unrest. It never happened. These messages become known as "Q drops" or "breadcrumbs".

Q followers also apparently believe that that Supreme Dick, Donald Trump, is essentially a messiah and that Hillary eats babies in the belief that infant stem cells will energise her in her quest for power. I am gobsmacked to see that what started as a political conspiracy theory on the internet has grown into an actual political movement with millions of followers. Many of the guys who storm Capitol Hill in January 2021, after Trump loses the election, are members.

And I am accused of belonging to this group of wackos? I mean, I can't even begin to defend myself against this bullshit … I try to find the connection. Aah, now I see it! Because I am *questioning* the Covid narrative, and because QAnon followers are also shouting doubts, I must be a card-carrying member. To my growing horror, I begin to realise that one of the many problems we are facing during this time is the total distortion of perspective through reductionism.

But, as time goes by, and I dig further and further to try to make the connection between independent thought and this sudden witch-hunt, and its increasingly bizarre connotations, I begin to suspect that it may be the exclusively "medical" approach to The Pandemic that is driving this myopic, black-and-white thinking. Many scientists, politicians and members of the media follow a "virus-centric" method in handling the virus, one in which the notion of avoidance of infection at *all costs* seems to railroad fundamental logic and basic values like civil rights and the fallout of economic devastation.

I notice, too, how my own "reductionism" plays out during the whole Joe Rogan Spotify saga. Although not a fan initially, I begin paying more attention to Joe when he's roasted for allegedly "spreading misinformation" after interviewing a Covid sceptic by the name of Dr Robert Malone.

Malone is an interesting figure in the pandemic landscape. In December 2021, he's expelled from Twitter for speaking out against what he believes to be some dubious science around the Covid-19 virus. Whether one agrees with him or not, Malone is not some airhead bozo. He is a highly qualified scientist who originally worked intimately with nine original mRNA vaccine patents. In 2020, he ran clinical trials for the Covid-19 vaccine. His voice deserves to be heard.

Malone is no stranger to being censored. Apart from his run-in with Twitter, he'd already been deplatformed from LinkedIn, his virtual "sin" having been to encourage people to question what we were putting in our bodies. He was subsequently accused of being "anti-vax" and promoting "vaccine hesitancy". With all the recent Facebook, Twitter, LinkedIn and YouTube purges, clearly certain Big Tech censors are working hand in hand with governments and Big Pharma. Sometimes even "fact-checkers" have an agenda.

The day after Malone is drop-kicked from Twitter, he's interviewed on *The Joe Rogan Experience*. At the time, it's the most downloaded podcast series in the world, with more than 100 million monthly listens and far more traction than most established media outlets. I had never listened to Joe. Now I make sure to download the controversial interview, which has of course been immediately ripped down by YouTube. As a result, it goes viral, with more than 50 million listens on Spotify, the platform that hosts Joe.

Within days, in early 2022, two "woke" artists – Neil Not-so-Young and Joni Mitchell, now on the other side of 80 – remove their music from the platform in protest against Rogan. Spotify's market capitalisation plummets by $2.1 billion over the following three days. Most mainstream media join the all-out attack in denouncing Rogan, dredging up any dirt they can dish on him.

I am left deeply disturbed. In my mind, Rogan has done nothing criminal in interviewing Malone in a bid to open the debate and ask important questions. But now I watch how the attempts to dilute his influence accelerate. The character assassination takes a sinister turn when he's accused of being a racist and using the "N" word in previous podcasts. A number of black celebrities, however, come out in support of him. And some of those who voice allegiance to Rogan, like Russell Brand (whose YouTube channel became hugely popular during The Pandemic, boasting almost six million subscribers), are now branded "right wing".

I am shocked. What kind of world have we descended into

where we are no longer able to question what is happening to our bodies, our minds and our rights? What has happened to good old debate? It feels as if I keep slipping further and further down a black tunnel into the endless pit of thoughtcrime.

Remember George Orwell's dystopian *1984*, published in 1949? The novel in which "thoughtcrimes" referred to politically unacceptable and unorthodox thoughts that contradicted the fascist Ingsoc ideology forced upon the citizens of Orwell's mythical Oceania? It was my setwork book in Standard Nine. Now, 70-plus years after its publication, against the background of so much noise, confusion and turmoil, it appears that those who are questioning "Big Brother Science" have to be silenced.

And then, much to my horror, I discover that I, too, am tainted by this scourge of myopic thinking. Once I read that Rogan has been accused of racism, my own reductionist mind tells me that if Joe Rogan can be seen as a racist, and if I show support for him, I too will be branded one! I consider erasing all mention of him from this book.

I experience similar fears after voicing support for Novak Djokovic in his attempts to enter Australia unvaccinated after receiving permission to do so from the officials of the Australian Open. My ever-watchful brother quickly posts links of Djokovic, photographed with a couple of Serbian war criminals, to my Facebook page, clearly alluding to the notion that if I am endorsing Djokovic, I must be a fan of the Serbian genocide. It feels like the "You Support QAnon" bullshit all over again.

This is the kind of mindfuckery the world is having to deal with now? What to think in this time of reductionist witch-hunting? I sense how insidious these thoughtcrimes have become: if I cancel Rogan, if I cancel Brand, if I cancel Djokovic … I may as well just delete myself.

✳

And so it is that the line in my brain that used to easily discern between truth and lies becomes increasingly blurred. It jitters and loops like a spastic colon. Like a smackhead jonesing, it feels as if my mind is withdrawing from stability and reason.

What am I to believe? What I know for sure, though, is that the virus is exposing the rot that's existed long before The Pandemic. Systems that have failed the people. The greed of the super-rich and privileged. Gaping class and economic disparities. Consequences of gross environmental abuse. Global political and Big Pharma rapacity and corruption.

Sometimes, I stay silent for days. I observe my Unbrave New World, like an ineffectual spectre. I become one of the New Dumb.

To keep myself from going mad, from becoming zombified, I decide to set off on a mission. I feel a little like some loony Nancy "Virus" Drew, but I am desperate for clarity and new perspectives. Because, no matter how hard I've tried to sanitise my hands, do downward-facing dogma, mask my face and comply, something just doesn't feel right. It really doesn't.

Chapter 27

HOW DID WE GET HERE?

On most mornings in the first year of lockdown, I'm reminded of waking up in my mother's house in 1999. Back then, in those early months of sobriety, my sorrow sobbed for the loss of my two babies, my husband, my home and everything that had once been familiar. I suffered from toxic grief for the drugs I could no longer use.

More than 20 years have gone by, and now my ache is for our old world – the one, with all its deep flaws, that's been snatched away. For everything that has been "flattened", despite being assured that "it" will only last for three weeks. I wake up displaced and go to sleep paralysed by panic. Overnight, it feels as though we have lost our connection to each other. Our smiles, our smirks, our laughing teeth, our grimaces of pain are all now hidden behind masks.

So, when I'm not trying to escape by bingeing on *Love Island UK,* begging Soul-Mat to have suicide pills on tap, or publishing books in a mad, work-work-work frenzy, I spend my time asking: *How the hell did we get here?*

I've always believed that to comprehend the present, we need to examine the past. Over the last two decades, since I got clean and sober, I've been trying to dig deep, to understand the microcosm of my inner recovery world. Over the last five years I've attempted to untether myself even more from the damages of my past in Soma ceremonies to "innerstand" myself and my world. To fix "us" up.

My curiosity to ask "why?" has its roots in my early childhood.

In 1971, the year after my father dies, Don McLean releases his eight-minute single "American Pie". I am only five years old and will hear the song for the first time only a few years later, on a seven single my sister brings into the house, to be played on our record player.

I'm immediately mesmerised. I will continue to listen to that song throughout my childhood. It's probably the piece of music that most influences me growing up. Little do I know at the time, but this is my first experience of popular culture that will introduce me to the notion of allusion.

Although I don't have the words for it back then, I instinctively sense the ironies in the song. And although I am too young to remember Buddy Holly, I will later discover that when McLean sings of "the day the music died", he is "alluding" to his hero who was killed in a plane crash in 1959. I don't know either, of course, that "The Jester" to whom he refers is Bob Dylan or that "helter skelter" speaks to the Manson murders, and that the girl he meets who "sings the blues" is Janis Joplin – I know none of these details – but I somehow sense that he is singing a song that is sad, a song about longing and disappointment.

For decades, McLean refuses to explain his lyrics, so "American Pie" becomes one of the greatest musical mazes ever composed. It's a song that many spend years trying to decipher. Some have even called it "a lyrical collection of conspiracy theories". It sure as fuck confused me, but it not only got me thinking, it also deeply *mystified* me – a synonym for "bamboozled".

Years later, after first hearing that mesmerising melody, I will discover that it is indeed a song about the profoundly dark social and cultural changes that swept through once "perfect" 1950s America. It is song about the loss of innocence and grief.

It is a song that tells us that the American dream is dead. It's a song that says things are not what they seem.

"American Pie" is the catalyst that makes me wonder about the bigger world in which we live. As I grow into my teens, I become more conscious and start to interrogate what I am told to believe. To question the stories we are fed through the propaganda of apartheid's Christian National Education and the Church.

In a rebellious bid to untangle myself from parental and pseudo-state guidance, I delve into my deeper psyche by smoking weed, confronting my dark side. At some point in my transition into adulthood, I come out on the other side, always questioning myself, my thoughts and the world. Interrogating what we are told, and the actual truth behind the lies.

So, it seems, I lost trust in authoritarian structures long before 2020. In fact, I abandoned my faith in the idea that life was reliable when, before I could even read, my dad unexpectedly keeled over in front of me. That was my cruel awakening to the notion that nothing is what it seems and that what we think we know and think we can trust is often an illusion that will eventually fall away.

✳

As lockdown is serially extended in 2020, I become obsessed with trying to look back in order to make sense of how we, as a world, got here. And to ask the question, "Why?" My instinct tells me to go back to the turn of the millennium. To the year 2001 and 9/11, to be precise. That, for me, is the moment I believe a seismic shift struck our world, the day when the United States of America's bastion of economic power crumbled into a heap of dust.

Pre-2001, back in the days of guys like JFK, Reagan and

Clinton, the American dream – on the surface, at least – is still one of hope, despite its many failings. I'm kind of taken in by it. I've grown up with the background patriotism of Bruce Springsteen belting out "Born in the USA". In South Africa, we are so influenced by American culture that our aspirations tend to resemble US sitcoms. But, after 9/11, the USA seems to transform overnight from the "land of the free and the home of the brave" into "The Land of the Angry and Petrified".

If you are old enough, you will probably recall where you were on that day. You will remember the images of the planes crashing into the North Tower of the World Trade Center. You will remember the ashy masses running for their lives. You may remember black-suited men, like ragged crows, leaping wingless from the top floors of the 110-storey tower to escape engulfing flames.

On that day, I had just walked out of an Iyengar yoga class in Parkview. A small group had gathered around a television screen. I moved closer. At first the footage resembled a clip from some Bruce Willis action movie. But then I noticed CNN's red news band running along the bottom of the frame. This was real. The volume was turned up. Now sweaty yogis, armed with rolled-up yoga mats, stood transfixed. Together we watched repetitive footage of a plane crashing into the North Tower. It was 8:46am in New York when it happened – it was now 3.05pm in South Africa.

The attacks on the Big Apple and Washington DC shake the world's foundation. It all feels so unreal … Almost 3 000 are killed in NYC. Another 184 die at the Pentagon and 40 lose their lives in Pennsylvania, where a hijacked plane crashes as desperate passengers try to take control of the aircraft and apparently fight off the hijackers.

Over the next few days, I am hypnotised by the news. Airports across the US remain closed. Security is beefed up everywhere.

America has been caught off-guard. We are all shell-shocked. The threat of Terrorism, with a capital T, now keeps me and the rest of the world awake at night.

Chapter 28

A WAR ON TERROR

"The object of terrorism is terrorism. The object of oppression is oppression. The object of torture is torture. The object of murder is murder. The object of power is power. Now do you begin to understand me?"
– George Orwell, *1984*

By September 2001, I've barely scraped together two years of sobriety. Most days are spent serving endless cappuccinos to wealthy Parkview mommies and saving coins from tips to pay the rent. An NA friend has lent me an enormous, old Telefunken television set and given me access to her DStv account. And so I watch CNN like it's church.

George Bush Junior, who so often looked half-asleep before 9/11, now seems to have a cracker up his ass. Suddenly, he wakes up and, behaving as if he now runs the entire planet, issues orders to take far-reaching action against all "outside threats". At a media briefing, he announces: "Freedom itself was attacked this morning by a faceless coward, and freedom will be defended."

Immediately, we are flooded with images of Osama bin Laden who has overnight become the world's most wanted man. Although I don't ever say as much, to me he looks strangely beatific, a bit like an Arabic Jesus.

The 9/11 attacks trigger something labelled the "War on

Terror" – a term that is entirely new to my vocab. That "war", however, will explode in reach to become an all-out battle, waged not only on terrorists, but also on everything that makes Americans scared. The fear is contagious. It spreads across most Western countries. But the US, like Neverland, is thousands of miles away from southern Africa, from me and my scuzzy flat in Melville. It will take years before I fully process the implications of 9/11 and what happened to our planet in the aftermath.

And so a sinister new age of monitoring is ushered in. The overreach to achieve "security" sees invasive surveillance laws introduced on an unprecedented scale. The US Congress races to pass the USA Patriot Act, which expands the FBI's powers to "search and survey". And that means everyone.

Less than two months after the Twin Towers come tumbling down, the US invades Afghanistan. I watch on CNN how Bush claims that this landlocked country has been harbouring al-Qaeda terrorists responsible for the massive 9/11 attack on American soil. Thousands of "terrorist militants" belonging to the Taliban and al-Qaeda are now hunted down like rabid dogs and either captured or killed. By November 2001, the Taliban has fallen. But, instead of then withdrawing and going off on their merry way, US troops will remain in Afghanistan for the next two decades until they finally leave in 2021, ending the longest war in US history.

During this time, something called the "Department of Home-land Security" is birthed. Overnight – although I only discover this some time later – ordinary Americans are now unable to prevent the US government from spying on or monitoring their phone calls, their emails and their homes. There is nothing they can do about it. The invasion of privacy spreads its tentacles into the financial industry. Banks are required to report "suspicious" customer behaviour in case they are "involved in terrorism-related money laundering".

Naively, most American citizens are so caught up in wanting to catch the baddies and lynch the murderous bastard Bin Laden that little do they realise they've given away all their rights to privacy, only to become suspects in the War on Terror themselves. If you're wearing a hijab or go to mosque, you're fucked.

I travel to the States in 2002 on a sponsored trip to write a magazine story on "Drug Courts in Boston". Because my passport still carries my Lebanese ex-husband's Arabic-sounding name, I'm dragged out of the arrivals queue at JFK. Along with a string of Muslim passengers, I'm interrogated about my intentions, my reasons for visiting the country I once revered as The Land of the Brave and Free.

In early 2003, about six months after my US visit, despite there being zero evidence of Saddam Hussein having collaborated with al-Qaeda in the 9/11 attacks, I watch on CNN as President Bush issues the order for America to invade Iraq: *For the peace of the world and the benefit and freedom of the Iraqi people, I hereby give the order to execute Operation Iraqi Freedom. May God bless the troops.*

The very next day, on 20 March, the US invades and, within three weeks, they manage to capture Baghdad. I remember watching the footage of the massive statue of Saddam Hussein being toppled from its plinth. I'd always believed Saddam was a bad, mad, fascist dictator – which, by most accounts, he was. And so, just as many others do, I buy into America's brash accusations that he's been "harbouring weapons of mass destruction".

Hussein, who has gone into hiding, is now a dishevelled, ragged fugitive roaming the hills of Iraq. When he's captured, just before Christmas 2003 near the small farming town of Ad-Dawr, close to Tikrit, I'm one of the many who celebrate America's victory. The US operation is called Red Dawn, named after that 1984 movie starring Charlie Sheen, who, like me, also became something of a fucked-up junkie.

The following year, the accusations of "harbouring weapons of mass destruction" are proven to be complete bullshit. This is when my heart finally turns against the United States of Hypocrisy. I now begin to see the light without the filter of the Stars and Stripes. I finally open my eyes to understand the havoc and suffering the bellicose King of Consumerism has wreaked on our planet. I realise how, underpinned by its imperialist policies and a "profit at all costs" economic game plan, America is driven by an insatiable hunger to dominate. Far from the democratic hero that its PR machine has worked hard to establish, I now see how the US is the world's foremost bully.

One of my favourite comedians, the legendary George Carlin, once said: "The owners of this country know the truth. It's called 'the American Dream' 'cause you have to be asleep to believe it."

It is here, in the richest country on Earth, that Big Pharma, Big Food, Big Science, Big Tech, Big Military, Big SUVs, Big Movies, Big Hair, Big Burgers and Big Lies have flourished.

In 2006, Hussein is executed by hanging for crimes against humanity. As I watch the spectacle on my church of misinformation, CNN, I wonder what would happen if the Iraqi people did the same and hanged the US president from the wall, just as they did to "dissenters" in Atwood's dystopian Gilead …

Quite incredibly, unlike the now dead Hussein, Osama bin Laden, America's real Public Enemy Number One, manages to evade capture for a full decade. Back in 2001, within days of the 9/11 attack, President Bush had announced that he wanted Bin Laden hunted down and captured – "dead or alive". A $25-million bounty is issued for information leading to his killing or capture.

There are rumours at one stage that he's been sighted down south in Fordsburg, Joburg, where I often go to enjoy good curry. I fantasise that I may spot him sipping a lassi. And although I sure as hell could do with the cash reward, I secretly hope they'll never find him.

By the time Bin Laden is allegedly killed in the early-morning hours of 2 May 2011, Bush has been replaced by Barack Obama.

Initially, I was thrilled that America finally had a black president who seemed like a good guy. He sure as hell could inspire with his "Yes we can" speeches. But it turns out that he's not exactly the peaceful prez I initially hoped he would be. In the years that Obama is head of state, more wars are fought by America on foreign soil than under any other US president.

I remember watching CNN that early morning in May 2011, spellbound as a hit squad of US Navy Seals under Barack's command penetrates Bin Laden's compound in Abbottabad, Pakistan. They allegedly execute him on the spot, along with four other people who "get in the way", including his 23-year-old son, Khalid. I feel sorry for his boy.

After the deed, there will be some speculation whether the man finally murdered as bounty for 9/11 is even really Bin Laden. I must say, I do find it weird that no photographic or DNA evidence of his death is made public. I'm disturbed that we never actually see his face. It feels too convenient that his body is allegedly taken to Afghanistan to be identified and then hastily tossed into the sea less than 24 hours later. Officials say this is out of "respect for Islamic customs". I mean, when have American officials ever given a flying fuck about Muslim people, never mind their traditions?

And just like that, the world's most wanted man disappears off the radar.

So you might ask, as I often have, if the murder of Bin Laden was staged, what could have happened to the world's most wanted man? A number of theories have circulated since 2011.

One possibility, promoted by the Iranian regime, claims that the US had captured Bin Laden long before the Navy Seals' raid. But they worried that if he was to face trial on home soil, it could result in a hung jury, or even worse, an embarrassing acquittal. And so, the story goes, they executed him, then staged the dramatic Navy Seals raid for a heroic, patriotic pay-off.

Another theory claims that Bin Laden had already died of renal failure years before 2011. And so like some sci-fi movie, they froze his body in liquid nitrogen, waiting for the right moment to stage his elaborate capture and claim a victory for the US. There are others, however, who believe he is still alive and working undercover for the CIA. These ideas might sound like a whole lot of twaddle, belonging to the same league as Q-Anon. But then again, when it comes to the good ol' US, anything is possible ...

Similar "conspiracy" scepticism erupted around the attack on the Twin Towers. In the two-plus decades after 9/11, there have been growing claims that the Towers were brought down by US dark forces in order to fabricate an excuse to go to war in the Middle East. I find this idea a tad too far-fetched to seriously entertain. I mean, how could a government be that evil and sacrifice close to 4 000 of its own people as an excuse to invade another country?

Along with all the Bin Laden claims, the 9/11 one will be dismissed by the establishment as a laughable "conspiracy theory", a term that will become tantamount to a swearword during The Pandemic. Others will call them "spoiler alerts".

✳

We will soon discover – unsurprisingly, I suppose – that the War on Terror does not come to an end after Bin Laden is captured. And during Barack Obama's presidency, the language shifts subtly. The War on Terror now evolves into "countering violent extremism".

It will dawn on me only much later, during The Pandemic, that over time, Fear has slowly changed its shape and form to become not so much a reason for a war against terror, but rather, instead of actually *fighting* the "Terror", Fear is used to *feed* and *nurture* the battle being fought in the name of "Freedom". And so, with the support of those wide-reaching invisible tentacles of the internet, a psychological tool called "global anxiety" becomes a weapon in itself, an unwritten policy.

Propped up by the huge, unbridled power of tech to monitor and spy on ordinary people, Fear keeps seeping into our veins and brains. Fear becomes part of our everyday normal.

I watch, I observe how panic-stricken I am by all of this. As the Covid death numbers keep rolling in, as my paranoid thoughts keep multiplying, I see how my hands tremble, clutching the panic button when I unlock the door to the new house. Fear is all around me.

Chapter 29

A MEDICATED WORLD IS EASY FODDER

"There will be, in the next generation or so, a pharmacological method of making people love their servitude, and producing dictatorship without tears, so to speak, producing a kind of painless concentration camp for entire societies, so that people will in fact have their liberties taken away from them, but will rather enjoy it, because they will be distracted from any desire to rebel by propaganda or brainwashing ... And this seems to be the final revolution."
– Aldous Huxley, "The Ultimate Revolution" speech, University of California, Berkeley (1962)

After two decades of terror-mongering, from the moment the Twin Towers implode in 2001 and by the time The Pandemic arrives, we are all scared. Very, very scared. It feels to me like we're in a subconscious state of free-fall fear, brought on by a cauldron of violence, confusion and mixed messages. Some might call it "a state of cognitive dissonance".

I'd often wondered what that actually meant. It always sounded very clever when people dropped the term into conversation. For those of you who, like me, were wondering, "cognitive dissonance" is: *The mental discomfort that results from holding two conflicting beliefs, values or attitudes.* Basically, "mind-fucked" or "bamboozled".

So, while all this fear was seeping into our veins, trickling into our psyches like wood-eating worms, many of us had become zonked out on bad television and wall-to-wall streaming services. We'd fallen deep into the clutches of social media. We'd become catatonic clickbait, puppets in a pantomime of digital falsehoods. That we were under surveillance had been seeded into our subconscious. Very few of us seemed to give an actual fuck.

Just by observing the people around me, the world had never appeared lonelier, more disconnected or more medicated. Our naive assumptions that apps like Facebook were created to provide us with connection and companionship had by now been smashed. Some of us had begun to realise that our profiles, our likes and dislikes, were all being mined and sold by internet overlords to corporates to track our desires and commercialise our humanity.

As The Pandemic spread, Big Tech appeared to accelerate its domain to take charge of censorship. It also drove division. Internal documents leaked by a Facebook whistleblower in 2021 revealed that content embracing "anger and hate" was considered the "easiest way to grow Facebook". That may explain why so many Facebook "friends", individuals I had never previously encountered, were tearing me apart back in 2020. In our desperate need to connect, we were, ironically, being driven by fuck-you-I-hate-you algorithms.

One day, as we rode the crest of amended Level 2, I decided to google "loneliness" stats. It wasn't long before I came across a number of global polls that seemed to prove my "disconnected" theory. They revealed that, when it came to whether people enjoyed their lives or were happy with the work they did, massive dissatisfaction and feelings of meaninglessness became evident. Data showed that in 2013, 63 per cent of people in 142 countries were so disengaged that they felt as though they were "sleepwalking".

Another analysis conducted more recently, in 2019, a year before The Pandemic reared its head, showed that only 15 per cent of people felt "engaged" in the workplace. I mulled over the stats. So, basically, at least 85 per cent of people felt like zombies at work? That blew my mind.

And, as we dragged ourselves into the second year of the lockdown, I envisaged how those stats must look now, after endless disrupted connections among people in every imaginable sphere of life.

I wondered, if we were all so disengaged, imagine how lonely we must be? It saddened me to discover that, in 2018, a Ministry of Loneliness was set up in the UK for the millions who felt stranded and alone. In 2021, a similar ministry was established in Japan. Straight out of an Orwell novel.

I kept thinking of that Beatles song, "Eleanor Rigby". As a child, I conjured up a vivid image when listening to it, of a spinsterly woman picking up rice in a church after a wedding. Dreaming of love, but always going home alone. John and Paul and George and Ringo sang "Aaah" in unison, and asked where "they" all came from – the lonely people. I often closed my eyes and imagined "them" dotted all across the world, alone in their boxes, eating two-minute noodles.

It was hardly surprising then that, as a result of this *other* pandemic of loneliness, without anything tangible on which to pin our fears, exacerbated by feelings of meaninglessness, the consumption of anti-anxiety and depression medication had exploded over the last two decades.

One in five people on the planet now suffered from a medicine chest full of anxiety disorders. For years, I'd self-medicated with whatever I could lay my hands on in order to quell my inner turmoil. I was the one in five. A bit of googling told me that in the UK the number of prescriptions for antidepressants had almost doubled in the past decade. Within the first year of The Pandemic, these figures increased exponentially, with psychiatric prescriptions skyrocketing. Thankfully, I was one of the lucky ones who'd escaped overzealous prescription-pumping psychiatrists. But almost everyone I knew was now on some kind of medication for "anxiety" or "depression". And at the root of it all sat Fear.

Then I happened to stumble upon an interview in which a Belgian professor, Mattias Desmet, mentioned the term "free-flow anxiety". This guy seemed to share my concern that this "fear narrative" had been gaining momentum in our psyches for years. I was thrilled that he appeared to agree with what I'd been sensing in my clutch for clarity. Hallelujah! Hello, Mattias! I desperately needed a thought ally. I suddenly felt less alone. There were others who felt the same, who shared my concerns.

We both believed that, by the end of 2019, as we stood naively on the precipice of an impending viral pandemic that would change everything we knew or regarded as "normal", we had reached a point that was a perfect storm for mass manipulation to take place. My brain caught fire when I read Desmet's observations on *why* so many people adhered to the new laws at the start of The Pandemic. This question had really been, err … plaguing me.

By the time Covid arrived, the Belgian prof suggested, for the first time in recent history, overnight, people were presented with a *receptacle* into which to pour their ever-growing fears. Suddenly, that "free-flow anxiety", which had been whirring around our depressed brains since 2001, without anything tangible to latch onto, had a point, a new collective focus.

I watched aghast as most media came to the fear-driven party in a spectacular way, using the rolling numbers of deaths and infections to dominate the news. ("Terror", after all, makes for great headlines.) I often found myself muttering to no one in

196

particular that it felt like we were watching the World Cup of Fucking Corona.

Now, on reading the Belgian professor's observations, it made sense to me. He suggested that when we, the citizens of the world, were called upon to unite, it was as if a heroic struggle suddenly emerged in which people could finally feel the heady sense of a collective struggle. We threw ourselves into a united battle of solidarity, with all of us human soldiers fighting "the evil pandemic".

For a moment in time, the dark sensation of disconnect and loneliness that swamped us seemed to evaporate. Instead of being overwhelmed by feelings of insignificance, we could now stand together as one world to fight the object of our collective anxiety – the Big Bad Virus.

"They switch from this very highly aversive mental state to a symptomatic positive state where they feel connected," said Desmet. "Their lives (which previously had little meaning) make sense again through this heroic struggle with the object of anxiety ... That's why people continue to believe in the narrative, even if it is utterly absurd."

He described this phenomenon as "mass formation hypnosis" and "mob psychology": "If you look at the Corona crisis and listen to the mainstream narrative, you will hear that everything is about solidarity. You have to participate, you have to accept the vaccine. You have to respect social distancing, because if you don't, you lack citizenship, you show no solidarity. That's the most crucial thing, always, in mass formation."

From my minuscule locked-down world, I was amazed to see how quickly and easily people got sucked into this global "battle". How swiftly swords were drawn. How we viciously began to "other" each other. And, added to the catfights on social media and dogfights around dinner tables in suburbia, in the background, I watched in horror as the machine that was driving the fear, worked overtime against anyone who questioned the science and the logic, or tried to connect the dots in what seemed a maze of contradictions.

Those who failed to comply soon became targets of shame and derision. Those who hesitated when told to take the jab without asking questions, were branded "anti-vaxers", "right wing", or "selfish". Some even called them "murderers", baying for separate spaces and medical apartheid.

In those very early days, while I was still in a state of deep mourning for our old world, the one that appeared to be dissolving, I tortured myself with dystopian nightmare scenarios.

What if it was true that a world Corona vaccination rollout plan was on the cards? A world in which, unless we complied, we would not be able to access services like banking, where we would not be able to shop, work, gather in groups, go to school, or attend book launches or the theatre? One in which, without these "passports", we would not be able to catch planes and travel? What if it was true that all of these new rules were tied into a global vaccination ID system that would allow even more tracking and surveillance? A social credit system that would force us to finally surrender what little personal autonomy we had left? What if there was some kind of "new world order" waiting in the wings to declare a new world government with a new global currency?

These thoughts, back then, seemed so paranoid that it was almost embarrassing to admit to. Like overly dramatic "future fearing" out of some far-fetched dystopian Orwellesque nightmare. I dared not voice them on Facebook. I tried to keep them to myself. Instead, I downloaded more episodes of *Love Island UK* lest I got stretchered off to a clinic.

Two years later, many of the "New Rules" had slunk in and materialised. It felt as if the goalposts of how we measured "normal" and "acceptable" had been shifted while we were sleeping (or swallowing our meds). While we stared at the ratatat-tat of stats. As we squirted endless dashes of hand sanitiser onto our raw, cracked, clean-clean hands. Locked down, adhering to Covid laws, tethered to curfews, masks and prohibitions, we let them.

Soon our memories of passionate protests and pledges to orchestrate change before The Pandemic dissipated in the shadow of forced compliance. Impotency set in. Eventually, we even lost our main impetus to fight the Big Bad Virus – we were far too busy fighting each other.

By the time some of the Covid rules were alleviated, we were so grateful to ditch our masks that we confused fresh air with freedom. I sometimes wondered whether "The Pandemic" had not been some sinister social experiment, orchestrated to test how far people could be pushed and how much the mice could be controlled.

I was filled with dread. Throughout history, when it came to totalitarianism, the division of people and the manipulation of truth had always been extremely potent tactics. And if ever there was a compelling example of this, it was the way the Nazis under Adolf Hitler totally reinvented not only the circumstances in pre-Second World War Germany, but also history itself through the deception of memory.

Chapter 30

TELL ME LIES, TELL ME BIG LITTLE LIES

My mother was a fan of Adolf Hitler. This was something I simply could not comprehend. I now realise that she was really just a victim, a sheep, a product of a system, a child who had grown up at the height of insanity in apartheid South Africa. A compliant daughter who was in awe of her strict German father.

At around the age of eight, I discovered the Holocaust in a set of Second World War encyclopaedias my mother had bought courtesy of a special offer from *Reader's Digest*. I spent many horrified hours crouched over the black-and-white pictures of skeletal Jews being carted off to ovens and gas chambers. Images of piles of cadavers littered my childhood nightmares.

"Hitler had the right idea," my mother would sometimes announce as she sat at the head of the dining-room table at Sunday lunch, glass of wine in hand – that's when she wasn't taking a dig at "the blacks".

As a kid, her admiration for the Nazis and distaste for black people shamed me deeply – so much so that I would often tell anyone who'd listen that I was Jewish, hoping to redeem what I feared would be my mother's fucked-up karma. With my fair, freckled skin, I could hardly tell strangers I was black.

But, as much as I found Nazism abhorrent, it also held a deep fascination for me. I was particularly drawn to the rise of Hitler and how it came to be that one man could hold such enigmatic power over an entire nation and get ordinary people to do such heinous things.

My mother often defended Adolf with a litany of defences: "He was the only one who managed to restore Germany to its former glory … While German men went off to fight in the First World War, the Jews stayed at home, made money and used and impregnated the German women."

Jesus.

I knew from history that it was the Great Depression of 1929 that really allowed Hitler to get to the heart of the German nation's core paranoia. The fear of "not enough" can drive people demented. Even before the kind of stuff my mother later relayed to us over Sunday beef and roast potatoes, a hellbent Hitler went on a mission to finger the Jews as the cause of all of Germany's economic hardships. Gypsies and homosexuals were also on his hit list. Although I'm not quite sure how my mother felt about the Romani, I suspect she was pretty homophobic.

Later, in 2020, with a renewed interest in "mass formation" and the Nazis, I found it interesting that during The Pandemic, fear was once again used to manipulate people. The Germans were led to believe that their salvation would be in the restoration of national glory and ethnic cleansing by removing the "unpure". I feared that, in the time of the Big Bad Virus, the "unpure" might point to all those who didn't "comply".

One day, during amended Level 3, I came across absurd footage on YouTube that had been shown at Nazi rallies. A crazy set-up revealed a fabricated discovery of antiquated relics that supposedly proved German cultural superiority and a blood linkage to ancient civilisations like Sparta. By using these constructed images, Hitler managed to create a false Theatre of Memory, inventing past events that spoke to the German people's need for a dream of a mighty future.

Never before in history had the masses shown their sheep-like mentality more than those who allowed Adolf and his deluded government to take the reins of Germany. What I didn't realise until recently is that, as gung-ho as Hitler was about *engineering* false memory, he was as passionate about *wiping out* true memories that reminded Germany of its failures. In fact, as Nazi soldiers marched through Europe, it was not just land that the Germans were seizing, but rather an actual *invasion of memory* took place, with instructions given to destroy all First World War memorials in Belgium and France.

And although our circumstances in 2020 were entirely different from those in Second World War Europe, I saw certain disturbing similarities in the way many of us responded during The Pandemic. We now appeared to erase memories of untrustworthy governments, leaders and certain media – in fact, we now placed all our trust and our very lives into their hands.

I understand that raising the issue of the "Nazi brainwash" here is risky. I'd tried to express something similar on Facebook in July 2020 and felt the wrath of the social media Stasi. But then I stumbled onto a far more recent case of mass gullibility in which a bamboozlement had taken place that exposed just how easy it was to con a whole lot of people. Even those with titles, badges and high-ranking reputations.

✳

When I first read about Elizabeth Holmes back in 2014, I was intrigued. At just 19 years old, this American girl, who'd dropped out of Harvard, had come up with a groundbreaking idea for what seemed like a miracle blood-testing device that would revolutionise the entire global health industry.

She claimed that the compact black box, cleverly christened the "Edison", could detect illness, including cancer, by using just a few drops of blood from a single finger prick. Her company, Theranos, planned to charge less than half the rates demanded by Medicare and Medicaid in the States. The Edison could potentially save the government $200 billion over the next decade.

Dubbed the world's youngest self-made female billionaire and the "next Steve Jobs", Elizabeth – who, like Steve, wore only black turtleneck sweaters in public – became the darling of the media. She graced the cover of *Fortune*, and the magazine named her one of the richest self-made women in the world. She made it onto *Time's* list of 100 Most Influential People. She spoke on panels with Bill Clinton. She was given standing ovations at TED talks. She could even quote Jane Austen by heart.

Investors couldn't get enough of the young blonde, blue-eyed Elizabeth. Especially rich old white men. I watched with glee as she managed to bedazzle a string of them – highly respected and powerful heavyweights who threw their money and support behind her scheme. Guys like Henry Kissinger, the former US Treasury Secretary, Secretary of State George Shultz and four-star-decorated Marine Corps General James Mattis were Elizabeth-struck. Even creepy media baron Rupert Murdoch invested £120 million in the company.

They were not alone. I was equally captivated, and celebrated her successes. A female tech start-up giant had finally landed! At last there was girl power right up there, rubbing shoulders with Big Tech's Zuckerberg-led hoody-bro club. And over the next few years Theranos would soar in value to $9 billion.

But then, in 2015, it all came crashing down when it emerged in a scathing *Wall Street Journal* exposé that the "genius" black-box, blood-testing device was a sham. All the Edison tests were, in fact, performed on Siemens machines, blood was being diluted, and unreliable, potentially life-threatening results were being sent to patients.

Elizabeth Holmes, with those piercing blue eyes and deep put-on-for-interviews voice, was a fake and Theranos was a sham. Yet, despite the damning evidence, many still refused to believe it.

"She got a huge amount of the benefit of the doubt, even after my first story came out," said John Carreyrou, the *Wall Street Journal* journo who exposed Theranos and Holmes. "People didn't want to think that this giant fraud had been perpetrated by a woman."

Finally, in 2016, after US regulators had banned Lizzie from operating any blood-testing service for two years, people began to wake up. Partners cut ties. Lawsuits piled up.

I could have kicked myself. There had been clear signs that the science around her claims was total bullshit, but we chose not to see them. Back in 2015, when a *New Yorker* reporter asked Holmes how the Edison actually worked, she had mumbled a vague explanation that sounded like something out of *Star Trek*: "A chemistry is performed so that a chemical reaction occurs and generates a signal from the chemical interaction with the sample, which is translated into a result, which is then reviewed by certified laboratory personnel."

So how could all of us, including the US's Food and Drug Administration, have been sucked into the whole Theranos farce so completely? How did Elizabeth Holmes manage to bamboozle so many powerful people for so long? Attract billions of dollars in investment money to what was clearly a harebrained scheme? Holmes was obviously entirely out of her depth, but it appears our need to believe her was stronger than both logic and science. Mine certainly was. Something called "confirmation bias" kicked in, and we focused on the information and data that supported our belief that the black-turtleneck-sweatered Holmes was the next Steve Jobs.

After she was charged with fraud, many claimed that Holmes showed no contrition and gave no indication or acknowledgement that she had done anything wrong. A few days after the company closed, she set off to the Burning Man festival with her new boyfriend, Billy, and appeared to be having the time of her life.

"Part of what makes them so convincing is that they've told so many lies and the lies have gotten so big that the line in their minds between what's true and what's a lie becomes blurred," said John Carreyrou. "That enables them to continue being able to say these lies with confidence."

And, naturally, we trust them.

In his book *The (Honest) Truth About Dishonesty*, American author Dan Ariely proves that what we believe depends on the "stories we tell ourselves" – textbook Elizabeth Holmes. Having studied the working of the brains of people asked to repeatedly tell lies, he says: "We saw that over time, their brains reacted less and less to lies, they were less sensitised." The results essentially revealed that, after a while, we believe our own and other people's lies. And so Ariely concluded that far from being objective, "truth" is an extremely slippery slope.

※

During The Pandemic, as I watch myself trying to get to grips with what the hell is going on, I suspect that the part of our brain that can be hoodwinked, or our penchant for turning a blind eye in order to keep a fantasy alive (our "confirmation bias"), is going into overdrive.

The thing is, many of those declaring themselves experts or guardians of Truth had historically been proven to be not just tricksters and liars, but also relentless aggressors against those who exposed the facts.

Amid this chaos and all these mixed messages, although governments, leaders and certain media houses were publicly claiming deep concern for our health and safety, track records revealed that many of them had, time and time again, shown us that they may *not* necessarily have had the people's welfare at heart, while simultaneously, pretending to.

Chapter 31

YE, THE PEOPLE, SHALL NOT SMOKE!

"It was a bright cold day in April, and the clocks were striking thirteen."
– George Orwell, *1984*

While Hitler was prepping for his rise to power in the late 1920s, having spent his earlier years painting mediocre watercolour postcards in Vienna, across the ocean in New York a guy by the name of Edward Bernays, aka the King of Modern PR, was dreaming up schemes to get women to smoke in public.

Back then, the tobacco companies – their products purchased and consumed primarily by men – had woken up to the fact that they were targeting only half the potential market. Although women did, in fact, smoke, most did so secretively, behind closed doors. Clearly, there was a tonne of money to be made from the fairer sex.

George Washington Hill, then president of the American Tobacco Company, was convinced that if the female smoking taboo could be broken, profits would double. "It will be like opening a gold mine right in our front yard," he said. And so he hired Ed to work some PR magic. Influenced by his uncle, Sigmund Freud's fascination with man's darker subconscious, Bernays believed that in order to turn the thinking that smoking was socially acceptable for only men, he needed to understand the deeper reasons why women were drawn to it. And so he approached a respected therapist whose research told him that, for women, a cigarette was a phallic symbol. Many women felt that, by smoking, they were given access to that male power.

Excited by this revelation, at the annual Easter Parade in New York on 31 March 1929, Bernays organised an almost Dadaist "happening". He hired a group of young debutantes to swan around in the crowds, openly lighting up and puffing on their cigs. He was fastidious in choosing the women: "While they should be good looking, they should not look too model-y."

The media was thus briefed that suffragettes were intending to use the parade as a form of protest, demanding their freedom as women. The march was supported by feminist Ruth Hale, founder of the Lucy Stone League, a women's rights organisation established in 1921 to fight for the right of women to not be forced to take their husband's surname in marriage. Hale called for multitudes of like-minded women to join in the march: "Women! Light another torch of freedom! Fight another sex taboo!"

And so, with the suffragette movement behind it, Bernays' carefully constructed publicity worked like a bomb. The story exploded, with major media houses publishing the news across the world.

Overnight, cigarettes were now associated with freedom and power for women.

Little did I realise how symbolic these cancer sticks would become in my own quest for liberty.

✳

On Sunday, 26 March 2020, almost a century after New York's suffragettes openly puffed away at their march for freedom, South Africa naively heads into what's been claimed to be "a three-week lockdown". And then Cooperative Governance Minister Nkosazana Dlamini-Zuma (one of the top dogs in South Africa's National Coronavirus Council) drops a smokeless bomb. In a monotone voice, she announces to the nation that tobacco is banned. What the actual fuck! This is a completely unexpected curveball for me and 11 million other smokers in South Africa.

"Are you for *real*? What the fucking fuck!" I scream at the live-streamed national broadcast. I head off to Facebook Live and rant, puffing away defiantly on screen. Us smokers are incensed.

In the month leading up to The Pandemic – for years, in fact – I had been debating giving up smoking, ever since my nicotine relapse in 2014 that broke 10 years of abstinence. But once NDZ announces the 21-day prohibition, my commitment to smoke rises to a whole new level.

Let me elaborate a little on how I became a smoker again after that little red Italian car crash. I managed to kick the filthy habit in 2004, and for 10 glorious years I was happily smoke-free. In fact, in my third book, *Crashed*, I wax lyrical on how I'd stopped smoking and how I would *never ever* do it again. Never say never. (I still carry some shame for making a dick of myself by blabbing off like that. But so be it.)

A few months after the crash, with PTSD still coursing through my veins and to celebrate the sale of my Joburg house, I puffed defiantly on a cigar. One is too many, they say, and a thousand is never enough …

A week before the three-week lockdown tobacco drought ends, President Cyril Ramaphosa announces that we smokers need not worry because, by 1 May, our nicotine fix would once again be made available.

And then, horror of all horrors, on 29 April, two days before the supposed emancipation of tobacco is to take place, Nkosazana Dlamini-Zuma does a massive flip-flop. In a few short sentences, she breaks the hearts of millions of local puffers by announcing that tobacco will in fact remain banned. Indefinitely. She backs her outrageous decision by claiming that 2 000 individuals submitted their opposition to making tobacco available, suggesting that "sharing zols" will endanger people's lives, and that smokers will take up too many hospital beds in the time of Corona.

And, just like that, South African puffers are forced to find devious ways and means of securing their fags. I, thankfully, had purchased a rather large stash of Raw, my preferred roll-up organic tobacco, the day before the start of lockdown. But by now I am literally on my last dregs. Come the morning of Thursday, 30 April, my supply is nada. Before Nkosazana betrayed us, I'd planned to camp out at my local tobacconist on Friday, 1 May, to replenish my stash, much like people do when a new iPhone is released. Queue really early. Be at the front of the line.

NDZ's announcement leaves me devastated. Of course, I am fully aware that my problems are privileged, First World ones. I know that people all over the country are literally starving, but the small-minded, needy addict steps to the fore. *I need my tobacco!* Once again, I take to social media, screeching my rage. I have a captive audience. Many who view my meltdown share my rant. Us smokers are reeling.

After much scrabbling through drawers and obscure dusty places, I find a two-year-old clump of stale, vanilla-flavoured Colt tobacco. Although the sweet smell sickens me, I am jonesing. I decide to microwave it to try to nuke away the nauseating aroma. For someone in recovery, clean and sober from drugs like heroin and booze, for more than 20 years, my behaviour is more than embarrassing. It reminds me of those days when I hunted down crumbs of crack between the car seats. I am fully aware that all my addict buttons have been pushed, but I am desperate for my fix.

At 8am that same Thursday morning, I receive a phone call from an old acquaintance, who now works for British American Tobacco SA. She's seen my rant on Facebook and is calling to ask if, by any chance, I'd be prepared to write some kind of affidavit on behalf of BATSA. I subsequently learn that South Africa's largest tobacco company is planning to take the government to court.

On any normal day, I would have thought long and hard about whether I wanted to get into bed with a company that had been accused of associating with organised crime, state capture and dirty politics, but my anguish to access tobacco overrides ethics and clear-thinking.

I am promptly informed that lawyers representing BATSA will contact me. And it's not long before they do. By Friday, my carefully constructed affidavit is submitted to a group of legal eagles at the law firm of Webber Wentzel, who are pulling all-nighters to pull the case together to submit by Monday, 4 May. I channel the suffragette Ruth Hale. I imagine myself the Joan of Arc of Tobacco. I am doing this on behalf of all of us 11 million smokers who, just like me, are also freaking the fuck out!

Chapter 32

HOW I SUED THE GOVERNMENT FOR TOBACCO

In my affidavit, as a "co-applicant" to sue Cyril, Nkosazana and the South African government, demanding that they release tobacco, I begin by explaining how my love affair with the substance started at the age of four when I smoked my first stompie. What I don't tell them is that, on discovering my misdemeanour, my furious mother washed my mouth out with Sunlight soap as punishment.

I do, however, tell them that I was 17 years old when I began smoking Camel Filter, and subsequently participated in an addictive relationship with nicotine for the next 20 years. During this time, I elaborate, I also became a heroin and crack addict. I don't tell them about the gang rape, about using drugs while pregnant, or how withdrawing from heroin feels like you're being drawn and quartered on a medieval torture rack as your muscles tear from your bones.

Instead, I explain how, after I finally got clean in 1999, cigarettes played a "huge part in me managing my recovery" for the first five years of sobriety: "I probably wouldn't have been able to kick smack and crack if I had not used tobacco products as a crutch. Smoking assisted me to divert my cravings for harder drugs, helping to calm me down and reduce my anxiety."

(I wonder whether Cyril and NDZ will actually read this, and if they do, what will they think of me?)

I then tell them about the miracle: that I managed to stop smoking for 10 years. I don't elaborate on the feelings of emancipation and pure joy I felt on kicking the filthy habit. Instead, I describe the serious car accident in which I was involved in, in 2014. I specify that I wrote off a R3.2-million Ferrari. I decide to leave out the part that I was test-driving the car at the time. How the crash occurred when I'd overtaken a slow-moving truck. I don't explain that because the traffic lights were obscured by a heavy growth of overhanging trees, I didn't realise I was heading into an intersection where the robot had just turned red, and so I landed up being T-boned by a seven-seater tractor-like Pajero. That kind of info might be too detailed for an affidavit.

What I do tell them is that the accident was life-changing. Not only did I come within an inch of losing my life, but the subsequent emotional, financial and legal fallout from the almighty crash also brought on a severe bout of PTSD. On the verge of a nervous breakdown, unable to sleep or stop weeping, I was subsequently hospitalised for three weeks at Crescent Clinic in Randburg. My treatment included taking Seroquel and Epitec for my PTSD. I don't tell them that while I was a patient I had a completely inappropriate relationship with a fellow sad-eyed inmate 16 years younger than me. That would have taken up just too many pages.

Instead, I try to explain to Cyril and NDZ that the psychotropics I was prescribed were supposed to assist with my extreme anxiety. Instead, on leaving the clinic and trying to reintegrate into "normal life", I soon found that the medication was severely fucking with my cognitive abilities. (The lawyers later change the words "fucking with" to "impairing".) And so, I tell them, within a few months of leaving the clinic, I decided to stop taking the medication. The prescribed drugs inhibited my creativity in particular. As a writer and publisher, I explain, I rely heavily on my brain to think clearly in order to earn a living. And so, during that time, I tumbled down the slippery slope of nicotine relapse.

I give a detailed account of how, believing I could just have a harmless puff, I subsequently began smoking Black Stone Cherry cigars to cope with my anxiety. At around R130 for a pack of five back in 2014, they soon became prohibitively expensive, so I opted to smoke organic tobacco, which I believed was a healthier option. I point out that it contains no chemicals or pesticides in its farming. I could write paragraphs on how normal cigarette paper is really toxic, but I decide to stick to the subject at hand. Finally off the mind-numbing psychiatric medication, with the aid of my rollies, I soon began to feel better and cope with the pressures of life again.

I hope that both Nkosazana and Cyril will get it, that no matter how many years a serious addict has been clean and sober, there is always the possibility of returning to destructive old habits. In my then 20 years of sobriety, I had seen many addicts with long-term clean time relapse and ruin or end their lives. I explain that, quite apart from the pleasure that smoking gave me, I believe tobacco effectively prevented me slipping back to those dark days when I was addicted to hard drugs. I point out, that no matter how much Nkosazana may hate smoking, as a free-thinking human being, I am practising my constitutional right by making a conscious adult choice to smoke tobacco.

My affidavit then clearly describes how my entire world was jolted when, inexplicably, the sale of tobacco was prohibited for a second time on the day Nkosazana did her flip-flop and once again banned our fix.

I really hope she reads this part: "I felt a deep sense of betrayal and a sudden lack of faith in government, who I had been strongly supporting during the initial lockdown. It felt like you guys had said one thing, and then broken your word. It felt as if the government was playing mind games with us smokers who have an addictive need for tobacco and tobacco products. This left me feeling depressed and powerless. In a single night I lost faith in my government as these measures to continue to ban tobacco appeared to be punitive, which led me to wonder how many more times the government would break its word."

Although I am nervous to disclose that I am contemplating securing tobacco on the black market, as this is tantamount to planning "a crime", it is an important part of my argument. I choose my words carefully: "I am fully aware that I can source illegal cigarettes as millions of smokers are flagrantly doing. But I have made a pact with myself not to do so as it feels that if I start trying to 'score' cigarettes illegally, it will remind me too much of a time when I was a desperate addict trying to 'score' heroin and crack cocaine."

For good measure, I also add how outlandishly expensive illegal tobacco has become on the black market: "I knew from friends who were smokers that there was a thriving illegal tobacco market. The prices being charged were extortionate. A single packet cost between R80 and R100 and, in some cases, I had heard of cartons of ten packets being sold for close to R2 000. Now that the sale of cigarettes was not permitted under Alert Level 4, and potentially not even under Alert Levels 3 or 2, I feared the prices may further escalate." (Which, of course, they do.)

I elaborate on how, at the time of submitting my affidavit, we are into our third phase of lockdown, which is an incredibly stressful time. This "new" normal has been a shock to all our systems. In the early days, I explain, I could hardly get out of bed, while on other days, a manic energy took over. Tobacco has effectively helped me cope. None of us knows when this is going to end – and, boy, does that turn out to be a massive understatement. I note that the ritual of rolling a cigarette, in the safety of my home, brightens my day. It lifts my mood and allows me to be focused and productive.

In conclusion, I state that the tobacco prohibition has had a severe impact on my psychological and emotional wellbeing, and, in particular, my ability to regulate my stress and anxiety. I can't for the life of me see any rational basis related to Covid-19 for the government to prohibit the sale of tobacco products, while allowing for the sale of sugar or coffee. In my experience, these are also stimulants that form part of people's daily coping rituals. The same, I explain, is true of prescription drugs used for anxiety and stress management, many of which may – as I have personally experienced – have addictive and sometimes even life-threatening and cognitive-impairing side-effects.

I further note that I find it ironic that the government cites the "sharing of zols" as a risk of spreading the virus as a reason for this prohibition, when "illegal" cigarettes, which are clearly widely available, are far more likely to be shared because of their exorbitant pricing.

It feels good to record all my feelings on paper. I hope that my rantings make some kind of sense and will be of some use in the case. So I email my affidavit to the Webber Wentzel legal team late that Friday afternoon.

By now my stale old stash of tobacco is finished. I have recently taken to ripping open sachets of chamomile and rooibos tea, rolling the contents into Rizla papers and puffing pathetically on the pungent leaves.

The legals at BATSA seem to appreciate what I have to say. The following day I receive an email asking me, "based on the strength of your testimony", whether I would consider becoming a "co-applicant" in the case. Before responding, I decide to check who my bedfellows would be.

The proposed list is as follows, in this order:
  British American Tobacco SA
  Japanese International Tobacco
  Melinda Ferguson
  Limpopo Tobacco Processors
  South African Tobacco Transformation Alliance
  Black Tobacco Farmers Association

I find this rather amusing. Little old ex-junkie me and all these huge corporations and alliances, suing the big bad wolf of the state. I am so up for this fight. I email back and reply with a resounding "yes".

Over the weekend the team of lawyers puts together a case on my behalf, tabling how prohibiting tobacco has severely infringed on my fundamental rights as an individual. They maintain that, as an adult, I should have the right to choose the products I use to cope with stress and anxiety. Through the tobacco prohibition, the government has, therefore, limited my autonomy and my "inherent human dignity" to make these choices – and it has done so without any justifiable basis since there are far less drastic means available to achieve its Covid-related aims.

I am thrilled to be a part of this landmark battle. I can't wait for Monday, 4 May, for the government to be served.

Chapter 33

MY FLICKERING TORCH OF FREEDOM

I come to believe that the Tobacco Case is far more important than simply allowing us smokers our right to purchase and puff on tobacco products. It addresses our fundamental right as human beings to the *freedom of choice*.

You have no idea how disappointed I am when on Tuesday, 5 May, I receive a mail from the BATSA lawyers to "regretfully" inform me that their client has "withdrawn". I am devastated. I put long hours into my affidavit and have been heavily weighing my bets on the strength of our case. I have hundreds of people, even thousands, on social media, rooting for *moi*, placing their hope in little old me to represent their cause.

I slink off to the microwave to nuke some more vanilla tobacco. Then I get a call from a friend. "I know you're struggling. I just want to tell you that there's a place in the CBD selling your Raw organic tobacco."

All promises to not "go black market" fly out the window. Within 20 minutes, I am downtown, combing the area for said supplier. I arrive at a bolted security gate. A man with dark glasses appears.

"Do you have any Raw?" I whisper between clenched teeth.

He glances nervously up and down the street and then waves me in. The deal goes down quickly. I purchase his last two packets for R600 (they usually cost R130 a piece).

"Let me know when you get more!" I say under my breath as I hand him crumpled notes and my business card. I scuttle back to the car and hide my stash under the driver's seat just in case I'm stopped in one of the many roadblocks set up to maintain Covid law. The shit may as well have been heroin.

Then, a few weeks later, an email pings into my inbox informing me that BATSA has come back on board. Oh, well, jolly good, but a little late, don't you think?

"What a bunch of fuckwits," I mutter.

Although I would love to tell them to go screw themselves – I'm still pretty incensed with them for dropping the case back in early May – by now us smokers are beyond climbing the walls. So I clamber down off my high horse, ditch my moral high ground and agree to sign up again. Not for a second do I, of course, believe they have my best interests or needs at heart. They've clearly come to their financial senses and worked out how much dosh they're losing. The legal tobacco industry is bleeding while the black market is screaming, "Lotto!" But I don't care. I want my tobacco!

The case is finally heard months later, on 5 August 2020, in the Cape Town High Court. Masked up and feeling darkly dejected, I sit in the Covid-manned courtroom and listen to the arguments from both sides. By this stage, I've lost all faith in rationality or the wheels of justice turning in favour of "we the people".

More than four months of the tobacco prohibition have passed. During this time, us smokers have all found ways and means of securing our stashes while prices on the black market continue to soar to outlandish levels. The year 2020 sees South African puffers – grandmothers, schoolteachers, miners, metal workers, shop assistants, artists and captains of industry – behaving like a bunch of crazed heroin fiends, trawling dark alleyways and dangerous ghettos to get their fix. Contrary to Nkosazana's assurances, very few of us have kicked the habit. In fact, the long months of prohibition have only served to increase our manic hunger to find ways and means to get something – anything – to smoke.

In court, our Webber Wentzel team, led by Alfred Cockerill SC, presents a compelling case and literally burns holes in the government's constitutionally unsound ban. I begin to feel cautiously optimistic, but also wary about grasping at hope. It's such a long time since I felt any.

But then, before judgment is even made by the bench of three, on 18 August 2020, the tobacco prohibition is miraculously lifted. I will always be of the opinion that, after watching the case broadcast via livestream and seeing their own weak arguments, the government and its advisors must have realised that they were snookered. And so, instead of losing face completely, they dropped the outrageous ban before the court even reached its decision.

Despite this being a case that sought "urgent relief", it would take almost four more months, after being heard in court in early August, before the verdict was finally announced on Friday, 11 December 2020 – close to nine months since this whole sorry smokeless debacle had begun.

Before the news is out in the media, I receive a mail from the legal team, stating that the Western Cape High Court has finally ruled that the ban on tobacco sales during the country's hard lockdown was "unnecessary and inconsistent with the South African Constitution".

Tobacco had won! Tobacco was now emancipated. Look, I am no Julia Assange, but I had at least done *something* to keep the fragile, dimly flickering torch of choice and freedom alight. But, in all honesty, I was scared. Petrified, actually.

What if they came for me? Bugged me? Followed me? Jailed me? During these tumultuous times, standing up for what one believed in and, even worse, taking a public stance, posed its own dark and sinister dangers. I mean, look what they did to Julian.

Chapter 34

THE BIRTH OF THE
TRUTH-BOMB MOVEMENT

"Those who would destroy us with lies will themselves be destroyed by the truth."
– Julian Assange, *Free the Truth: Free Assange* documentary

I had a soft spot for Julian Paul Assange from the outset. The Australian hacktivist who established the whistleblowing platform, WikiLeaks, in 2006 was a brainy shit-stirrer and reminded me a little of a sly silver fox. I read somewhere that his hair had gone white at the age of 15 after a science experiment with a cathode-ray tube went wrong. I guess it was no surprise that I was drawn to his rebellious cause. I'd always found myself on the side of the black sheep, having been cast in that role for much of my life.

Seven years after the Twin Towers imploded, a burst of bright light shone onto our terrified world. It was razor sharp and threatened to expose the Deep State's criminal secrets. From where I watched, it had enormous potential to realign our planet's moral axis and the balance of power as we knew it.

It all began in 2008 when a group calling itself "Anonymous" launched an arsenal of cyber-attacks on certain governments, corporations and the Church of Scientology. For decades, I'd been suspicious of Scientologists, who regularly tried to recruit me when I was a drama student at UCT. Besides, some famous members, like Tom Cruise, were downright weird. So I was pretty stoked when I read that this Anonymous group had brought down the cult's website, and used Julian's WikiLeaks to publish all these compromising secret documents for us to feast on. I became an instant fan of these unidentifiable guys wearing Guy Fawkes masks, inspired by the movie *V for Vendetta*. They actually reminded me a little of the baddie in *Scream 2*. It felt as if they were covertly messing with established power, and that thrilled me.

But it's only in 2010, when I am deep in relationship-addiction mania with a guy who consistently threatens to cheat on me, that WikiLeaks shoots spectacularly into the headlines. Shockwaves reverberate across the planet with the unleashing of a series of sensational leaks.

The info is provided by a trans soldier, Chelsea Manning, formerly known as Bradley. (Back then, I hadn't given the whole transgender issue much thought, so occasionally I'd sometimes misgender Chelsea and call them Bradley. These days, I'm a lot more careful for fear of being roasted or cancelled by the Pronoun Police.)

Up until now, the US's PR machine had been working hard to pose as the heroic victim avenging the attacks of 9/11 on American soil. But then everything changes on 5 April 2010, when Assange shows 39 minutes of grainy black-and-white footage to a packed room at the National Press Club in Washington.

The documentary is titled *Collateral Murder*. I watch the shocking video on YouTube. Filmed from an Apache military helicopter, it reveals American and British soldiers behaving as though they're performing in a simulated video game. Without hesitation, they fire their weapons at unarmed Iraqi civilians going about their daily business. The shooters also mow down a foreign journalist armed only with his camera, as well as his driver. In the end, 18 innocent people are murdered. Two children – five and 10 years old – on their way to school are also severely injured in the crossfire when their father stops to try to pick up the injured in his van.

Assange tells his audience at the National Press Club that he and his WikiLeaks team worked day and night for weeks in order to break the US military's encryption on the video. While he protects his source, we will later learn that the footage was supplied by 23-year-old Chelsea Manning.

Collateral Murder is broadcast across the world and causes both outrage and mayhem. It rips the scales from our eyes on what this war is really about, blowing to smithereens all illusions of the US's right to be in Iraq. It sickens me. None of the killer soldiers will ever be brought to book or charged with war crimes. None of the victims' families will ever be compensated.

History will later show us that *Collateral Murder* causes the US government and military more reputational damage than all the other secret documents combined that WikiLeaks will go on to publish. It catapults Assange into the role of both rock-star hacktivist hero and traitorous villain. He becomes the foremost global threat to state secrecy.

WikiLeaks and Jules are now on a roll. Next up is the *Afghan War Diary*. Considered at the time to be the biggest leak in US military history, the shit totally hits the fan when *The Guardian*, *The New York Times* and *Der Spiegel* publish the explosive leaks in July 2010.

In the month before my second book, *Hooked*, is launched, I remember being addicted to reading blow-by-blow accounts of how thousands of Afghan civilians had been killed and how their deaths had remained undocumented in this bloody, senseless war in Afghanistan. *The New York Times* described the leaks as "a six-year archive of classified military documents [that] offers an unvarnished and grim picture of the Afghan war".

I had deep respect for these WikiLeaks hacktivists who, along with Chelsea, were risking everything to inform us of US war crimes. These were crazy and dangerous times. Bin Laden was still on the loose and, in my view, many Yankees, including their government, had become a bunch of trigger-happy psychopaths. At this stage I sincerely believed that Assange, Manning and WikiLeaks (which played the role of a societal safety valve) would win the next Nobel Peace Prize.

Naturally, a lot of people in high places were extremely pissed off when all this compromising info emerged. And then, the following month, in August of 2010, something really shocking happened.

I was completely blindsided when I read that while he was on a public speaking trip in Sweden, Julian Assange had been accused of rape and sexual molestation. Jeez! How could I have been so wrong? I had really held him up as my hero, one of the few good guys.

Stories calling Assange a "narcissist", "rapist" and "sexual deviant" were now published across the globe. Overnight, his reputation was obliterated. Overnight, my feelings for the Aussie hacktivist flip-flopped and, along with most of the rest of the world, I now denounced him as a sex criminal. (This all happened seven years before the #MeToo movement really took off, before we got used to the idea that we were surrounded by misogynists, paedophiles and perverts.)

While Assange vehemently denied the allegations, over the next few years I took a wary step back. I watched from afar as he became more and more tied up in legal red tape and one court case after another as he tried to defend himself against what he described as "trumped-up charges".

It would be some time before I began to suspect, cautiously at first, that his character assassination might have been orchestrated by the CIA and the US and Swedish governments, as well as other players he had embarrassed via WikiLeaks who had so much to lose.

But, much to my surprise, the Aussie didn't let up. In fact, his personal troubles seemed to fire up his determination. He continued to soldier on with his mission to "correct the truth". Over the following year, he would publish the sensational *Cablegate* files and *The Guantánamo Files* a month before Bin Laden was "deleted" in 2011.

From the very start, the Guantánamo Bay detention camp in Cuba had freaked me out, but now we were being shown how prisoners – including children, the elderly and mentally disabled – were brutally tortured and coerced to confess while detained at the Bay.

By the time Assange walked into the Ecuadorean embassy in London, seeking political asylum, it was June 2012. He was now not only hounded after the sex-crime allegation, but he was also pretty certain that, given the chance, the US would do everything in its power to extradite him across the Atlantic to face serious charges of espionage.

Luckily for Jules, Ecuador's then liberal president, Rafael Correa, took pity on him. The welcome mat was laid out, the doors were flung wide open and, for the next seven years, he became the embassy's houseguest.

By this stage, I was firmly back in the silver fox's corner. My hunch that there was something seriously amiss with those rape allegations would prove to be spot on. But I would only truly see just how dark the vilification of Assange was after I read the book *The Trial of Julian Assange*, released in 2022, by Nils Melzer, the UN's Special Rapporteur on "Torture and Other Cruel, Inhuman or Degrading Treatment or Punishment".

As I suspected, it turned out that neither of Assange's "victims", two Swedish women, known as "A" and "S", ever, in fact, alleged that Julian had raped them. Their concern was that they had both had consensual but unprotected sex on separate occasions with him, and wanted him to take an HIV test. At the time, he appeared reluctant to do so, although he agreed to a test at a later stage as he was "currently too busy" with the *Afghan War Diary*.

S thought she could force him to undergo the test by going to the police. A joined her at the station to offer support. The police subsequently compiled statements where the term "rape" was introduced into the narrative, despite both women insisting that this was not the case. S subsequently refused to sign her statement, but the allegations were nevertheless released to the media via the Swedish prosecution. Within hours, Assange was vilified across the world as a "rapist".

For the following 12 years, the sex-crime allegations would cause untold reputational damage for the Aussie and effectively distract the rest of us from the real dark crimes he would continue to expose via WikiLeaks. According to Melzer, the Swedish prosecutors never had a semblance of a case against Assange – nor, it seems, the slightest intention to actually investigate "the crime" because they knew there was "nothing there".

✳

By 2013, while Jules was still safe behind the gates of the Ecuadorean embassy in London, across the Atlantic, things were not going well for Chelsea Manning. After she'd collaborated with WikiLeaks by disclosing nearly 750 000 highly classified documents, she'd been incarcerated without trial by the military for three whole years following her arrest in 2010.

When her trial did finally commence and conclude on 21 August 2013, she was sentenced to 35 years in prison. That was just a day after my birthday, so I was still feeling pretty fab about my life that week. As the "trans traitor" was marched off to the maximum-security US Disciplinary Barracks at Fort Leavenworth, where her torture would really begin, little did I realise that my own year of mayhem was about to unfold. I would crash that R3.2 million Ferrari just 10 days later.

It's around this time that the third hero in the Truth-Bomb movement arrives on the scene. While Chelsea is facing three decades in prison, Jules is locked down in the Ecuadorean embassy and I am about to be catapulted into a disciplinary hearing at work for crashing the Italian stallion, Edward Joseph Snowden steps into the spotlight. Despite having serious post-crash PTSD, I soon become obsessed with this young, serious-looking, bespectacled and soft-spoken geek.

The documents Edward unleashes through WikiLeaks are essentially highly classified proof of massive collusion and espionage within this *thing* called the "Five Eyes Intelligence Alliance". Up until now, I wasn't even aware that this secret alliance even existed. I soon discover that Five Eyes represents a covert agreement between Australia, Canada, New Zealand, the UK and US to work secretly with the National Security Agency and various telecommunications companies to spy on ordinary citizens.

Snowden goes on to describe the collaboration as a "supra-national intelligence organisation that does not answer to the known laws of its own countries" – sounding incredibly 007 to me. The leaks subsequently create colossal fallout for all the nations that are involved.

Overnight, just as it was for both Manning and Assange, Edward Snowden becomes "an enemy of the state", hunted down by US law enforcement. (My impending "crash" hassles prove to be much milder; I am only persecuted by HR.)

Snowden is now on the run for his life. So Julian, still safely ensconced in his Ecuadorean embassy "guesthouse", helps Ed find refuge in Russia.

A few months later, I check myself into a clinic to have

that nervous breakdown. During my mentally precarious incarceration, I don't follow the news. I am too zacked out on psych meds.

Chapter 35

THE DARKNESS FIGHTS BACK

"Once the deceived become aware of their deception, they are no longer deceived."
– Nils Melzer, Al Jazeera podcast *The Take*

By 2015, the year I go on my first psilocybin journey to embark on my own search for light, WikiLeaks – or "the Light Keepers", as I prefer to call them – has unleashed more than 10 million documents into the public domain. It's as if a torrent of bitter gospels has been given flight. To many, the truth is blinding. But secrets and lies continue to be exposed. Assange describes the leaks as "a giant library of the world's most persecuted documents".

But what really accelerates the hunt for Assange is the WikiLeaks publication of a set of the US Democratic Party's hacked emails in September 2016. And we all know what happens when you fuck with America on its home turf.

Ironically, the leaks help the Orange Clown, Donald Trump, win the presidential election. While he had previously called for nothing less than the death penalty for Assange following the publication of the Afghan and Iraq war diaries, he now characteristically suffers periodic memory loss, does a total about-turn and publicly claims: "I love WikiLeaks."

But, within three months of his invasion of the Oval Office,

Trump does another predictable flip-flop. He gets his attorney-general, that creepy guy, Jeff Sessions, to announce that Assange's arrest is a "priority" for the US. But he doesn't stop with Assange.

Trump then turns his wrath on Chelsea. A few months earlier, as Obama was leaving office, he had signed a decree to release her. For seven years she'd been fighting for her life and sanity in maximum-security lock-up. But if the world's most famous trans prisoner thought for a minute she was home free with Obama's pardon, she soon experiences the full wrath of the Trump administration that is out for revenge. The Orange Clown labels her "an ungrateful traitor" who "doesn't deserve her freedom". No longer protected by clemency, she is rearrested and jailed a year later for refusing to testify before a Special Grand Jury investigating Assange. And, as far as Snowden is concerned, Trump calls the truth fugitive "a spy who should be executed".

Across the pond, in London, things suddenly start to get super shit for Assange. His Ecuadorean protector, President Rafael Correa, leaves office and is replaced by a dude called Lenín Moreno who turns out to be a proper fascist. President Moreno soon makes it clear that he is cooperating with Trump and Washington and considers Assange an "inherited problem".

For six years Assange had been living in a tiny, cramped space in the embassy. I'd come across a few pictures of him surrounded by the computers from which he ran WikiLeaks. I remained in awe at how he'd managed to work from there. Now, under the orders of the new right-wing president, the bastards decide to cut off his internet and install a jammer to prevent him from accessing the web via his phone.

I begin to fear that Assange will now go loco, knowing first-hand how fragile our minds can be and how easy it is to cross the line into insanity. I also am fully aware of how addicted I am to the virtual highway, so if I'm so reliant on it, imagine how obsessed the driver of Wikileaks must be? Not only is he now deprived of access to his virtual life's work, but he's also forced into solitary confinement with no outside visitors allowed.

Assange has no choice; he steps down as editor of WikiLeaks. For a man whose only outlet has been to connect with the world and pursue his mission to tell us the truth via the World Wide Web, the loss of access indeed proves to be catastrophic for his mental health.

I watch in dismay as CCTV footage is broadcast around the world, showing a caged-in, dishevelled "prisoner" trying to exercise, manoeuvring no more than a few centimetres up and down on a scooter in this tiny, chaotically messy room. It looks as if he hasn't shaved or changed clothes in weeks. Many in the mainstream media mock him. And over the next few months his appearance and mental health will continue to decline. I fear that the Deep State has finally won, that he is completely broken. I feel powerless and depressed for the future of Truth in our world.

The tide of revenge has clearly turned on the Light Keepers, and I strongly suspect that, behind closed doors, there's now an accelerated and orchestrated effort to break and destroy Assange. Like the relics of Ozymandias, once the Ruler of the Realm of Truth, once the Soldier of Conscience, Assange is now crumbling.

A month later, in April 2019, Ecuador officially withdraws Julian's asylum.

I watch President Moreno spew his vitriol against the Australian on CNN. "We've ended the asylum of this spoiled brat. From now on we'll be more careful in giving asylum to people who are really worth it, and not miserable hackers whose only goal is to destabilise governments."

He's clearly no longer welcome as a "houseguest"... Appalled,

I switch to Sky News as Assange, who now looks like a deranged and unkempt madman, is forcibly dragged from the embassy, having been arrested by gung-ho British cops. He's carted away to the dark dungeons of Belmarsh Prison, also known as "Britain's Guantánamo". An hour later papers are served on the prisoner, demanding his extradition to the US. Perfectly orchestrated.

Assange's torturous treatment and ensuing arrest sends a sinister message to all who seek the truth, and bodes far-reaching consequences for investigative journalism. It is a clarion call against the free press. Here is a less-than-subtle warning to all those who dare to stand up against the Deep State. "This is your fate. Watch our power, and shiver. Don't fuck with us. You will be obliterated."

And, just like that, a few months later, in November 2019, after nine long years, Swedish authorities finally drop all rape investigations against Julian Assange. I mean, really. By now it's blatantly obvious that the entire fiasco was no more than a fabrication to discredit him and distract us from his truth-bomb mission.

As the world goes into Covid-19 lockdown, on 12 March 2020, just two weeks before South Africa finds itself in an official State of Disaster, there is at least a smattering of good news. Chelsea Manning is released after a year in jail. Two weeks earlier she'd tried to kill herself in her cell. Who could blame her?

By June 2020, unable to trap Manning, the US now puts all its energy into its bid to extradite Assange.

By the time this book goes to print, UK Home Secretary Priti Patel approves Assange's extradition, after various failed appeals. If convicted in the US, he will face a sentence of 175 years in solitary confinement in a maximum-security prison. Game over.

"The only real threat posed by WikiLeaks is that it challenged the impunity of the powerful," reiterates Melzer in his book *The Trial of Julian Assange*.

I know I may be incredibly naive in still holding hope that history will one day honour the damning exposés and massive upheavals that these three – Assange, Manning and Snowden – visited on those in dark power. But, for now, both Assange and Snowden are regarded as "terrorists". Chelsea seems to be the only one who's managed to resume a semi-normal life – that's if you don't count the scars of PTSD and torture. The last time I looked, she'd shacked up with Clare Boucher, the singer also known as Grimes who is the ex of Elon Musk, the billionaire king of Tesla. Snowden remains in hiding.

Chapter 36

NOT WITH A BANG BUT A WHIMPER

I guess I have to thank the downtime during lockdown for affording me the opportunity to keep gathering info on my "What the actual fuck is going on?" mission. My obsession to read and research serves as a compelling distraction from depressing death stats, manic property searches, *Love Island UK* and the new Omicron and Zedicron mutations.

I must say, before I started fitting together all the pieces of my "How the fuck did we get here?" puzzle, studying timelines and correlating events, I didn't realise how big a role the info Assange and Manning unleashed would play in *almost* igniting a serious people's revolution across the globe.

And nowhere does that play out more beautifully than in the Arab Spring of 2010 – also known as the "WikiLeaks Revolution".

Until I delve deeper, I am unaware that the call for freedom that sweeps through North Africa and the Middle East is as a *direct* response to the publishing of those hundreds of thousands of highly classified WikiLeaks documents.

I am truly taken up by the winds of change as I watch the people rise. One by one, corrupt leaders are toppled – Hosni Mubarak, Zine El Abidine Ben Ali, Ali Abdullah Saleh – like dominos, they all fall down.

The call for justice is contagious.

The people have finally found their voices! Real change to previous power structures is possible! It gives me hope that if the need and opportunity arise, we as citizens of this planet can indeed all mobilise.

And so I watch, eyes shining, as the heady energy of protest and freedom spreads across the oceans.

Like millions of ordinary people, I'd been horrified that so many corrupt bankers and financial institutions had "gotten away with it" after the global economic crash of 2008/2009. I'd angrily watched countless documentaries and newscasts detailing how ordinary people had lost everything, their properties repossessed, lives destroyed, due to the greed of bankers. Having been homeless once, I knew how they felt in the Depression of Dispossession. And so, much like the sensation I had as I sat glued to the uprisings during the Arab Spring, when the Occupy Wall Street movement takes off a year later, it too holds great hope that the people are finally taking a stand and saying "no" to corrupt power. That things indeed can change.

Exactly a decade after the Twin Towers go down, in September 2011, thousands gather in Zuccotti Park in the heart of New York's Wall Street Financial District to rally against gross economic inequalities, greed, corruption and the sinister influence and power of money in politics. My heart surges in glee as I turn up the volume on my television to hear the deafening roars that demand that corrupt bankers – who had largely escaped any legal consequences connected to the global crisis – be brought to book.

I even get an Occupy Wall Street T-shirt, displaying the slogan "We are the 99%", referring to the massive divide of income and wealth inequality between the wealthiest one per cent and the rest of the US population. In South Africa, that schism is far deeper.

But what really excites me is that in all these civil movements, the social media apps that we all have on our phones – Facebook, Twitter, Instagram and WhatsApp – are the tools the people use to connect and mobilise at the heart of the revolution! These are the days of innocence and heady hope, when we still believe in the purity of these networks. These are the days before Big Tech censorship, before we become aware that with every like and comment, our information is being mined, surveilled and monetised.

Amid an explosion of banners, slogans, social war cries and marches, for a moment in time I truly believe that the ordinary people of our world have grown wings, standing up for what is right; that we are taking back our power and that a new world, free of oppression, corruption and forced surveillance, one in which there will be greater economic equity, is indeed on the horizon.

But, tragically, the heady hope and brilliant ambitions promised by all these movements kind of fizzle out and, before the end of the second decade of the millennium, many have ended "not with a bang but a whimper".

By 2018, the Arab Spring is known as the "Arab Winter". In most of the countries that tasted freedom, counter-revolutionary forces have gained power and corrupt old regimes are replaced by corrupt new regimes. On Wall Street, it's business as usual.

Chapter 37

CAN'T GET YOU OUT OF MY HEAD

"Covid has been like lightning on a dark night. Suddenly you see what has been there the whole time."
– Adam Curtis, *Can't Get You Out of My Head*

Once I finish the last season of *Love Island UK*, the one in which The Flack is achingly absent, I tell myself to get a life and find something a little more brain nourishing to watch. And so I move on to my next obsession: British filmmaker Adam Curtis. In his brilliant eight-hour BBC documentary series, *Can't Get You Out of My Head* – which I've watched at least five times – Curtis says, "Clearly, nothing is working. The systems are broken. Inequality is ruinous. A huge number of very angry people want genuine change. Yet no one can even imagine what that change could be."

When I watched the doccie for the first time, I actually paused it at that point and wrote that sentence down. It touched something deep inside. It held so much truth in explaining my feelings of impotency.

Like Curtis, I'd spent megawatts of brainpower wondering why all these "people's" movements, which held so much potential and promise, had not succeeded when it came to actual transformation – indeed, why some had outright failed.

Curtis puts it down to "a lack of sustained vision", where

movements that on the surface looked as if they could make a profound difference, had no real follow-through or plan. So, basically, once the placards came down and the slogans got tired, there were no alternative structures on offer.

Curtis then goes on to express how these "failures" of sustained vision and meaningful change have affected the psyche of "we the people": "This theory was going to have a very powerful effect in the future because it would lead to a profound shift in how many people understood the world. Because what it said was that, in a dark world of hidden power, you couldn't expect everything to make sense, that it was pointless to try to understand the meaning of why something happened, because that would always be concealed. What you looked for were the patterns."

Again, his words touched a deep nerve. They explained why I constantly felt so discombobulated, why I constantly found myself in a loop, trying to answer the elusive "why?".

Even before The Pandemic, but especially during this time, I'd clearly become increasingly obsessed with searching for meaning, for patterns, for reason in a world that felt like it had gone mad. A world that appeared to be strangled by hidden power. A world that was bamboozling me at every juncture.

Then one day in early 2021, in the midst of amended lockdown Level 3, something dawned on me. It felt profound, like a slap in the face.

While I agreed with Curtis's theory that real change may have been aborted because of a lack of follow-through after the protests had died down, I found his reasoning a little too simplistic.

And so I began to wonder whether the "anti-movements" and the Truth-Bomb brigade had, in fact, been much closer to actually securing meaningful transformative shifts in the established power than what Curtis suggests ...

There was no denying that these forces of resistance – Assange and Co., the Black Lives Matter movement, the Occupy Wall Streeters – had all disrupted the agenda for control. There was no denying that WikiLeaks had caused deep embarrassment for those who governed us. In fact, it was so much more than just embarrassment; dark secrets and heinous crimes were brought into the light. Those who had been exposed were enraged. They must have wanted revenge.

The patterns now showed me the gargantuan lengths that "hidden power" was prepared to go to in order to snuff out and cauterise those who had disrupted the herd. We only had to look at what they did to Assange – the billions of dollars they spent in their 12-year mission to entrap, discredit and extradite him in order to make him pay for exposing their shadiness, their crimes and their lies.

To tell the truth in this world had become increasingly dangerous. I found myself living on a planet where investigative journalism had become confused with criminality. I saw how the real villains prospered, while those who risked their lives to expose their crimes were persecuted.

Even writing this book sometimes froze me. Over and over again, I'd watched how those exposing deception had been imprisoned, exiled or assassinated. The bad guys always seemed to get away with it.

And then, of course, "we the people" played our complicit role in our silence and lethargy. Most of us were too complacent, too zonked out, afraid or confused, to risk publicly supporting those who disturbed the status quo.

By now I was deep in the maze of trying to make sense of my data and patterns. I had even taken to pasting little sticky notes all over my locked-down fridge – you know, like they do in those true-crime detective series?

And so I began to wonder ... What if, as we were heading into

2020, those in real power – the ones who controlled the world's resources, who funded governments, corporates and institutions in order to dictate global policies and agendas – decided to "do something" extreme to put an end to any further disruptive resistance?

What if they were sick and tired of "the people" – who had over the past decade been getting more and more out of line with their uprisings, their marches, their banners, their provocations, their *V for Vendetta* masks, their damning exposés? What if they felt a vengeful need for a deep reset to return power to those who had lost control because "the people" had become too noisy, too clever, too powerful?

Indulge me here for a second. This is merely rumination. For now, please keep those keys to the thoughtcrime prison jangling in your back pocket.

So – #DeepBreath – could it be possible that a "deadly virus" was allowed to escape a lab in Wuhan "by accident", precipitating a global lockdown? Creating a scenario in which emergency laws could be introduced, people's movement could be restricted, and new surveillance and medical legislation could be instituted? Extreme measures that granted unprecedented control over all of us, to those who were pulling the strings of our world in order to re-establish and "reset" the power "balance"?

Was it possible that, with the arrival of the virus and global lockdowns, we the people were forced to don our masks and coerced to hand over what little power that we thought we still had in exchange for the "promise of protection"? Don't get me wrong, I know the virus is real and of course has killed people, but that is not the point.

Despite the risk of being carted away to thoughtcrime prison as a dangerous "conspiracy theorist", this idea made some kind of scary sense to me. Perhaps I was really losing the plot, but in my desperation for clarity and answers, this notion felt entirely plausible … Because, by the time The Pandemic hits us, there is no denying that the world is in big fucking trouble.

Under the illusion of "democracy" and "free markets", the powers that be, particularly the US – still led by Donald Trump in 2020 – is greedier, more militarised, more globalised, more authoritarian and sophisticated in surveillance tech than ever.

The Pandemic just might have been another perfect smokescreen for a new seizure of power. Just like 9/11? I will even venture as far as to suggest that perhaps the "event horizon" of Covid-19, which quickly spread across global borders, may have been used as a diversion to establish harsh regulations that gave unbridled power to those who ruled the world.

And because terror had been coursing through our veins for the past two decades – because our world had been steeped in the Era of Fear since 9/11, and because those Light Keepers who had tried over and over again to tell us the truth were now in prison, on the run, in hiding, being extradited or dead – the majority of us were too afraid, too depressed or too medicated to question or resist. We had become immune to being lied to.

And, besides, our focus had conveniently shifted. We no longer had the energy to ask "why?" We were too busy trying to protect ourselves from a killer virus, trying not to die. Or fighting with each other.

I happened to stumble upon what I believe to be a prescient interview with Truth fugitive Edward Snowden, published in the first year of lockdown in *Vice* magazine:

"It seems that [Coronavirus] may be the greatest question of the modern era around civil liberties, around the right to privacy … As authoritarianism spreads, as emergency laws proliferate, as we sacrifice our rights, we also sacrifice our capability to arrest the slide into a less liberal and less free world. Do you truly believe that when the first wave, the second wave, the 16th wave of the Coronavirus is a long-forgotten memory that these capabilities will not be kept? That these datasets will not be kept? No matter how it is being used, what is being built is the architecture of oppression."

Chapter 38

LET IT GO

In NA I was taught to "let it go", to accept my powerlessness over people, places and things. To surrender to the concept that "I am an addict". That's how I got to stop, to put down the drugs and booze. That's how I realised I could no longer successfully use. And so, by doing this, I was granted my first keyring to the Kingdom of Recovery, where I no longer spent interminable days withdrawing and scoring.

But, as The Pandemic grinds on, feelings of powerlessness swamp me, and they are not the healthy kind that once led to freedom and serenity. I grow increasingly obsessed. I keep looking for more and more patterns, searching for a thread that will bring me clarity and revelation. Instead, I find an expansive and sinister web that threatens to erase me if I don't comply with what's being touted as Truth.

I desperately want to feel like I belong, that I am on the "right" side ... Yet everything during this time feels so goddamn polarised – hyper-real, painfully magnified and, at the same time, terrifyingly opaque. I am constantly disoriented by people I once considered "woke", enlightened, intelligent and rational, who are now postulating whack theories and shouting crazy reactionary statements. I know that there are those who are just as confused by me. The things we thought we knew about each other before The Pandemic are now twisted and blurred.

Left has become Right has become liberal has become fascist.

It's as if open-mindedness and kindness have left the building, as though something has been added to our municipal water, a divisive potion called Vitriol and Judgment, with a smattering of Dumb, that has recalibrated our brains.

Whatever "side" we find ourselves on, in the end it feels as if none of us really know what the actual fuck is going on. Or who is really in charge anymore. We, the people, sure as hell aren't. As the months drag by, as year one becomes year two, I feel suspended, waiting for the next announcement. For the next rule. The next wave. The next viral variant. The next virtual stab in the back.

What we do perhaps have in common is our fragility. And our fear of death. And no matter what side we find ourselves on, deep down, most of us are dazed and confused.

By the end of 2020, my entire belief system has spectacularly crumbled like the Tower of Babel. The world I once knew appears to be crashing down all around me. I miss people. I miss not being able to touch and hug each other. I long to inhale a stranger's muggy breath. I long to spend real time with Monica in our magical Soma healing house. I am sick of seeing only masked humans in queues and flat people on flat screens. I'm even a little sick of Soul-Mat.

Remember that REM song, in which Michael sings so beautifully about being trapped in a corner, and not knowing whether he can "do it" – you know, the one about losing his religion? How life is bigger than you? How every waking hour he's choosing his confession? Well, that's me in my corner. Choosing my words carefully. Panicking about whether all the dread fantasies that flail around in my brain will come true. Like a hurt, lost and blinded fool, I'm losing my mind.

But what I do know is that in order to hold onto a fragile sliver of hope, I – like some ancient crusader – need to take a risk and step into the unknown in search of something more. Despite all my best attempts at figuring "it" all out, my piles of research, my obsessive reading, my quest for patterns and my hundreds of sticky notes, flapping sadly on my fridge – my brain is still a mush of tangled tapeworms. I am more bamboozled than ever. I know I am not going to find "it" on Facebook, or on Twitter, nor in a conspiracy theory, or on Sky, CNN, Showmax, Amazon or Netflix.

And that's when I urgently start looking for that "escape" house. At this stage, I've pretty much given up on joy and freedom.

PART FOUR

IN SEARCH OF JOY AND FREEDOM

"We shall meet in the place where there is no darkness."
– George Orwell, *1984*

Chapter 39

A NEW YEAR'S JOURNEY

Mere anarchy is loosed upon the world,
The blood-dimmed tide is loosed, and everywhere
The ceremony of innocence is drowned;
The best lack all conviction, while the worst
Are full of passionate intensity.
– William Butler Yeats, "The Second Coming"

It's New Year's Eve. I stare at the date on my phone's calendar that will bridge 2020 with 2021. It does not feel like the start of a fresh year to me. There's dread and a sinister stench in the air. Where the first half of 2020 has indeed been a challenge, there have still been tinges of hope that things will go back to some kind of "normal". By July 2020, I'm still naive enough to imagine that, by Christmas, Covid-19 will be a thing of the past. Surely, it can't go on for a whole bloody year? But it does. The year 2020 drags itself towards its end, like Yeats's slouching beast to Bethlehem.

Things fall apart; the centre cannot hold.

On New Year's Eve, Soul-Mat and I decide to do a Soma journey in our lounge. It's been a lifetime since we travelled to the Great Beyond. The mushroom ceremonies at Monica's house in Somerset West are now but distant memories. Gatherings of more than 10 people are outlawed, so for the first time in years, the Healing House has closed its physical doors. Besides, who wants to delve into the depths of one's soul in a room where everyone's faces are plastered over by masks when the whole point of a psilocybin journey is to unmask the self?

So, as a result of the Covid restrictions, Soma has gone online for the past year; journeyers now stay at home, each in their own separate spaces, connected via a WhatsApp group at night and a Zoom meeting in the morning to share their experiences.

In our candlelit lounge, we silently mix our mushroom sacrament with sweet honey tea. We dim the lights and settle on mattresses on opposite sides of the room. For a moment, I acknowledge how much I have grown over the last five years. I think back on those early days when I literally clung to Soul-Mat in terror.

I search for the Soma playlist and press Play on my phone connected to a Bluetooth speaker. We close our eyes. The first song fills the dark night. Leonard Cohen. "Anthem."

His deep, comforting voice booms.

Urging us to ring the bells that still can ring.

Urging us to forget our perfect offering.

There is a crack ...

I feel my heart beating. I long for it to split open and connect with something. Anything.

I can't deny that I'm anxious. What if I go completely psycho? So much has happened this past year. Is my mind even still in one piece?

Darkness settles. It takes a while for the mushrooms to kick in.

Time shifts. I go under.

Tonight, The Doors I travel through are without visual patterns or shapes of otherworldly promises.

After some time, I hear a clear and commanding voice:

Now I will show you the suffering of the world.

I'm hovering above a planet seething in plague and fire.

Locusts swarm and circle in a dirge of darkness. Revealed to me is human suffering in its many forms: slaves, masters, wars and death. Death. Death. Death. There is so much death. Mountains of cadavers pile up. From high above, I am shown suffering through the ages – from the time of the great Egyptian pyramids when slaves are whipped as they break their backs under huge stones, to the religious Crusades of blood and mayhem. Swords and horses, ripped-out bones and seared flesh. I see women screeching, witches burning on pyres. I watch the insane and the demented, the tortured and the reviled. The deadly plagues of Black Death sweep through shadowed alleyways; corpses are piled up high on horse-drawn carts.

I see black bodies packed on ships, sardine slaves.

War after war, limbless men bleeding out on battlefields. From high above, I see Wilfred Owen's First World War trenches, the lines, entrenched in memory from high-school poetry, now spitting sharp like gunfire.

Gas! GAS! Quick, boys!—An ecstasy of fumbling
Fitting the clumsy helmets just in time,
But someone still was yelling out and stumbling
And flound'ring like a man in fire or lime —
Dim through the misty panes and thick green light,
As under a green sea, I saw him drowning.
In all my dreams before my helpless sight,
He plunges at me, guttering, choking, drowning.

I watch.

There is no end to the suffering. There is no end to this journey.

I observe this palette of pain, suspended high, swinging from above the Earth like a girl in a rococo painting, a mute spectator. The fresco of torture over time is an extended "Guernica".

Now I see The Plague of 2020 – the masked masses. I see vast wastelands of famine. The planet's people, the foodless,

253

are starving. A mother's breast wrinkled and parched of milk. A child's sunken skull, huge eyes pleading for a morsel of bread. People locked up. All in cages, faces contorted in Munchean screams.

The suffering of the world is a mirror of your own.

I hear the voice loud and clear.

The age of worshipping money is gone. All that is left is the search for joy and freedom.

By the end of the journey, those two words remain, carved into my heart and mind like the stone-etched inscription on my father's tombstone.

Joy. Freedom.

✳

Hours later, I walk out into the night with Soul-Mat. We stand, silent, on the edge of our balcony that opens onto the midnight skyline. The stars above are 3D silver filigree. Then the sound of military helicopters circling the city drone in from the distance. As the worldly clock strikes 12, the spluttering of a handful of pitiful fireworks attempts to limply celebrate, on the dark horizon of Cape Town. The vigilant 'copters, growling louder now, make a mockery of any whelp of a New Year's celebration.

I find my voice. "Do you see it?" I whisper to Soul-Mat.

We stare at the horizon. We teeter on the tipping point of our world. We are the last two survivors on a broken planet. I lean in closer to tell him that tonight I saw the writing on the sky's blackboard.

"Darling, we need to get out."

He takes my hand. Gunfire explodes.

"Everything is broken." My voice is conspiratorial, as if some draconian power might overhear us. "It's going to get a lot worse before it gets better. I saw it, in my journey. We are in the fucking *Handmaid's Tale*, Mat. It feels like this is the final battle for freedom."

The helicopters drone louder; searchlights cut through the dark night of the New Year's sky.

He squeezes my hand. I know he knows it too.

On New Year's Day, after a few hours' sleep, with my *Pain of the world* journey still fresh in my mind, I go online and house-hunt as if our lives depend upon it. Because they do.

I don't really know what kind of place I'm looking for, but what I do know is that I want to be able to escape from the city with its helicopters and sirens, its hunger and despair, with all its aching reminders of its inequalities and hypocrisies. Cape Town is a cruel, cruel mother for those who have nothing, a place where white privilege stinks.

The luxury and choice that are mine, to search a property website, do not escape me. But this is not the time to allow guilt to overwhelm me. I must go. Get away. If I can find a place high up in the mountains where I can tear off my mask and breathe, perhaps I can wash away my displacement and unravel this dark and heavy mind of mine. I cannot fucking bear the thought of another year inhaling my second-hand "protected" breath.

Two days later, we find the cabin. Less than three months later, The Woman is killed. Four days after her body is found, the "escape from The Pandemic" house officially becomes mine.

What the actual fuck? How could my house of freedom now have become my prison, literally overnight? How short-sighted of me to imagine that Freedom and Joy do not have a price tag.

Chapter 40

JOE

Seven days after The Woman is murdered, I start searching puppy-rescue groups on Facebook. Although I've been trying to ward off the paranoia, I am in pieces. My safe spot in heaven has been dismembered. I can't stop dwelling on The Woman who was so brutally killed just two doors away. I've made peace with the idea that I will never own a gun. Perhaps a furry, four-legged child will keep me safe? I discuss the idea with Soul-Mat because I know I won't be able to parent alone. If I am to become a dog mother, our pup will need a dog dad.

We have both had our hearts broken by collies lost through circumstances beyond our control. Years later, our sadness still cuts deep. But now our fear of dog death fades as we start our search.

As when I am trawling property sites, my capacity to home in on puppy-rescue groups is immense. It doesn't take long before I find The One. There are three of them: Suzuki, Honda and Ducati. I'm immediately drawn to a photograph of Ducati, who has a crooked little ear and the saddest, most pleading eyes I've ever seen in a dog. It feels like his big, brown eyes are literally drilling into me, saying, "Mommy, come get me." I show Soul-Mat the pic. He gets zapped too.

I know that he will be "Joe" before we even meet him. We don't want our dog child to be named after a motorbike.

It all happens so quickly. I sign forms and submit pics of the puppy-safety set-up in our house that I have had to hastily construct. Adopting a dog has been the last thing on our minds. I get the green light and soon I am WhatsApping Joe's foster mom, a student in Stellenbosch. We need to move rapidly. I am obsessed that someone else is going to get him.

At 10am on Wednesday, 14 April 2021, we set off for the university town in a big Kombi that I'm reviewing. I'm so hyped up I haven't even thought of taking along water or a box in which to contain him. We have puppy food at home and a plastic tub that I've fashioned into a bed with pillows and a soft, red, shiny furry blanket to keep him snug.

With a tiny, skinny Joe on my lap at the Stellenbosch digs, we are shown a video of the puppies being found by one of the students on a garbage dump in Elsie's River. Joe, just a few weeks old, started his life on the wrong side of the tracks. Watching him stumble around amid the debris on his shaky newborn legs, I can't help but be reminded of how I too once ended up homeless on a rubbish heap all those years ago. Now it's my turn to do the rescuing.

Little does this boy know that his life is about to spectacularly change. As is mine.

Soul-Mat drives while I sit in the second-row seat with the 10-week-old boy on my lap. He whines throughout the entire 40-minute journey back home to Cape Town. He is inconsolable. We have had to remove him from his brother, Honda, and I am certain that he is yelping in pain from the separation. A huge part of me wants to go back and pick up his sibling, but we can't. We aren't even really prepared for one new puppy.

I stroke him, whisper words of comfort, cosset him, but however hard I try to placate this little boy, nothing seems to be working. He just wails and cries. The drive back home seems endless. The more I try to soothe him, the more he yelps and moans. He is literally screaming.

"He hates me, Mat. He hates me …" I am close to tears.

The minute we touch ground, we feed him.

He vacuums up a bowl of food in five seconds flat. His yelping and screeching miraculously stop. He is fucking starving! That's why he's been wailing so much – he doesn't hate me! He doesn't hate me.

"Joe needs protein," announces Soul-Mat. "He is severely undernourished."

My nutrition expert shrink jumps into action. "Flax-seed oil, and chicken and eggs and mince."

Joe is a wolf in puppy's clothing. He hoovers up food as if he's never been fed. Joe becomes an angel boy after he's eaten. He loves to gobble, he loves to talk; he is the most vocal puppy I have ever heard. After hoofing down his 5-star, fit-for-a-prince cuisine, Joe, potbellied, loves to sleep.

Soul-Mat and I are doting parents. Joe snoozes between us. He is the baby we never had together. We stare at our child, misty-eyed.

✳

Joe is so tiny and defenceless. He needs constant attention. Day in and day out, as I shadow him, I am terrified that something will happen to him. I am a mad mother, always behind him, obsessed that he will stumble off a step, trip into our pool that has no cover, tumble off the upstairs balcony, wiggle through the gate … I can't leave him alone for a second. Is he hungry? Is he thirsty? Is he sick? Is he cold?

Within the first two weeks, I am so exhausted that I sometimes wonder whether I've done the right thing. In frantic moments, I am wracked with guilt when I fantasise about giving him back. *You can't return a puppy you've adopted, Melinda!*

Soul-Mat is there to help, but he is not nearly as involved or neurotic as I am.

I can't leave the house.

I can't leave Joe's side.

It feels like I am having an extended panic attack.

Am I good enough? my insides scream.

I no longer have the time to dwell on our messed-up world, to click on the news, to follow death stats, to watch the president's "family talks" or trawl social media. Joe changes my brain.

Instead, I am thrown back to those dark, twisted days, more than two decades ago, when I doubted my every anxiety-stricken move as I tried to mother my babies. As I watch myself running after Joe, I am constantly reminded of how I struggled to be a parent to human babies, of how desperately inadequate I felt caring for those two helpless souls. Back then, at least I had an escape – I could get high. The fear of making a mistake froze me up so badly that I took the furthest seat in the back of the bus and watched my husband take over.

Now, 22 years clean and sober, I am in super-sharp present mode. I scurry after Joe, trying to compensate for all those shameful days when I was unable to function as I watched smack-gouged from the sidelines, smoking reality away in a haze of avoidance and denial.

And, in rare moments when I do sit down and just watch Joe sleep, when my breathing slows, I experience periods of stark clarity in which I'm forced to confront my concrete-heavy baggage of the past: the full and ugly truth about my lack of maternal skills when it came to taking care of my own flesh and blood.

Who would have guessed that a furry, four-legged rescue pup would now gift me the opportunity to start again on a fresh page, to become a conscious mommy and confront the shame that I'd been trying to stub out for years?

And sometimes, as I cradle this potbellied boy in my arms, my own mother, who has been dead for 17 years, comes to sit beside me.

Chapter 41

BAD, BAD MOTHER

"How could you have left your children for drugs? What kind of mother turns her back on the flesh and blood she has birthed?"

These are the fundamental questions that have plagued my soul ever since I got clean. Having been graced with the opportunity to mother little puppy boy, I am finally able to start trying to untangle the remorse, confront my guilt and be honest with myself about that dark time. Perhaps I can finally, *finally* forgive myself?

For years I have tried to explain to others how, after my mother-in-law took our two boys away and my husband was sent to a five-star rehab back in early 1999, my heroin- and crack-addicted heart was so shattered that I believed I had no other option but to go on a major drug mission to drown my sorrows and satiate my cravings.

This is partly true.

The thing is, I could have chosen the other path. I could have confronted the debris of my life back then and stopped, just as my husband did. I could have begged to go to rehab. Just as Amy didn't. But like that tortured blues girl, I also screamed, "No, no, no!"

And so I am forced to finally admit the deeper truth: I *needed* to leave them. And not only did I need to, I *wanted* to. There, I've said it, in all its bleak cruelty.

From the very outset, I was tortured by the concept of motherhood.

I grew up acutely aware of my own mother's disconnect as a parent. I watched her grind her life away, heaving, sighing, muttering and snarling under the burden of it. Drinking the nights away to try to forget it. From a young age, I observed how her needs, desires and dreams, had been snuffed out by us, her four vampire children who had sapped and sucked from her body and her mind. As a teenager, I made a vow to myself that pregnancy was something I would never allow. Having children was not part of my life plan. As I grew older, I became increasingly repelled by the notion and was ridiculously fastidious when it came to contraception.

And then, bang. A broken condom. A Catholic husband. A two-blue-lines pregnancy test. Every fibre in my being resisted.

The nine-month first pregnancy played out against a sinister background: two parents in deep drug addiction. To appease the guilt, I tried to go to rehab. I relapsed three hours after checking myself out of the clinic. And then suddenly, within weeks, now back in the tentacles of addiction, that soccer ball in my tummy became a real-life baby that I tried to embrace, to cradle, only to discover that my arms were as unreceptive as dead, broken twigs.

Once he was born, my anxiety trebled, quadrupled. It had no bounds. I had none of that inborn "motherly instinct" all other mothers seemed to have. It took every ounce of strength just to move my darkly depressed body, to attend to his needs. A cry would send me into a spiral. What did he want? What was he saying? Was he sick-hungry-sad-wet-soiled, hungry-sick-wet-soiled? I had no clue, no fucking clue at all. My husband took over. I watched from the sidelines – a mute, uninvited spectator. The shame within grew like terrible weeds.

By the time our second son arrived, less than two years later, I was truly frozen.

As I held that second positive pregnancy test in my trembling hand, I felt gravely ill. The nausea that engulfed me was an even deeper terror than the first. Because this time, I could see the entire movie playing out, frame by gritty frame. There could be no denial that our second son would be born to parents who were both using heroin and crack. This reality upped my dread to such an extent that my only solution was to think of ways to top myself. But how could I end my existence when I was the host to this embryo embedded in me, which depended on me for its very survival?

I was faced with what appeared at every juncture to be an insoluble conundrum. I would have to wait the pregnancy out before choosing my own ending. Nine months dragged by.

I clearly remember, after going through labour and finally birthing our new son, staring out of the window like Plath in "Tulips", her famous "hospital" poem. She speaks of how she didn't want any flowers. How she only wanted to lie with her hands turned up and "be utterly empty".

I stared into nothing, wondering whether I would succeed by jumping off the Klerksdorp hospital's single-storey building to splat on the pavement. I suspected that, at best, I may break a leg or two. By now my shameful failure was irreversible. There was absolutely no evidence to suggest that I had been able to take care of our first son. And now there were two.

I did not jump. Instead, I dragged myself back to the Klerksdorp heroin horror house. I would only realise years later that one of the main reasons it was so hard to kill myself during that time was because, by becoming a mother, my self had already been obliterated. The Me BM (Before Mothering) had been sucked away. There was simply nothing left to assassinate.

So why didn't you just stop?

It is a question I hear often. And I have tried to answer it many times.

The only riposte that feels true is this: *Because I didn't want to. Because the craving to get high was as huge as a killer whale, far greater than the desire to mother ... Love no longer resided within me. Only Fear.*

When my boys were taken from me and I went on my suicide mission to Hillbrow, back in the winter of 1999, for a moment in time what I felt, as I discarded the shackles of motherhood like an unwanted chainmail cloak, was freedom. I skipped down the yellow bricks of Soper and Abel roads. Like mad Dorothy, I raved through drug hotels in a dervish of gluttony. After years of being constricted, it was as if all that crippling anxiety had finally lifted.

It was just me now.

Just me.

In my hunger for oblivion, I tried to smoke away all that guilt and buried rage that throbbed within like septic episiotomy stitches. I sucked on pipes laden with crack just as a newborn devours its mother. I was finally untethered. The freedom of being childless, severed from the umbilical cord of anxiety, gave wings to my Doc Martens. And so I got high.

Deep down, I had been wanting to leave for a long time, trapped in my junkie marriage, playing fake housey-house, and trying to act the part of "mother" but failing dismally. The irrefutable evidence of my collapse was laid out on The Last Supper table for all his family to see.

And when I finally crashed, when I finally got sober, all that latent shame I'd been shoving down a crack pipe came roaring in. If feelings could kill, I would be dead today.

✳

I never got the chance to ask my own mother: Did you ever actually want children? Perhaps, like me, she too ended up having to unwillingly grow unruly beings in her ever-distending, stretch-marked belly.

What I know now, however, is that her resentments were contagious, seeping into every corner of our childhood home. Once I became an angry, rebellious teenager, I met her halfway and tried to hurt her as much as her anger and dishonesty hurt me. I hurled up her painfully measured-out plates of food, bunked school and screeched off on my own mission of self-destruction.

"You are my biggest disappointment," my mother will tell me when I arrive back at her house in 1999, aged 33, penniless and suicidal.

Apart from the addict gene, her grudge-to-mother is the primary curse that I inherit. For many years, I blame her style of mothering on her drinking, just as I blame mine on my drugging. But whereas she died still aching to reach for a wine glass, I had managed to arrest my substance addiction. Surely, I would now have the opportunity to put the brakes on this genetic voodoo and become a present and loving mother? Clean and sober, I assume that, in recovery, I will suddenly develop a magic button that will activate my nurturing brain.

It doesn't happen.

Sure, I become more conscious, more driven to be a provider and pay my half. To rent a flat to shelter my boys, to buy a house to protect them ... but that miraculous switch, the one called "maternal instinct", evades me.

I try to "fake it till I make it". I perform the tasks. I cook and clean. I drive them to school, buy groceries, do homework and pay school fees, but I take every opportunity to retire into my own head, my own space.

My sister wrote a song for our mother in the late 1980s, Titled "Bay of Bombay", it is a poignant piece about a woman staring out the window, dreaming of faraway Bombay, her fingers "rubbed raw from the clothes she cleaned and ironed".

That was our mother. I swore that I would not be her. But she found herself into me anyway. I am just like her.

And then, years later, after a particularly painful Soma journey, I will miraculously find an ember of compassion and insight. I will finally understand what it must have been like for the woman who birthed me, who was not able to choose a creative or fulfilling life, who had neither the outlet, nor the excuse of checking out with, "I need space. I am writing."

For 17 years after I got clean, while performing my three-days-a-week parental duty stipulated in our divorce arrangement, I imagined that my boys would not notice my crippling inability to engage. Turns out, they did.

It all comes to a head in a mighty explosion less than two years before the onset of The Pandemic.

Chapter 42

THE AFTERMATH OF *SMACKED*

My sons fly up to visit Soul-Mat and me in July 2018. Almost two years have passed since my *Pain I caused others* Soma journey. I am in the early stages of birthing this book and in a state of terror at the thought of having to write about my healing work with psilocybin mushrooms lest I be judged. As much as I miss my boys and am looking forward to their visit, I am in deep word-building mode. I long for silence. I know I will need to quell that familiar part of me – the writer one – over the next few days.

On day three, I'm a tad over-enthusiastic when they announce they want to see a movie. I give them money. I am drowning in unwritten words, commas and full stops. Finally, I can get back to my book lover. I'm relieved to hear the movie's a long one – that should give me at least a few hours of writing space.

Less than 20 minutes after I hear the car pull off, my phone rings.

My eldest son's panicked voice: "Mom, we have a puncture."
Nooooo.

I have just started a new chapter; I'm on a roll. I don't spare my irritation at the intrusion.

"Boy, you're old enough to drive, you need to sort this out, just go to the garage across from the parking lot and ask someone to help."

Phone call sorted, back to the writing.

Three minutes later, the phone rings again.

"Mom, the garage has closed down. What do I do?"

Fuck. Fuck. *Fuck.*

"James, what am I supposed to do? Don't you know how to change a tyre? Can't you google or ask someone in the parking lot? Just try to sort something out."

Back and forth, the anger spills out between us. He cuts the call.

I inhale. Try to get back to the writing. Mother self must be obliterated.

"Write as if the world is dead around you," I always tell my authors. But, as I burrow back into my string of thoughts, *What the fuck is wrong with you?* I hear the other self reprimand. *They need you. Your boys need you. You are so fucking selfish.*

So I send an attempt-at-peacemaking WhatsApp: "Go to the movie. We'll sort it out afterwards. Sorry for fighting with you, my boys."

Silence. At last.

For the next three hours I am left alone. But, instead of connecting to a waterfall of longed-for words, I am wracked with guilt and remorse. I crawl into bed and watch two episodes of *Humans* back to back. You know, "the series-numbing effect". The anaesthetising sermons of our age. I have a never-ending supply of streaming to obliterate unruly feelings. *Orange is the New Black*, *Game of Thrones*, *Breaking Bad*, *The Affair*, *Narcos*. Back then I have yet to discover *Love Island UK*.

I don't mean to fall asleep, but a flickering screen can do that to me. I wake with a start. It's 5pm. I feel clod-heavy, having fallen asleep at the wrong time of the day.

I check my phone. There is a string of messages from my sons and a picture of the sad, flat tyre.

I try to call. Seven times. Their phones are off. Now it's getting dark. They're punishing me with their silence. I grab the car keys and decide to head out to where I think they must be stranded. Another call to them goes unanswered.

I'm coming. I send a WhatsApp. As I'm reversing down the drive, I get a curt response: *We have fixed it.*

I start preparing dinner. I'm making Thai chicken. Maybe they'll forgive me when they taste their favourite, my pathetic attempt at a peace offering. This is not how this holiday was supposed to turn out. I know I have not handled this well at all.

When they return, it's dark and cold out. The mood is thick, laced with undercurrents of my then 18- and 20-year-olds' anger.

"You okay? Did you manage? Did you fix it?" My awkward concern, dripping in guilt, stutters out.

Finally. "Our dad helped us. We phoned him."

Daniel, my youngest, glares daggers at me. "We needed you and all you could say is 'Sort it out'."

A night of old wounds unfolds. A punctured tyre is the catalyst.

Dan takes the floor, his olive-brown eyes flashing in accusation. He proceeds to pin me to my cross of inadequate mothering. His rage is calm and succinct. In his soliloquy, my crimes are laid out like a manic cash register spewing purple ink-stained till slips of proof.

I am told how I have always shown more love to and favoured his elder brother. He has a list of evidence: how I dawdled on having curtains put up in his room when I bought the new house in Orange Grove while his brother got his straight away. How I always dished bigger servings for James when they were younger, how when he experienced night terrors when he stayed at my house, it was always his dad he called, not me. How when he was made head boy last year, I went on social media and told my 5 000 Facebook friends of his achievement before I even called to congratulate him. How I am more concerned with how my "fans" and "followers" see me than I am about my sons … The accusations rattle on. Each one lodges bullets deeper into my bad, black mother heart. I don't even attempt a defence. In some way, I know that I am guilty of them all.

You're a fraud, a fake, a fucking terrible mother, the voice within taunts – the one I have listened to all of my addict life. It is a voice I have tried to heal in my recovery. It's evidently still buried in a dark chamber of my heart, triggered now to come back on this night to heckle me.

I dissolve into victim mode. I try to claw my way out of this assault of accusations, to defend myself: "Your father has alienated you against me. I never stood a chance. He got clean before me and he's been punishing me ever since."

My pleas for my son to listen, to understand me, fall on deaf ears. Dan flashes those eyes at me and, in a cold, calm voice, he demands that I do not interrupt.

"It's my turn to talk, 'Mother'." I can almost hear those parentheses.

I obey. I watch him, me now relegated to silence as he commands his space. I am unsure whether to feel admiration for this boy, this young man, my son whom I nurtured like a little unwanted bean in my belly, who has now turned out to be so strong and impressive, or deep shame as his words bullet through me.

Then he drops the bombshell – the words I have been dreading for years.

"I read your book. I read *Smacked* in January."

This is his ultimate accusation. The crowbar in the coffin.

Fucking hell.

"I told him not to—" James interjects, always the protector of his younger sibling, always carrying far too heavy a burden of responsibility for his brother.

When I write my addiction memoir back in 2005, I have no filters for how my words will affect those in my life: my sons, their father, my brother and sisters. I write as if I am indeed the last person alive on this planet. As though everyone else has perished in a mammoth car crash. I am hellbent on telling *my* truth – the hard and vicious underbelly of addiction and how I fucked it all up and mowed down whoever got in my way.

Over the years, I have been asked many times: "What will you do if your sons read the book?"

I adopt the ostrich approach. Head in the sand, I simply can't bear to think of it.

I've also been told that when *Smacked* was published back in 2005, my sister wrapped it in brown paper to shield her children from reading about their scandalous junkie aunt. I think they read it anyway.

So, as my boys grow up, I attempt the opposite – a sort of twisted, reverse-psychology approach. There are times when I encourage, even instruct them to read my memoir, knowing full well that they will in all likelihood do the exact opposite. To my relief, my sons ignore my book, which is openly displayed in a prime spot on my heaving floor-to-ceiling bookshelves.

Now my youngest has read it. While most parents share with their kids childhood fairy tales of Snow White, Cinderella and Little Jack Horner, I have left my two boys with the harrowing hell tale of my shameful smack and crack addiction.

"I know you wanted an abortion when you were pregnant with me." Daniel stands tall above me, directing his laser-sharp eyes at my fallen self.

The words I wrote in *Smacked* now flood back. They are cruel chunks of truth-blows:

If seeing those two blue stripes appear on the home pregnancy test had made me weep when I discovered I was pregnant with my first son in 1996, this time I was sent into a deep and dark depression like some forlorn, pillaged oil well in Iraq.

I am comatose by the news. I am not handling mothering one child; how will I take on another? I do not have a bank card, or an ID book. I do not drive. I am relying totally on handouts from my husband's family and, even though I veer in and out of denial when it comes to my drug use, seeing those two accusing blue lines, I know for certain that I can't do this. I am a fucking junkie. How can I be growing another child?

Neither of us can do this. I implore my Catholic husband to consider an abortion. Abortion has just been legalised in South Africa – a few months earlier, in February of 1997. But my husband will hear none of it. I have lost total control over my life and body; the only thing left to do is kill myself.

Now, 18 years later, I try to explain the state of disaster that was sweeping through our home in 1997/1998. "I was so freaked out when I fell pregnant with you. I saw no future with your dad. We were both bloody addicts – how were we going to bring another being into this world? We were nothing more than these two messed-up children; we couldn't even take care of ourselves, never mind two babies."

I now have to go to the place of darkest confession. There is no turning back.

"Dan, I know there's always been this thing between you and me, this ghost of unsaid words ... I have been tortured by such shame all these years, praying that you will never know that, during my entire pregnancy with you, all I heard, every waking day as you grew inside me, was a voice that urged me to end it all. I didn't want to kill you, my boy. I hated myself so much I just wanted to kill me."

I am weeping now.

"So," I gently try to tell my son between sobs, "if you felt an unwantedness from me as you were growing up, you were right. You didn't imagine it. You must have sensed it before you even took your first breath ... I just couldn't face bringing you into this world. I was so fucked up."

271

This is the most difficult admission I have ever made to another human being. The lies we tell our children in the desperate hope that they will, somehow, be better off not knowing the truth tend to fester and grow. There is no way out.

"My mother withheld so much from me. Sometimes the biggest lies are those left in silence. Even though I have dreaded you reading about this in my book, somewhere deep inside I think I wanted you to eventually discover the truth – the record of my shame – so that one day the feelings of abandonment that you carry inside, the questions that gnaw your bones, could be answered so that you wouldn't have to go out into the world blaming yourself for all your missing pieces."

But now, as I stand in all my naked horror in front of my boys, somewhere amid this dredging up of dark history I suddenly remember another moment between us … when, soon after my youngest was born, I quite unexpectedly found myself attaching to his beautiful little new self.

"By this stage, your father and I were no longer sleeping in the same room. At night, your dad would take your brother into the spare room and look after him during the night, while I was left to take care of you. Even though we woke most mornings withdrawing from heroin, I loved having your tiny body next to me, waking up to feed you, seeing your face in the early morning. Even though we were these desperate addicts, snivelling and shivering, thinking of ways to score to deal with the pain, I found a love for you inside me that I never knew was possible. So when you were just seven months old and your grandmother took you and your brother away from me and your dad on the pretext of taking you out for an ice cream, it felt like my insides had been torn out by a hyena."

I remember the words I wrote in *Smacked* and I know that, having read them, he must be aware of every raw detail of what happened to him on that godawful day:

My mother-in-law looks at my filthy tracksuit and unwashed hair and sniffs as I pack the bottles and nappies for the boys' ice-cream outing. She is a picture of Sophia Loren elegance. Never a hair out of place. The queen lioness of the town.

I am relieved at the promise of a break. Maybe we can drive to Joburg and score. As her huge 7-Series pulls out the drive, the tin foil is out, and within minutes we're en route to Joburg to Smack Crack Lalaland.

By late afternoon, comfortably numb and back in Klerksdorp, there's no sign of our boys. My husband tells me his mom is going to keep them for the night. I'm happy – a rare baby-free night. Besides, we still have a few more hits to get lost in.

By 4pm the following day, there is still no sign of the boys. I am getting worried. My husband seems nonplussed. Then, suddenly, it hits me: She's taken them. Oh God, she's taken them. And he is part of the plot.

"Motherfuckers!" I scream. I tear out the house and begin running towards the palace on the hill, where my two sons are being held. It takes me 15 minutes to get there. By the time I collapse down the drive, filled with luxury cars, my husband's car pulls in.

Panting like a mad dog, I throw myself against the big wooden front door, ringing the bell, bashing my fists against it. Finally, she opens it. She's kitted out in evening wear; expensive jewels adorn her ears and white swan neck. Behind her stands Emily, one of her two "servants" – she's holding my baby. He sees me and breaks into a gurgle, stretches his arms out towards me. I lurch towards him.

"Get out of this house, you drug-addict whore. Get out!" my mother-in-law screams. "You will never see these children again. Never."

As I push past her, smashing at her million-dollar made-up face, trying to grab my son, I am felled by my husband, dragged

273

out the palace, thrown into the car. My howls are drowned by the screech of brakes."

I take a deep breath.

"After you two are taken away from me, I go insane," I tell my boys. "Your dad goes to rehab the following day while I am dumped at my sister's house in Joburg. I am absolutely broken. In one small day, in just 24 hours, I lose both of you and your father. I am now on an all-out mission to die. I soon find myself walking the streets of Hillbrow, lost. I believe your grandmother's threats that I will never see you again. The only thing I can think of is to use as many drugs as I can lay my hands on to get high; then I plan to jump off that big tower, Ponte. It's only much later, after I get clean – years later, in fact – that I see that your granny was our guardian angel, the one who saved all our lives by taking you both away from us. At the time, though, I could feel nothing but rage. Deep, blinding rage. You see, even though I was an addict, I think the pain of loving you and knowing how much I was fucking up was what drove me to do what I did. It's probably really hard for you to understand, but it felt like my love for you had the power to kill me."

I can't breathe. I am weeping uncontrollably. "I'm sorry I'm sorry I'm sorry."

Somehow, I am up on my feet. They allow me to embrace them. We are wet from tears.

When all has quietened, when the sobs have receded and the air hangs clean with confession, Dan finally speaks.

"Mommy," says my beautiful youngest boy, "you have no idea how much I really do respect you. You were raped – I read about it in the book. You lost everything, you landed up homeless. But you managed to pull it all together. You got clean, you write books, you became a publisher."

He wraps his arm around my sunken shoulders.

"I know it hasn't been easy. There have been times that I have hated you. But now I see that I have also learned the best from you."

"A few years ago, we wouldn't have been able to talk to you like this," says my eldest, his arms enfolding us both. "Now, at least you are listening to us."

They are right. I am listening more and more. My ears are opening and my mouth is learning to slow down. I keep shovelling up heaps of debris. And once the digging starts, those layers just keep on unfolding … Then, just as I think I'm "better", I discover new mounds of wounds that need to be cleared and reconstructed.

But tonight has filled me with hope. I am fixing my *self* in Truth. And, in the recalibration of my broken parts, we three are slowly reconnecting. Like filaments of beautiful fungi.

Chapter 43

RECEIVING FIRE

"What matters most is how well you walk through the fire."
– Charles Bukowski, *What Matters Most Is How Well You Walk Through the Fire*

During lockdown, I happen to stumble upon the book *Stealing Fire* by Steven Kotler and Jamie Wheal. The title refers directly to Prometheus's theft of fire, which is symbolic of "knowledge", an action that almost got him killed by the fire-keeper god, Zeus.

What really gets me hooked is the section on technology and pharmacology, which I devour. The book describes how many of the great tech minds of our time, in places like Silicon Valley, have for a number of years been participating in the consumption of various "illegal" psychedelics. They have done so in the hope of attaining higher states of consciousness, in order to open their minds to innovation, to help solve some of the world's greatest challenges and to outwit their competition. For a long time, for many highly stressed creatives, in order to work long hours and stay alert, the go-to fixes were Adderall, cocaine, Provigil and Ritalin – all of which are addictive drugs and can have serious side-effects from long-term use.

I am often asked where I find all my energy.

"Don't you ever get tired?", "How are you able to do so many things simultaneously?" or my favourite: "You better rest, else you are going to burn out." Before I sat down to write this book, I very rarely told people the true source of my "work ethic" – it had simply felt too complicated to explain and, at times, even dangerous.

I deeply believe that psilocybin has opened my neural pathways, allowed me to tap into an unlimited creative well. It's helped me connect to a deeper spiritual source. It's facilitated life-changing insights into the many wounds of my past that had imprisoned me since early childhood.

Prior to 2015, despite claiming 16 years of sobriety, and stashing every one of the accompanying 12-Step keyrings, it often felt as if I was host to a bleeding ulcer, trapped in immovable pain and multitudes of character defects.

I'd always had a pretty solid work ethic, but over the last seven years my productivity has felt a lot like an out-of-control fynbos fire. To date, I have published more than 70 books, written three more titles to add to my memoirs, edited hundreds of thousands of words, read piles and piles of submissions and worked with so many prospective writers in workshops that I've lost count.

At any given time, I am juggling at least five book-publishing projects, flitting from city to city, reviewing cars, running an Airbnb, flipping back and forth between a multitude of tasks, gobbling up work as if it's fuel for fire. I cannot help but connect the source of this bottomless energy to my first psilocybin journey back in March 2015. The night the cork to my brain popped. Back then, it felt as if an ember had ignited, silencing my obsessive, controlling brain. From that point on, I experience my mind awakening and receiving fire. On that journey, something profound transpired, and I was able to access a deeper, more connected part of my *self*. The Doors have been swinging open wide ever since.

In my reading on psychedelics, I discover that I am not alone.

Travelling to the Great Beyond has helped many other bright and productive souls. Way back in the 1950s, before Silicon Valley ever existed, along with people like AA's Bill W, both Francis Crick and James Watson – the duo who discovered the double-helix structure of DNA – admitted to taking LSD and subsequently attributed many of their scientific insights to their "acid" experiences.

Gabor Maté, probably the most globally respected voice in the addiction and recovery community, is an outspoken advocate of healing the self and mind with plant and fungi medicine. Then there's Tim Ferriss, respected author of *The 4-Hour Workweek*, who openly admits to using large doses of psilocybin and ayahuasca for self-exploration and inner healing.

Before Steve Jobs died, he described how his experiences with LSD had largely shaped him into the man he became with the ideas he had birthed to revolutionise our tech world. In his biography, *Steve Jobs*, he referred to Bill Gates as "unimaginative" and suggested his billionaire rival could have benefitted if "he had dropped acid once".

And then there's a most unexpected fan of travelling to the place of "innerstanding", Mike Tyson. These days, the much-beleaguered former heavyweight boxing champion is a staunch proponent of psilocybin mushrooms. At one point, he was regarded as one of the most feared and violently irrational fighters on the planet. In 1992, before I'd even had my first hit of crack, I remember him being jailed for rape. And who can forget the 1997 "ear incident" with Evander Holyfield in which Tyson tore off a chunk of his opponent's ear during a championship brawl? He was subsequently disqualified and the next few years saw his life imploding into street fights, cocaine addiction, suicide attempts and bankruptcy.

But then Tyson found magic psilocybin, and what followed was deep healing.

In an email interview with *The Guardian* in 2021, he said: "I believe if I'd been introduced to the benefit of psychedelics for therapeutic use early in my professional career, I would have been a lot more stable in life. I had a lot of public outbursts and they were all mental-illness related. Prescription drugs meant I didn't feel like myself, but with psychedelics I feel I'm a happier, lighter version of me."

Today Tyson is unrecognisable from the violent, irrational beast we once knew. These days he's a successful and deeply insightful podcast host and cannabis entrepreneur. Not only has his career been revived, but his psyche has undergone a complete renaissance. "It's like a dream. I think somebody is going to wake me up and say, 'Get your ass back in the [jail] cell' or something. It's [psilocybin] just an amazing medicine."

And then, of course, there's the mind-blowingly innovative billionaire Elon Musk, the founder of Tesla and SpaceX and currently the planet's wealthiest man. For years, I'd been wondering whether Elon did psychedelics. I mean, how the hell did he come up with all those groundbreaking ideas? In 2021, he made a statement that made global headlines: "I think, generally, people should be open to psychedelics. A lot of people making laws are kind of from a different era, so I think, as the new generation gets into political power, I think we will see greater receptivity to the benefits of psychedelics."

While I am light years away from being anywhere close to thinking like a tech innovator or planning to colonise Mars, reading these testaments verifies what has been happening in my own life since I first took psilocybin.

✳

It's easy for me to compare the changes I've been experiencing to when I was using hardcore drugs – those dark days when

I imbibed whatever I could lay my hands on to try to "fix" those wounds, to stop the bleeding. But I prefer to concentrate on the differences I've experienced with psilocybin, compared to the time I took pharmaceutical drugs when I was already in long-time "recovery". Just three months into my popping-psychiatric-pills-twice-a-day period, I had lost all my fire. Days felt same-same, undifferentiated. I shuffled around like a zombie. My impulse to write, to create, was buried in some far-off memory. I began to forget where I had left my keys, whether I had locked the door or turned off the stove.

For most of my life, I'd woken up before dawn, around 4am, like clockwork. Now I overslept, waking up thick-brained and dull-headed, eyes gunked closed. It was if I had died inside, imprisoned now in a flat-lined waking existence. But even the horror I experienced in my medicated brain felt dull and second-hand. I was numb.

Now, with each passing year of working with psilocybin, with each life-shifting insight, I am increasingly aware of the twisted attitudes within the medical establishment. I question the draconian legislation and law enforcement in many countries around the world that have all contributed to our tragic ignorance – those responsible for outlawing healing agents like psilocybin and misrepresenting them as "dangerous and addictive drugs".

How absurd it is that mushrooms – these miraculous fungi that carry the magic key of consciousness, ego death and transformation – sit beside deadly heroin and crack? I have been a slave to both these killer substances. I have first-hand knowledge of what it's like to be a desperate addict. I often wish that these lawmakers, doctors, psychiatrists and governments would ask someone like little old me – I *know* the difference.

As a result of many years steeped in some sort of addictive behaviour, I have spent three decades talking to – and paying

– various therapists. New Age healers. Psychics. Card readers. Energy realigners. I've even walked into (and out of) a number of churches. I have more than 20 years of 12-Step meetings under my belt. All my efforts have been attempts to alleviate my psychic pain. Up until I opened The Doors, I had never really fully understood or gotten close to the *source* of the hurt inside.

With psilocybin, it feels as if I have stumbled upon a miracle healer and am now able to find many of those deep and transformative answers in a single night – in contrast to the decades I spent unsuccessfully trying to address my debilitating issues. It feels like I am finally in recovery – which, by the way, is generally defined as "a return to mental health".

The decision I have taken to work with fungi medicine is a very personal one. It's definitely not for everyone. Like the person I was before I embarked on my first experience, many people are terrified of relapsing. Others are afraid of losing control, going mad, crossing an imagined threshold, never to return. Many sceptics are petrified by the idea of no longer relying on their psych meds.

And so, with all that I am learning, I never actively encourage others to do what I am doing. There are, of course, many ways to achieve enlightenment and healing. Some are drawn to meditation, yoga, long-distance running, cycling or fasting. For me, it's been pretty simple. I heard magic fungi knock on my soul's door and I answered by opening my heart.

From personal experience, authentic transformation is never a quick fix or a magic button. Realisations are only as powerful as one allows them to be. If the hard work is not embarked on and continued, they can evaporate and dissolve in some meaningless "ecstasy chase", all amounting to nothing.

But these days, unlike the petrified "me", the tethered "me", the one I was before my first journey, steeped in the sludge of ego and denial, now there is no turning a blind eye. It's as if

I have liberated the spirit of reflected pain and, in turn, I feel the slow release of being unbound. Of being able to face the shadow self in the mirror, the one from which I once tried to escape. To finally love myself and others, and truly forgive.

Nothing is constant. There are many days when life gets a little murky and there are times when I forget to love. Sometimes, when resistance sets in and my ego and self-will rule my world, when I return to old behaviour, it feels as though my self-awareness is on vacation and that I will never change. It is oh-so-hard to break inner patterns and toxic behaviour.

And, besides, nothing is ever constant perfection – it is in our imperfection that we own our humility and touch the magic of connected humanity. As the wise old sage Leonard Cohen tells us in "Anthem", there's a crack in everything, because, "that's how the light gets in".

Chapter 44

FINDING THE DRAGON

"He is no hero who never met the dragon, or who, if he once saw it, declared afterwards that he saw nothing. Equally, only one who has risked the fight with the dragon and is not overcome by it wins the hoard, the treasure hard to attain."
– Carl Jung, *The Heroic Journey*

Before I finish writing this book, I watch a documentary titled *Dosed*.

The main character, Adrienne, is a struggling heroin addict aching for her fix as she trawls the drug-infested alleyways of Vancouver. She could be me in 1999. Vancouver could be Hillbrow. No matter the geographical location, these desolate ghettos always look the same when desperation is the driver.

A friend of Adrienne, a documentary filmmaker, encourages her to try to get clean by using psilocybin and iboga. And so we watch her struggle. I am particularly drawn to the parts where we witness Adrienne's work with mushrooms. We literally see her waking up and finding release from her crippling addiction to smack.

As I observe, entranced, a part of me wonders what would have happened if I'd had access to psilocybin when I was trying to get clean? Instead of having to waste so many dark years shivering and shaking in my many failed attempts to withdraw alone, in the shadow of my own and societal shame? I think of all the isolated addicts who have struggled and died from their addiction.

I come away from the doccie inspired by Adrienne, who not only allowed herself to be filmed in her most broken and vulnerable moments, but she's had the courage to stand up, own her journey and inspire others with hope.

But, afterwards, I also feel deeply sad.

Why have I allowed my fear of disclosure to silence me for so long? Is it really due to some misguided notion that I will lose my credibility? My imagined "Queen of Success" dethroning as this traditional 12-Step recovering addict? What dark "enemies" have I conjured to stop me from owning my fire?

As synchronicity would have it, on the same night after watching *Dosed* I stumble upon a YouTube plant medicine seminar. Gabor Maté is the keynote speaker, delivering a lecture titled "Manifesting the Mind".

In his address, he describes a woman who has journeyed with psychedelics and her experience of finding her "dragon". She says that if she cares too much about what other people think, she will lose her "dragon", her real and powerful self.

Her words hit home. That's it. *That's it!*

All the anxiety and the twisted energy I have been wasting on what "others" might say about my work with Soma medicine, what "they" may say about my thoughts on The Pandemic, have been tantamount to losing myself. To losing *my mind*.

How ironic. Here I am, doing all this aching work to heal my damaged self. To release anger, shame and resentment. To reconnect with my essence. To source self-forgiveness. To try to make peace with those I have harmed and those who have hurt me. And yet here I am spending so much of that healing energy in fear of what some unknown, imagined committee might think of me.

The really dangerous enemy is the one that exists within: the one who stops the self from telling its truth, from shining, from prospering, from daring to be free and participating in the Kingdom of Joy.

I realise I have run out of excuses. I can no longer confuse fear and timidity with self-preservation. There has never been a better time for me – just as Adrienne, Julian, Edward, Chelsea and Monica did – to stand up to share my beliefs. It's a light-bulb moment, a switch of mindset, a key to unlock and undo this block that's been paralysing me for so long. I make a commitment to myself to soldier on in the telling of my truth.

I only wish I'd had the courage to do it earlier.

※

Another magically synchronous event unfolds just days before I am to submit my manuscript to my editor. I come across a post on Facebook detailing meetings for a 12-Step recovery fellowship known as PIR, which stands for "Psychedelics in Recovery".

Ever since I first began working with psilocybin, I've longed to share my experiences of strength and hope in a group with other recovering addicts using psychedelics to heal. Is this the opportunity I've been aching for?

I am just in time to join a Zoom meeting scheduled for 1pm EST. As it starts, I'm thrilled to hear that the Twelve Steps and Twelve Traditions in PIR are the same as the ones I've been so familiar with in my old NA 12-Step meetings. Admittedly, they are worded slightly differently, and seem more compassionate. For the first time in seven years, I share truthfully at a 12-Step meeting. I am convinced Father Bill is smiling down on us.

Later that night, I discover that PIR was founded in 2016 as a tiny splinter group for people who, like me, were unable to openly discuss their psychedelic experiences in traditional fellowships for fear of judgment and recrimination. The website went live in 2019 and, during the first year of lockdown, PIR meetings went online. During The Pandemic, attendance mushroomed. There are currently a growing number of real-life meetings in no fewer than seven US cities and about 20 online meetings a week. My eyes shine with joy as I note the dates and times on my Google calendar.

What a gift I have been given.

I have finally found my recovery tribe.

There's a revolution of the mind on the rise.

✳

We are living in a world that is clearly broken, overflowing with billions of suffering people. We are a spiritually parched planet. Unable to access authentic connection, we're caught in our corporeal prisons. Our deeper impulses to "fix" ourselves, or to "touch God", have devolved into a desperate dervish of drinking, drugging, psyche meds, shopping, gaming, toxic sex, anaesthetising series-streaming, an obsessive reliance on the internet, the "news" and social media. People are angry, lost and lonely. There are wars and mass shootings all over the planet. The violence is an explosion of unresolved pain. The world clearly needs healing.

I can no longer hide in the shadows. The shadows are where I once scored and bled. The shadows are the demons I battle when I journey, those that I bring into the light.

I can no longer hold on to the magic healing fire I've experienced and keep it to myself. Because, if there is anything I have learned from psilocybin, my 12-Step meetings, my new PIR fellowship, lockdown and life itself, it is that you can only keep what you have by giving it away.

Chapter 45

HOLD YOURSELF

"As soon as we left the ground, I knew I myself had to fly."
– Amelia Earhart (after her first solo flight in 1921)

27 March 2022
One year later

I am at the new house with Joe on the one-year anniversary of The Woman's death. I am here to pay my respects to the stranger I never met, but whose brutal departure forced me to consider many things and helped me tackle my darkest fears in writing this book. A year on, no one has been arrested for the murder two houses away. I don't dwell too much on it anymore. Besides, I am also here to celebrate 12 months of owning my cabin.

I am not sure Joe is really cutting it as the watchdog I imagined him to be when I rescued him as a puppy. The only time he really barks is when he spots his own reflection in the glass sliding door that leads onto the deck. And when he does, his woof echoes across acres of wild fynbos and bounces against the mountains, and so he barks and his bark barks back. But Joe has become my boy child, my dear loyal friend. And all the while, during the many hours I've been tunnelling away on this book on my precious deck, his warm body pressed against my feet, he has become my sweet muse.

Where I once thought I'd saved him, he has in fact rescued me.

Time has a way of compelling me to look back to see the differences in how I once felt and how I feel now. The changes the clock brings are often imperceptible. They creep up on us in the dark, when the world is asleep and no one's watching. Change is an invisible silver thread that moves within, fixing, darning and sewing up the jagged inner snags, the black holes and missing pieces. In many ways, it's a lot like the way mycelium works, spreading a network of fine white filaments that create fungi, which are everywhere on our planet. In 1998, a 9.65-square-kilometre stretch of honey fungus was discovered in the Blue Mountains in Oregon. It's believed to be the largest living organism on Planet Earth, big enough to cover 1 350 soccer fields. Mycologists estimate it is anywhere between 2 400 and 8 650 years old.

✳

My doors are wide open tonight. It is dead quiet outside. The gentlest breath of wind whispers through the fynbos. There are signs of life in the distant houses dotted against a black night sky sprinkled in star-glory. My elderly neighbours, who were gagged and tied up a year ago, are here to say farewell to the last rays of summer before they return to Europe. There's a new owner in the slate-grey coffin house who has decided to change its colour.

I switch on the light that illuminates my Buddha statue in the garden at night. The Buddha says: "No one outside ourselves can rule us inwardly. When we know this, we become free."

Buddhists also believe that struggle is a gift, that if you go with the flow of adversity, you will find wisdom on the other side. You may even find joy. I have found much joy in the one who sits besides me on the deck, who smiles softly like a dolphin and pants while I breathe in the quiet of the night. Good boy.

My heart is still tonight. I am safe here. I feel free.

Just as writer Arundhati Roy suggested when she penned an essay in the early days of The Pandemic, it feels indeed as if I have, over the last few years, stepped through a brutal but magical doorway, to imagine new worlds and slowly shake off the baggage of the past.

"Historically, pandemics have forced humans to break with the past and imagine their world anew," wrote Roy. "This one is no different. It is a portal, a gateway between one world and the next. We can choose to walk through it, dragging the carcasses of our prejudice and hatred, our avarice, our data banks and dead ideas, our dead rivers and smoky skies behind us. Or we can walk through lightly, with little luggage, ready to imagine another world. And ready to fight for it."

Going through The Doors, shifting through this "portal" over the last few years, has taught me many things. But perhaps, if I have to choose one, it's that *I can change my mind*. Literally. Because it's all in my head.

In my mission to get down and dirty and rescue my self, to understand what has happened in our world, much like when a doctor pulls out a distressed baby during its birth, I have travelled to dark places where I sometimes thought I might die from the pain of confronting my past and the brokenness of our world. But, after all those years of running from my vulnerabilities, imagine my surprise when I discovered that the only way to mend ourselves is to embrace the truth head-on. And so I keep opening that door and finding a silver thread that I now follow towards the universal house of hope and healing.

I am not the same she I was two years ago when I begged Soul-Mat for suicide pills as we went into lockdown while our world was falling apart. I am not the same she I was one year ago, the one who felt as if her dream of heaven and escape had been decimated when The Woman was killed. And I will not be the same next year when who knows what might happen. And so, just for today, I won't beat myself up for sometimes being a failed human. I will try not to waste any more of my precious life fearing what others might say. I will try not dwell too much on death or mutations of a virus, or torture myself with "whodunnit?" when it comes to The Pandemic.

In the grander scheme of time, long after the Covid crisis is over, life will continue. People will keel over from heart failure, just as my father did. People will surrender to cancer, like my mother did. People will drown. People will hang themselves. People will lose their jobs. People will go to bed hungry at night … But people will also dance. They will laugh, they will love, and they will live.

I will weep again. I will feel trapped again. But I will also have days when I am able to taste the sweet nectar of joy and freedom as I watch the eagles soar above and feel kindness and love for my deceased mother who also loved feathered fliers.

﹡

I'm often asked why I head off alone to my magic cabin so often without Soul-Mat. Surely couples should do everything together?

And so I find myself contemplating the concept of "alone".

A-lone. Solitary. Single. Unescorted. Unattended, unchaperoned, partnerless, companionless.

The Latin word is *solus*.

It has a tragic tinge to it. *Sol us*: Without us.

The truth is, Soul-Mat and I both enjoy being on our own. Since our souls collided eight years ago, I have learned much about love minus the sugar-coating and rose-tinted specs. Between the sweet periods of tenderness and heavenly connection, there are also times of fire and brimstone. Of deep pain and disappointment.

There are days when wounds are ripped open, moments when we are thrown out of every imaginable comfort zone. And sometimes the ache is so huge that we both long to run and say, "No! Enough. It is enough now. Please. No more! This is not the perfect love we signed up for that day we fell in love at the airport!"

And then there are days of growth and devotion. When we finish each other's sentences, read each other's minds. There is never stagnation. There is always change. This is the way in which love carves a path that brings us back to each other. Sometimes limping and seemingly defeated. Sometimes ecstatic, flying and whirling. There are rewards when we bravely toil for our hard-earned space of trust, of deep love, forgiveness and healing.

He is the one with whom I hope to grow old, grey and wrinkled. When I glance in the mirror, that's already happening. And one day, we will die. I hope I go before he does, so that I don't ever have to face the grief of losing Soul-Mat. But it might happen the other way round and I will then be left all by myself. That makes me very sad.

To mark one year of owning the house, tonight I decide to do a Soma journey on my own.

I would be lying if I said I don't feel a little afraid. There is no container, no group to hold me. No Monica. No Soul-Mat. Joe has drifted off to sleep. He is making little snoring noises under the duvet.

I am *solus*.

Hours later, having journeyed through The Doors, I come out on the other side reminded that I am safe, that I am everything I need. That I am enough.

Hold yourself, the voice whispers, *in pain and joy and in the dark days of incarceration. And so you shall hold others. For in the end we will all be alone together. Connected.*

And so I do.

AFTERWORD

Becoming a book mother

"When I die, my deeds will follow along with me – that is how I imagine it. I will bring with me what I have done. In the meantime it is important to ensure that I do not stand at the end with empty hands."
– Carl Jung, *On Life after Death*

When I wrote it back in 2005, I had no idea that my debut memoir would all but incinerate my relationship with certain members of my family. What happens after *Smacked* reminds me of the line by Polish-American writer Czeslaw Milosz who won the Nobel Prize for Literature in 1980: "When a writer is born into a family, the family is finished."

Memoir can be mercenary.

I've often wondered whether, if I'd known back then the killing power it would have over my blood brother and sisters, would I have written my book as I did? My brutal blame treaty, a projectile retch of my life as a junkie, an intimate exposé of how I destroyed everything and everyone in my path in order to get my fix.

Back then, before the book had even been conceived, I was a woman hardly breathing, crawling on my belly like disgraced Eve exiled from Eden. Teetering on the edge, I clutched at anything that would give me a sense of purpose, a reason to keep the death urge at bay. So, like a line cast out to a soul swept away by the furious ocean, the publishing deal I was offered to write *Smacked* became my gift, my unexpected reason to stay alive. And so I wrote.

Before the book was conceived, my sons had been the only motivation for me to get clean and stay clean. Shattered as I was, I certainly did not believe I deserved saving. But then, suddenly, without the aid of my narcotic fixes or my husband to lend support, I struggled even more with the blinding demands of single motherhood. So when the opportunity to write the book came along, it miraculously felt like I had something to individuate myself from all my past failures.

Smacked was mine. Writing the book and then seeing it in its published form offered me something wondrous that I had not experienced for years: the freedom to just be *me*. My book was my fresh new baby. It was my second chance, an opportunity to rewrite my life. Ironically, once I held it, safely captured in black ink on white pages, this harrowing story of mine felt untarnished and untainted in contrast to all the real-life disasters of my past. Somehow, I had managed to transmute my shame into a piece of art. But I often wonder, was I even human when I wrote it? Was I even alive back then when I birthed my book?

I know that I did not think too much when I scrawled down my sordid story. What I mean is that I did not deliberate over my choice of words, which spilt from my broken guts onto the page. I just wrote.

I had a five-month deadline. I did not consider the people I would implicate. Possessed, I toiled day and night as if the world was dead. I expelled my words in a fury. When it was done, I came up for air. I knew I had told my truth. And in that I felt some vague sense of achievement.

But after *Smacked* hit the shelves and unexpectedly went on to become a bestseller and did much to redeem me in the eyes of the outside world, its aftermath was a Hiroshima for my family. Instead of healing over time, my inner circle progressively collapsed.

The strange thing was that I had hoped my book would make them proud of me – I, who had caused my sisters and brother so much shame. They had seen me at my worst, a skeletal smack and crack whore screeching on the streets of Hillbrow. Possessed, on a hellbent mission to score another hit. Surely, the new me was an improvement?

Many years later, I see now how deluded I was. I see how absurd my hope of reintegration into the family circle was. How could I expect them to love and re-embrace me, take me back into the fold, when my explosive words had damned them? When my pen sword had destroyed their memory of our mother, their illusion of our family? By their horrified responses, my book appeared to have caused even more irredeemable damage than my addiction had.

My "sorrys" did not stick. My attempts at amends were aborted trumpet calls rebounding off padded, soundproof walls.

It would take almost two decades for me to fully comprehend what *Smacked* had done to my brother, my sisters, their children and mine. How the words we write can never be taken back.

To my family, if you ever read this, I am truly sorry for the pain my words have caused you.

While I have learned to live with the consequences, I have also, ironically, grown stronger because of them. And while I sometimes wish them to be different, I also don't. *Smacked* was my life raft. It became my space rocket and I deeply love my book. Today, I accept that writing my first memoir was the price that needed to be paid for my rebirth.

And so, I guess, because in many ways I lost my family – my siblings (our mother and father were both gone by the time *Smacked* came out) – and because I am not exactly a textbook mother to my sons, I transition to become a parent of a different kind.

I become a book mother, a midwife of words, a kind of self-appointed matriarch to an ever-growing, heaving bookshelf of writers. I never planned any of this. But when the opportunity falls into my path and the doors are flung wide open, the way forward is revealed. I miraculously discover that I am rather good at publishing and nurturing creatives.

Real-life mothering had always been a mammoth internal war between *their* desires and *mine*. It had been a constant battle between the selflessness required to nurture those who originated from half of my DNA and my own magnificent dreams. At each step of the way in the parenting of my own two children, my needs always had to be put on hold. Deleted, in fact.

Now as a book mother, I am able to sense my writer kids' needs. I can read their frowns. I understand their fears. I can take them by the hand and lead them out of danger and comfort them when they doubt themselves or weep. I find I have never-ending space in my heart to embrace them, to nurture and love them. Unconditionally.

This kind of mothering is joyous.

Why was it so hard to do the same with my own sons when they were children?

Perhaps the answer lies in the word "selfish". *Self-ish* – used so often as an insult. But what does the word even really mean?

The traditional definition of *selfish* /ˈsɛlfɪʃ/ as an adjective is: (of a person, action, or motive) lacking consideration for other people; concerned chiefly with one's own personal profit or pleasure.

So, here's the thing … With every writer I have either worked with or published, I have done so not just for their benefit, but also because it pleases *me* deeply. There is a pay-off. And I don't mean money.

Publishing is always a financial gamble – sometimes your horse comes in and sometimes it's an also-ran. There are times when it doesn't even leave the stalls. Of course we all hope to profit from the venture but, more often than not, bringing a book to life is like risking a daring dance in front of a crowd of strangers.

It is a birthing process without the bloody mess of contractions and seeping episiotomy stitches. And, although there is plenty of hard labour, it is ultimately an act of love. In the making of this baby, mere ideas and concepts become a waterfall of words. And so a book is birthed from start to completion. Creation. Joy.

After those final contractions, once the baby is delivered, the author and publisher get to hold their precious child, their book, to cherish and, hopefully, profit from it. And I, the midwife, can take a step back to bask in the glory of this miracle even before a single copy is sold.

When I publish a book, it becomes an addition to my imprint, to my identity, to my ever-growing book family. I display each and every one of them on a dedicated bookshelf just as a mother lines up photographs of her children.

For so long, guilt and shame accompanied this real-life mother/child tug of war. What a relief, what freedom it is to finally forgive myself for my human failings and have a label to attach to the core of my inadequacies: *self-ish-ness*.

So a book mother I am. And the stretchmarks I now carry form silver streaks in my ever-expanding mind.

ACKNOWLEDGMENTS

My darling sons James and Dan, you are truly my beautiful, wise teachers. Thank you for forgiveness, for the love you have bestowed on me and for allowing me to be your mother.

Monica, my spiritual mother, thank you for your deep and life-changing wisdom. You have taught me so much, but especially about kindness.

Thank you to my dear friends, Martine and Meg, for always being there for me. Meg, your support as I hit the last wobbly will never be forgotten.

Thank you, Bridget and Maggie, who gave me my publishing wings. Erika, Marga, Eloise, Ilse, Nicky and the rest of the team at NB, thank you for helping me to take wing and fly.

To my designer, Wilna, you are the best. Your dedication and incredible work ethic are heaven-sent. Jaco, your exquisite photos make my heart sing.

To my editor, Sean, your insights made all the difference. I appreciate the huge amount of work you have done on this special child of mine. Riaan, thank you for your invaluable feedback and for your amazing eagle eyes as my proofreader.

To all the writers I've published and worked with, you are my shining stars.

Pumla, that "talk" gave me the courage I needed. Kagiso, thank you for "innerstanding".

Thank you, Melissa and Viv, for helping to make the cabin even more beautiful than it already was; Charles, for taking care of everything; Troy and Ighsaan for being the ones I turn to; Nelia for answering that call when you were still on holiday. Thank you all my other "neighbours": Jos, Greetje, Les, Hassan, Flip, Eugene, Conrad, Dickie, Angelique, Danie, Dot, Malcolm, Ben, Joubert, Thalita, Hans, Xandra and Doortjie. Tineke, thank you for my piece of heaven. You are an angel.

To my Dog Park Misfits, Michelle and Liam, thanks for all the puppy play dates.

Precious Joe, I am not sure whether you'll be able to read this, but I know you know just how much we love you. Woof.

Mat, I am deeply moved by the way you have held me in the writing of this book. Darling soulmate, I am grateful for every word you read, for every single overly repeated "fuck" you counted, but most of all, for staying at my side through dark days. I love you, Matty.

MY RECOMMENDED READING LIST

1984 – George Orwell
American Kleptocracy – Casey Michel
Ariel – Sylvia Plath
The Big Book – Bill W
Brave New World – Aldous Huxley
Chasing the Scream – Johann Hari
Crystallising Public Opinion — Edward Bernays
Drugs without the Hot Air – Professor David Nutt
Empire of Pain – Patrick Radden Keefe
The Great Reset – Klaus Schwab
How to Change Your Mind – Michael Pollan
In the Realm of Hungry Ghosts – Gabor Maté
The Laughing Heart – Charles Bukowski
Media Corruption in the Age of Information – Edward H. Spence
The Myth of Sisyphus – Albert Camus
Permanent Record – Edward Snowden
Profiles in Corruption – Peter Schweizer
The Psychology of Totalitarianism – Mattias Desmet
The Real Anthony Fauci – Robert Kennedy
*Stealing Fire: How Silicon Valley, the Navy SEALs, and
Maverick Scientists Are Revolutionizing the Way We Live and
Work* – Steven Kotler and Jamie Wheal
The Trial of Julian Assange – Nils Melzer
The Tyranny of Growth – Malcolm Ray

MY RECOMMENDED WATCHLIST

Can't Get You Out of my Head – Adam Curtis (YouTube)
The Century of the Self – Adam Curtis (YouTube)
Collateral Murder – WikiLeaks (YouTube)
Dopesick – Danny Strong (Hulu)
Dosed: It's Not Magic, It's Medicine – Tyler Chandler
Dosed 2: The Trip of a Lifetime – Tyler Chandler
Fantastic Fungi – Paul Stamets (Netflix)
The Handmaid's Tale – (Showmax/Hulu)
How To Change Your Mind – (Netflix)
HyperNormalisation – Adam Curtis (YouTube)
Utopia (2013) – Denis Kelly (BBC)
The Wisdom of Trauma – Gabor Maté

ALSO BY MELINDA FERGUSON

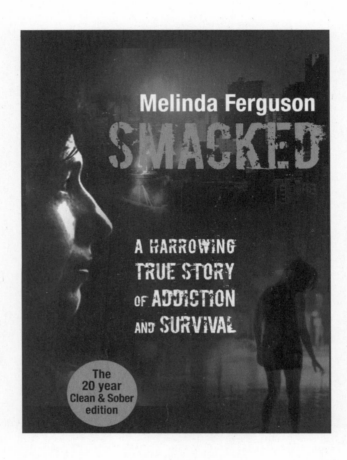